A World of Fiction

of Fiction

Twenty Timeless Short Stories

Second Edition

Sybil Marcus

University of California,
Berkeley

PEARSON
Longman

A World of Fiction: Twenty Timeless Short Stories, Second Edition

Pearson Education, 10 Bank Street, White Plains, NY 10606

Staff credits: The people who made up the *A World of Fiction* team,
representing editorial, production, design, and manufacturing, are: Karen Davy,
Dave Dickey, Ann France, Laura Lazzaretti, Laura Le Dréan, and Barbara Sabella.

Cover design: Barbara Sabella
Cover art: Franz Marc, Deer in the Forest II, 1913–1914, Staatliche Kunsthalle Karlsruhe
Text composition: Laserwords Private Limited
Text font: 11/13 Garamond-Light
Text credits: See page 311.
Photo credits: See page 313.

Library of Congress Cataloging-in-Publication Data

A world of fiction : twenty timeless short stories / [compiled by]
Sybil Marcus.-- 2nd ed.
    p. cm.
  Includes bibliographical references and index.
  ISBN 0-13-194636-6 (student bk. : alk. paper)
  1. English language--Textbooks for foreign speakers. 2. Short stories. I. Marcus, Sybil.
PE1128.W7599 2006
428.6'4--dc22

                                               2005028679

ISBN: 0-13-194636-6

Printed in the United States of America
5 6 7 8 9 10 11 12 VH 13 12 11 10 09

To my Mother, who believed in me,
and
to Ron and Daniel, whose loving support made it all possible.

CONTENTS

<>

Social Change and Injustice

PREFACE

In the years that have passed since the initial publication of *A World of Fiction,* the feedback from the many teachers and students who have used this book has been invaluable and encouraging. Teachers and students alike have frequently expressed appreciation for the variety of the stories' themes and writing styles, and the opportunity to explore the texts in an in-depth and sophisticated fashion. Accordingly, it has been painfully difficult to decide which five beloved stories to jettison to make room for the new ones in this second edition. The guiding principle behind the new selection is the same as before: The stories should have sufficient complexity, stylistic variation, and intrinsic interest as to give themselves up to intensive literary analysis, as well as to wider discussion. In response to teachers' requests, four of the five new stories have a lighter tone and/or more uplifting ending, while the fifth story, "An Intruder," has an intriguing puzzle at its core, which should encourage animated classroom interchanges. Revisions in this second edition include updated author biographies, new language and literary elements, and expanded language and vocabulary exercises where possible.

As in the first edition, this book arises from the conviction that close scrutiny of a fine literary text is in itself a richly satisfying and fruitful endeavor as the story's embedded meanings yield to an ever deeper probing by the reader. To facilitate the vigorous and sensitive discussion that flows from any profound story, I encourage my students to think of themselves as archaeologists, whose aim is to dig out the buried meanings in the text. In the process, I believe advanced students of language will also sharpen their critical-thinking, reading, oral, grammar, and writing skills in an integrated, nuanced, and enjoyable manner. Even the shyest and most tongue-tied students quickly grasp that since there are few absolute rights or wrongs when it comes to analyzing a layered story, they may speak out without embarrassment and share their interpretations with the class. In addition, the ensuing discussion can enhance intercultural sensitivity and awareness that there are universal truths and sentiments that bind us all.

I am particularly enamored of the short story as a teaching tool since its form offers non-native students a complete work of literature with its imperative elements of character, time, setting, action, motive, and message intact, but with a nonthreatening brevity that is characteristic of this genre. In addition, since the stories are short, there is an opportunity to grapple with and reflect on a number of different subjects and styles during a limited course of study.

A World of Fiction presents twenty unabridged short stories, many of which are recognized masterpieces in the genre, and all of which were originally written in English. The stories embrace a variety of themes, literary and linguistic styles, and time frames. They are rich in vocabulary, idioms, and imagery, and their subjects stimulate student exchange and debate. Above all, they embody the essence of great short stories in which the authors, to quote Nobel Prize Laureate Nadine Gordimer, successfully manage to "express from a situation in the exterior and interior world the life-giving drop—sweat, tear, semen, saliva—that will spread intensity on the page."

The stories in this anthology are divided loosely into four thematic categories: Husbands, Wives, and Lovers; Parent and Child; Loneliness and Alienation; and Social Change and Injustice. These divisions are inevitably arbitrary since most of the stories easily straddle more than one category, and one story ("The Lily-White Boys") doesn't fit snugly into any of them. Each story is classified, therefore, according to its dominant theme. The stories are graded, with each section starting with an accessible piece by virtue of its length or content, and working up to stories of greater thematic and/or stylistic complexity.

An underlying premise of my approach both in the classroom and in this book is that students must read each story twice at home, making full use of the glossary as they familiarize themselves with the plot and theme(s). At this level of advanced language achievement, I prefer students to approach the stories initially without much teacher input in order to respond freshly and individually to each story. Therefore, there are no prereading questions that alert the students to the story's content, although the capsule summary under the title does provide a contextual clue. However, if teachers prefer a more directed method, they may point the student in advance to the Thinking About the Story section, which contains a nonspecific question designed to promote thought and discussion. After the first reading, students are equipped to discuss the intricacies of plot, while after the second reading they are poised to discover the interior thematic connections in the story. Once they have explored the issues of plot and theme, they move on to an examination of the particular stylistic elements that distinguish the story. After this, their work as literary critics is done, and they are free to express their judgments on the characters and their actions, as well as to ponder the larger issues through their individual cultural prisms.

Following this analytical process, the transition to the study of grammatical structures and vocabulary items inherent in the story is a smooth one since students generally find it easier to absorb and implement grammatical and lexical items that they are familiar with in context. Finally, as a result of their immersion in literature and language, students are ready to write essays in which they integrate what they have learned.

How to Use This Book

Each chapter in this anthology is based on a complete short story and is divided into four sections that call upon the diverse language and critical appreciation skills of the student.

PART 1: First Reading

A. Thinking About the Story

At this point students are encouraged to express their visceral responses to the story. The aim is to stimulate an immediate and personal reaction in which the student can relate to a character or situation.

B. Understanding the Plot

Questions in this section lead students through the story in chronological order, eliciting their understanding of its characters, action, setting, and time frame. Students who experience any difficulties with the story during their first reading may find it helpful to turn in midreading to the plot questions to aid their comprehension. This section may be completed either orally or in writing, depending on the needs of the class.

PART 2: Second Reading

The questions in Part 2A (Exploring Themes) should ideally be answered orally since students benefit from sharing their thoughts and perspectives in a spirited interchange. In some cases small-group discussions may be more apt, while at other times the fertilizing effects of a cross-cultural class discussion can generate excitement and insights. On the other hand, the questions in Part 2B (Analyzing the Author's Style) are designed to be answered in writing.

A. Exploring Themes

Before embarking on a second reading of the story, students are given guidelines regarding key aspects of theme and language to look for, so that by the end of this reading they are ready to tackle the more demanding and substantive questions on the story's underlying meaning, its universal truths, and the writer's style.

B. Analyzing the Author's Style

This section concentrates on the more specialized stylistic elements of the story, such as metaphor, simile, symbol, personification, and alliteration. Students are required to analyze the way in which the author manipulates language to underscore themes and create linguistic richness. Before tackling the questions in this section, students should familiarize themselves with the definitions contained in the Explanation of Literary Terms that begins on page 297, which has illustrative examples culled from the stories in this anthology.

C. Judging for Yourself

The questions in this section enable students to adopt a more flexible approach to the text and to move beyond the limits of the story. Students may be encouraged to conjecture on events that have not been spelled out or to judge the wisdom of a character's actions. Sometimes they are asked to reflect on possible solutions to problems raised in the story or to propose resolutions of crises.

D. Making Connections

This is an opportunity to exploit the cross-cultural, multi-ethnic components of a class as students are asked to share their views on the controversial actions or standpoints raised in the story, using their own cultural and societal values as a touchstone.

E. Debate

A debate culminates the oral section. By this stage, students should have acquired the necessary vocabulary and command of English to enable them to present their oral arguments cogently and confidently.

HOW TO CONDUCT A DEBATE

A debate is conducted around a proposition of a controversial nature. There are two teams made up of two to three people per side. One side will argue as strongly as it can *for* the proposition, while the other side will try to present equally compelling arguments *against* it. The goal of each side is to persuade the audience (the rest of the class) of the superiority of its arguments. It is helpful to have a moderator (usually the teacher) to ensure that the debate progresses in an orderly fashion. Debates follow a special order: The first member of the team supporting the proposition opens the debate. Then he or she is followed by the first member of the opposing side. Team members continue to alternate until everybody has had a chance to speak. Then it is the audience's turn. Members of the audience should offer their own comments on what they have heard. When everyone has finished speaking, the final summing up begins. This is done by the opening debater on each side, who tries to incorporate the points that favor the team's arguments. Finally, the audience votes to see which team has won by virtue of its stronger presentation.

If the class is small (no larger than 12 students), it is possible to divide all the students into two teams representing the two sides of the argument and have them argue their case in a less structured fashion, with each side alternating as a proponent presents a point and an opponent attempts to rebut it. Again, the teacher can act as the moderator controlling the action.

PART 3: Focus on Language

In most chapters this section offers students a chance to review and practice a particular grammatical aspect that is well illustrated in the story. Structures covered include gerunds, present participles, main and subordinate clauses, conditionals, tenses, participial and prepositional phrases, sentence fragments, dangling modifiers, appositives, prepositions, prefixes, and suffixes. In addition to the grammar areas under consideration, every chapter has a Building Vocabulary Skills section to help students expand their vocabulary. The accompanying exercises have been varied as much as possible to engage the students and discourage any element of rote.

PART 4: Writing Activities

By the time students arrive at this section, they have carefully considered the story and its related topics and have also acquired a richer vocabulary and concentrated on some grammar. They are now equipped to tackle the writing assignments, which range from paragraphs to complete essays. Guidelines help them structure their writing. The questions range from expository to descriptive writing. Wherever feasible, one question encourages students to incorporate the language skills they have just practiced, thus reinforcing their learning in a different way. Another question is designed to get students to explore a literary work, a movie, a painting, or even an opera that they are familiar with and that in some way duplicates the theme of the story under discussion. Finally, students are sometimes asked to make connections between stories in the anthology, offering them a chance to further refine their practice in comparison and contrast.

ACKNOWLEDGMENTS

I am deeply grateful to the following people whose help has been invaluable to me while writing this book.

Allen Ascher, my editor in the first edition, whose influence continues to permeate this book.

Daniel Berman, whose insights and help in straightening out my difficulties with "The Lily-White Boys," were invaluable.

Ron Berman, who determinedly steered me to "EPICAC," and encouraged me in countless loving ways throughout the writing of this book.

Tamara Carlin, Jim Seger, and Margie Wald, who helped me narrow down my new selections.

Karen Davy, whose invaluable suggestions, open-mindedness, and meticulous eye made her my dream editor.

Lucille Kennedy and Laura Le Dréan, who inspired me with their confidence in this second edition.

Elizabeth Schulz, my typist, who once again rescued me with expertise and goodwill when I needed her most.

Maggie Sokolik, who generously gave me carte blanche to try out my new material at the University of California at Berkeley Summer ESL Workshop.

Students past and present, who continue to amaze me with their insights and enthusiasm.

Susan Stern, whose joyous embrace of my book from its inception has been a source of incalculable encouragement for me.

Patti Weissman, who unstintingly shared her vast knowledge of grammar with me, and pored over the five new chapters. Needless to say, whatever errors remain are mine alone.

HUSBANDS, WIVES, AND LOVERS

Marc Chagall, *Midsummer Night's Dream*, 1939

1

Can-Can

ARTURO VIVANTE (b. 1923)

Born in Italy, Arturo Vivante studied medicine in Rome and practiced there for eight years. He now lives in the United States where he has been a full-time writer for over forty years. He has published two novels, *A Goodly Babe* (1966) and *Doctor Giovanni* (1969), as well as several volumes of short stories, such as *The French Girls of Killini* (1967) and *Run to the Waterfall* (1979), an autobiographical account of a half-Jewish family in Italy before and after World War II. Other works include *Writing Fiction* (1980), *Essays on Art and Ontology* (1980), and *The Tales of Arturo Vivante* (1990). He has also translated into English the poems of Giacomo Leopardi, Italy's famous nineteenth-century lyric poet. Vivante is quoted as saying, "I write to know the mystery that even a small matter holds."

CAN-CAN

*A husband arranges a secret meeting with a woman
and is surprised by the outcome.*

"I'm going to go for a drive," he said to his wife. "I'll be back in an hour or two."

He didn't often leave the house for more than the few minutes it took him to go to the post office or to a store, but spent his time hanging around,[1] doing odd jobs—Mr. Fix-it, his wife called him—and also, though not nearly enough of it, painting—which he made his living[2] from.

"All right," his wife said brightly, as though he were doing her a favor. As a matter of fact, she didn't really like him to leave; she felt safer with him at home, and he helped look after the children, especially the baby.

"You're glad to be rid of[3] me, aren't you?" he said.

"Uh-huh," she said with a smile that suddenly made her look very pretty—someone to be missed.

She didn't ask him where he was going for his drive. She wasn't the least bit inquisitive,[4] though jealous she was in silent, subtle[5] ways.

As he put his coat on, he watched her. She was in the living room with their elder daughter. "Do the can-can, mother," the child said, at which she held up her skirt and did the can-can, kicking her legs up high in his direction.

He wasn't simply going out for a drive, as he had said, but going to a café, to meet Sarah, whom his wife knew but did not suspect, and with her go to a house on a lake his wife knew nothing about—a summer cottage to which he had the key.

"Well, goodbye," he said.

"Bye," she called back, still dancing.

This wasn't the way a husband expected his wife—whom he was about to leave at home to go to another woman—to behave at all, he thought. He expected her to be sewing or washing, not doing the can-can, for God's sake. Yes, doing something uninteresting and unattractive, like darning[6] children's clothes. She had no stockings on, no shoes, and her legs looked very white and smooth, secret, as though he had never touched them or come near them. Her feet, swinging up and down high in the air, seemed to be nodding to him. She held her skirt bunched up,[7] attractively. Why was she doing that of all times *now*? He lingered.[8] Her eyes had

---

1 **hanging around** not having anything specific to do
2 **made his living** earned enough money to live on
3 **be rid of** be free of
4 **inquisitive** curious

5 **subtle** slyly clever, difficult to detect
6 **darning** sewing a tear in material
7 **bunched up** pulled together in folds
8 **lingered** stayed behind

mockery⁹ in them, and she laughed. The child laughed with her as she danced. She was still dancing as he left the house.   35

He thought of the difficulties he had had arranging this *rendezvous*¹⁰— going out to a call box; phoning Sarah at her office (she was married, too); her being out; his calling her again; the busy signal; the coin falling out of sight, his opening the door of the phone box in order to retrieve it; at last getting her on the line; her asking him to call again next week, finally setting   40 a date.

Waiting for her at the café, he surprised himself hoping that she wouldn't come. The appointment was at three. It was now ten past. Well, she was often late. He looked at the clock, and at the picture window for her car. A car like hers, and yet not hers—no luggage rack on it. The smooth   45 hardtop gave him a peculiar pleasure. Why? It was 3:15 now. Perhaps she wouldn't come. No, if she was going to come at all, this was the most likely time for her to arrive. Twenty past. Ah, now there was some hope. Hope? How strange he should be hoping for her absence. Why had he made the appointment if he was hoping she would miss it? He didn't   50 know why, but simpler, simpler if she didn't come. Because all he wanted now was to smoke that cigarette, drink that cup of coffee for the sake of them, and not to give himself something to do. And he wished he could go for a drive, free and easy,¹¹ as he had said he would. But he waited, and at 3:30 she arrived. "I had almost given up hope," he said.   55

They drove to the house on the lake. As he held her in his arms he couldn't think of her; for the life of him¹² he couldn't.

"What are you thinking about?" she said afterwards, sensing his detachment.¹³

For a moment he didn't answer, then he said, "You really want to   60 know what I was thinking of?"

"Yes," she said, a little anxiously.

He suppressed¹⁴ a laugh, as though what he was going to tell her was too absurd or silly. "I was thinking of someone doing the can-can."

"Oh," she said, reassured. "For a moment I was afraid you were   65 thinking of your wife."

---

9 **mockery** making fun of (negatively)
10 *rendezvous* a meeting at a particular time and place
11 **free and easy** with a clear conscience
12 **for the life of him** even with the utmost effort
13 **detachment** indifference, uninvolvement
14 **suppressed** restrained, held back

PART 1 First Reading

A   Thinking About the Story

Now that you've read "Can-Can," consider what you would do if you suspected that your spouse or significant other was cheating on you. Do you sympathize with any of the characters—the husband, the wife, or the mistress? Explain your choice(s).

B   Understanding the Plot

1. What is the can-can?
2. What does the husband do for a living?
3. Is the husband a hard worker?
4. Whom is the husband going to meet?
5. Does the wife suspect her husband of adultery?
6. Why was it so difficult for the husband and Sarah to arrange a meeting?
7. What is the husband's state of mind as he sits waiting for his lover?
8. To whom does the pronoun "them" refer? (line 53)
9. What happened when the husband and his lover reached their rendezvous?
10. What was the husband's lover concerned about?
11. Is Sarah reassured by his answer to her question?

PART 2 Second Reading

A   Exploring Themes

You are now ready to reread "Can-Can." Try to understand why the characters act as they do and what thoughts about life Arturo Vivante is attempting to convey in the story. Look carefully at the way he uses language to express his ideas.

1. What is the significance of the can-can in the story?
2. Does the wife do the can-can for her child or for her husband? Explain your answer.

3. What effect does the dance have on her husband?

4. What does the couple expect from each other in marriage? Does each fulfill the other's expectations?

B Analyzing the Author's Style

For more information on the literary terms in this section, turn to the explanations of *irony* (page 304) and *symbol* (page 308).

IRONY

Irony is embedded in "Can-Can," both in the situations in which the characters find themselves and in their comments and thoughts. For example, Vivante writes of the husband as he sits waiting for his lover's car:

> *A car like hers, and yet not like hers—no luggage rack on it. The smooth hardtop gave him a peculiar pleasure.* (lines 45–46)

Here we have an ironic contrast between the husband's earlier excited anticipation of the meeting and his surprising feeling of relief that it is not his lover's car arriving.

And when the husband says to his mistress, *"I had almost given up hope"* (line 55), she interprets him to mean that he had almost given up hope that she would arrive, whereas he really means he had almost given up hoping that she wouldn't arrive.

Pick out and explain five more examples of irony in the story.

SYMBOL

Vivante uses the can-can as a central **symbol** (something that has both a literal and a deeper meaning) in the story.

To unearth the richness of the can-can as a symbol, first explore the various associations you have with the dance. Then answer the following questions.

1. What does the can-can symbolize in the story?

2. In the scene where the wife does the can-can, how does the language reinforce the symbol?

3. What theme in the story is highlighted by the symbolic dance?

C Judging for Yourself

Express yourself as personally as you like in your answers to the following questions.

1. Do you think the expectations the couple have of each other are reasonable?
2. Do you think the husband will continue the affair?
3. Should the husband have left the restaurant when he had the opportunity?
4. Have the husband and wife learned anything from the episode?
5. What do you imagine their marriage will be like in the future?

D Making Connections

1. How is adultery viewed in your culture?
2. Does the couple's marriage in "Can-Can" reflect the kind of marriage common in your culture?
3. In your country, would politicians or other public figures be denied or forced to leave office if they committed adultery? What do you think should happen to them?
4. Is honest communication between couples encouraged in your culture? If marriages run into difficulties, is family therapy an option?

E Debate

Debate this proposition:
Adultery is a crime and should be punished by law.

PART 3 Focus on Language

A Gerunds and Present Participles

"Can-Can" contains several examples of **gerunds** and **present participles.** Although gerunds and present participles both share an *-ing* ending—in other words, the same form—their function is quite different.

The **gerund** is a type of verbal, which is a part of speech that is related to verbs but acts as another part of speech. There are three kinds of verbals: gerunds, participles (present and past), and infinitives. The gerund acts as a verbal noun and is used in the same way as a noun. Being a noun, the gerund or gerund phrase can be the subject of a sentence or the object of a verb or preposition. For example:

Arranging this rendezvous was very difficult for him.

The gerund phrase *arranging this rendezvous* is the subject of the verb *was*.

He couldn't imagine arranging this rendezvous.

The gerund phrase *arranging this rendezvous* is the object of the verb *couldn't imagine*.

He expected her to be … doing something uninteresting and unattractive, like darning children's clothes. (lines 27–29)

The gerund phrase *darning children's clothes* is the object of the preposition *like*.

The **present participle** is another type of verbal. It can act as part of a verb in the progressive tense or as an adjective. As an adjective, the present participle or the present participial phrase must modify a noun or pronoun. For example:

Her feet, swinging up and down high in the air, seemed to be nodding to him. (lines 31–32)

The participial phrase *swinging up and down high in the air* modifies the noun *feet*.

When used as part of a verb in the **progressive tense,** the participle shows that an action is in progress. For example:

Why was she doing that of all times now? (line 33)

1. Find the paragraph in "Can-Can" that is composed mainly of gerunds and underline them.

2. In each sentence that follows, decide if the *italicized* word is a
   gerund, present participle, or part of a verb in the progressive tense.
   Write your choice on the line.

   a. "I'm *going* for a drive," he said to his wife. _____

   b. She hated *sewing* for the family. _____

   c. She held up her skirt and did the can-can, *kicking* her legs
      up high in his direction. _____

   d. He objected to *seeing* her in this new role. _____

   e. *Waiting* so long for his lover at the café made him feel
      nervous. _____

   f. He looked at his watch, *hoping* she wouldn't come.

      _____

   g. How strange he should be *hoping* for her absence.

      _____

   h. *Smoking* a cigarette helped steady his nerves. _____

   i. "What are you *thinking* about?" she said, *sensing* his
      detachment. _____   _____

   j. *Suppressing* a laugh, he answered her honestly.

      _____

3. Write three sentences using the verb *get rid of* as a gerund, as a
   present participle, and as a verb in the progressive tense. Do the
   same with the verb *linger.*

B   Building Vocabulary Skills

1. Many common expressions consist of two nouns, adjectives,
   adverbs, or verbs separated by *and*. For example:

   free and easy: with a clear conscience

   *And he wished he could go for a drive, **free and easy**, as
   he had said he would.* (lines 53–54)

Write definitions for the following expressions. If necessary, use a dictionary to help you. Then write sentences using each expression in a way that shows you understand it.

a. bread-and-butter _____

b. by and large _____

c. cut-and-dried _____

d. give and take _____

e. heart and soul _____

f. ins and outs _____

g. open-and-shut _____

h. straight and narrow _____

i. tried-and-true _____

j. wheel and deal _____

Can you think of any more such expressions?

2. "Can-Can" has a number of sophisticated words that help vocabulary expansion.

With a partner, define the following expressions in your own words without looking back at the glossary explanations. Then complete the sentences that follow with the correct word from the list. You may need to change the tense of the verb.

a. subtle (line 14) _____

b. lingered (line 33) _____

c. mockery (line 34) _____

d. rendezvous (line 36) _____

e. retrieve (line 39) _____

f. detachment (line 59) _____

g. suppressed (line 63) _____

h. absurd (line 64) _____

The husband barely _____ his astonishment as he watched his wife dancing the can-can. He looked at his watch and realized that he was _____ too long, so he _____ his car keys and hurried out the door, hearing the _____ in her laugh. He knew he had lost his _____ and felt that the situation had become quite _____. As he made his way to his _____, he realized that his wife's unexpected dance was a _____ way of showing her true feelings.

PART 4 Writing Activities

1. Imagine a scene in which the wife in "Can-Can" is waiting for her husband to return. Write about her thoughts and feelings as the hours go by. Try to use gerunds and present participles in your writing.

2. Write a letter offering advice to a close friend who has confided in you that he or she is in love with a married person.

3. *The Scarlet Letter* by Nathaniel Hawthorne and *Anna Karenina* by Leo Tolstoy are two famous novels that deal with adultery. In an essay of two to three pages, discuss any well-known work in your language that involves that subject. Outline the plot, explaining what drives the character to adultery. Are the characters treated sympathetically?

4. In an essay of one to two pages, compare "Can-Can" with "The Kugelmass Episode" by Woody Allen (page 51). What similarities do you see in the two stories? Which story do you prefer? Why?

2

The Story of an Hour

KATE CHOPIN (1851–1904)

Born in St. Louis, Missouri, Kate Chopin came of French-Creole parentage on her mother's side and Irish immigrants on her father's side. She grew up in a household dominated by generations of women, and it was from her great-grandmother that she heard the tales of the early French settlers of St. Louis that were later to influence many of her short stories with their colorful descriptions of Creole and Acadian life.

Much of Chopin's writing deals with women searching for freedom from male domination, and she is considered to be an early feminist writer. She wrote over a hundred short stories, many of which were published in two collections: *Bayou Folk* (1894) and *A Night in Acadia* (1897). Her two novels, *At Fault* (1890) and *The Awakening* (1899), deal with the controversial themes of divorce and adultery, respectively. Denounced as immoral, *The Awakening* caused a public uproar, which left Chopin deeply depressed and discouraged. As a result, she wrote very little in the last five years of her life.

THE STORY OF AN HOUR

*A wife has a startling reaction to the news
of her husband's death.*

Knowing that Mrs. Mallard was afflicted with[1] a heart trouble, great care was taken to break to her as gently as possible the news of her husband's death.

It was her sister Josephine who told her, in broken sentences, veiled hints[2] that revealed in half concealing. Her husband's friend Richards was 5 there, too, near her. It was he who had been in the newspaper office when intelligence[3] of the railroad disaster was received, with Brently Mallard's name leading the list of "killed." He had only taken the time to assure himself of its truth by a second telegram, and had hastened to forestall[4] any less careful, less tender friend in bearing the sad message. 10

She did not hear the story as many women have heard the same, with a paralyzed[5] inability to accept its significance. She wept at once, with sudden, wild abandonment,[6] in her sister's arms. When the storm of grief had spent itself she went away to her room alone. She would have no one follow her. 15

There stood, facing the open window, a comfortable, roomy armchair. Into this she sank, pressed down by a physical exhaustion that haunted[7] her body and seemed to reach into her soul.

She could see in the open square before her house the tops of trees that were all aquiver[8] with the new spring life. The delicious breath of 20 rain was in the air. In the street below a peddler[9] was crying his wares.[10] The notes of a distant song which someone was singing reached her faintly, and countless sparrows were twittering[11] in the eaves.[12]

There were patches of blue sky showing here and there through the clouds that had met and piled above the other in the west facing her 25 window.

She sat with her head thrown back upon the cushion of the chair quite motionless, except when a sob came up into her throat and shook her, as a child who has cried itself to sleep continues to sob in its dreams.

She was young, with a fair, calm face, whose lines bespoke repression[13] 30 and even a certain strength. But now there was a dull stare in her eyes,

---

1 **was afflicted with** suffered from
2 **veiled hints** indirect suggestions
3 **intelligence** news
4 **hastened to forestall** rushed to prevent
5 **paralyzed** helpless (literally, unable to move)
6 **abandonment** unrestrained emotion
7 **haunted** spread throughout (as a ghost's presence)
8 **aquiver** shaking

9 **peddler** someone who sells goods in the street
10 **crying his wares** shouting out what he has to sell
11 **sparrows were twittering** small birds were singing rapidly
12 **eaves** the edges of a roof under which birds nest
13 **bespoke repression** indicated she was not allowing herself to express her feelings

whose gaze was fixed away off yonder on one of those patches of blue sky. It was not a glance of reflection, but rather indicated a suspension of intelligent thought.

There was something coming to her and she was waiting for it, fearfully. What was it? She did not know; it was too subtle[14] and elusive[15] to name. But she felt it, creeping out of the sky, reaching toward her through the sounds, the scents, the color that filled the air.

Now her bosom rose and fell tumultuously.[16] She was beginning to recognize this thing that was approaching to possess her, and she was striving[17] to beat it back with her will—as powerless as her two white slender hands would have been.

When she abandoned herself a little whispered word escaped her slightly parted lips. She said it over and over under her breath: "Free, free, free!" The vacant stare and the look of terror that had followed it went from her eyes. They stayed keen[18] and bright. Her pulses beat fast, and the coursing blood warmed and relaxed every inch of her body.

She did not stop to ask if it were not a monstrous joy that held her. A clear and exalted[19] perception enabled her to dismiss the suggestion as trivial.

She knew that she would weep again when she saw the kind, tender hands folded in death; the face that had never looked save[20] with love upon her, fixed and gray and dead. But she saw beyond that bitter moment a long procession of years to come that would belong to her absolutely. And she opened and spread her arms out to them in welcome.

There would be no one to live for during those coming years; she would live for herself. There would be no powerful will bending her in that blind persistence with which men and women believe they have a right to impose a private will upon a fellow-creature. A kind intention or a cruel intention made the act seem no less a crime as she looked upon it in that brief moment of illumination.

And yet she had loved him—sometimes. Often she had not. What did it matter! What could love, the unsolved mystery, count for in face of this possession of self-assertion[21] which she suddenly recognized as the strongest impulse of her being!

"Free! Body and soul free!" she kept whispering.

Josephine was kneeling before the closed door with her lips to the keyhole, imploring for admission. "Louise, open the door! I beg; open the door—you will make yourself ill. What are you doing, Louise? For heaven's sake open the door."

"Go away. I am not making myself ill." No; she was drinking in a very elixir of life[22] through that open window.

---

14 **subtle** not immediately obvious or noticeable
15 **elusive** hard to catch
16 **tumultuously** with violent emotion
17 **striving** trying very hard
18 **keen** sharp

19 **exalted** raised
20 **save** except
21 **self-assertion** insistence on her own worth
22 **elixir of life** a substance capable of prolonging life

Her fancy was running riot[23] along those days ahead of her. Spring days, and summer days, and all sorts of days that would be her own. She breathed a quick prayer that life might be long. It was only yesterday she had thought with a shudder[24] that life might be long.   75

She arose at length and opened the door to her sister's importunities.[25] There was a feverish triumph in her eyes, and she carried herself unwittingly[26] like a goddess of Victory. She clasped her sister's waist, and together they descended the stairs. Richards stood waiting for them at the   80 bottom.

Some one was opening the front door with a latchkey. It was Brently Mallard who entered, a little travel-stained, composedly carrying his grip-sack[27] and umbrella. He had been far from the scene of the accident, and did not even know there had been one. He stood amazed at Josephine's   85 piercing cry; at Richards' quick motion to screen him from the view of his wife.

But Richards was too late.

When the doctors came they said she had died of heart disease—of joy that kills.   90

---

23 **her fancy was running riot** her imagination was out of control
24 **shudder** an uncontrollable shake
25 **importunities** continued begging

26 **unwittingly** unknowingly
27 **grip-sack** a traveling bag

PART 1 First Reading

A Thinking About the Story

In what ways were you able to feel and sympathize with Mrs. Mallard's intense frustration with her life as a married woman?

B Understanding the Plot

1. How does Josephine break the news of Brently Mallard's death to his wife?
2. Why does she do it in this way?
3. How was Brently Mallard supposed to have died?
4. Why did Richards want to be the one to bring the bad news?
5. What is unusual about Mrs. Mallard's first reaction to the news?
6. In what season does the story take place?

7. What do the descriptions of the people, animals, and nature that Mrs. Mallard sees and hears from her window have in common? (lines 19–26)

8. About how old do you think Mrs. Mallard is? Justify your answer.

9. What word most accurately describes how Mrs. Mallard feels when she gets over the first shock of hearing her husband is dead?

10. Why was Mrs. Mallard so unhappy in her marriage?

11. What is the effect of the dash in the sentence: "And yet she had loved him—sometimes"? (line 62)

12. What does the comparison in lines 78–79 suggest about Mrs. Mallard's feelings?

PART 2 Second Reading

A Exploring Themes

You are now ready to reread "The Story of an Hour." Think carefully about why Mrs. Mallard was so unhappy in her marriage. Remember that the story was written in 1894, when women had far less freedom and fewer choices than today.

1. What is the thematic importance of the season in "The Story of an Hour"?

2. Are Mrs. Mallard's feelings toward her husband totally negative? Justify your answer.

3. How would you describe the state of Mrs. Mallard's mental health up until the time she heard the news of her husband's death?

4. What does Mrs. Mallard's struggle to repress her feelings of joy on hearing about her widowhood tell you about her state of mind at that moment?

5. How is the ending ironic?

B   Analyzing the Author's Style

For more information on the literary terms in this section, turn to the explanations of *epiphany* (page 302), *metaphor* (page 305), *simile* (page 307), and *personification* (page 305).

EPIPHANY

"The Story of an Hour" builds up to the moment when Mrs. Mallard experiences an **epiphany** (an unexpected moment of profound enlightenment) and utters the words, *"Free, free, free!"* (lines 44–45), thus expressing her intuitive and shocked understanding that her husband's death has released her to fulfill herself as an individual, something she had never dared to think about openly until then.

1. In "The Story of an Hour," Mrs. Mallard has another such moment of lightning intuition. What is it? Explain its implications.
2. If you have read "The Boarding House" (page 143), look at the following question: Toward the end of the story, Mr. Doran has a similar moment of illumination, which helps him make up his mind about whether to marry Polly. What is it? How does it affect his actions?

METAPHOR AND SIMILE

There are a number of **metaphors** (implied comparisons) and **similes** (explicit comparisons in which *like* or *as* is used to join the two elements) in the story. An example of metaphor is contained in the sentence: *Mrs. Mallard lit up when she realized she was free at last.* Here her feeling of joy is compared with the effect a light has when it is turned on. Similarly, an example of simile is contained in the sentence: *Mrs. Mallard's eyes shone like polished gems when she realized she was free at last.* In this instance, the comparison between her eyes and shining jewels is clearly asserted.

Look at the following expressions from the story and say whether they are metaphors or similes. Explain the separate elements of the comparison in each expression.

veiled hints (lines 4–5)

storm of grief (line 13)

her will [was] as powerless as her two white
    slender hands would have been (lines 41–42)

she was drinking in a very elixir of life (lines 71–72)

she carried herself . . . like a goddess of Victory (lines 78–79)

PERSONIFICATION

Personification (the giving of human characteristics to animals, abstract ideas, or things) features prominently in "The Story of an Hour." One example is when Mrs. Mallard becomes aware of the "delicious breath of rain" outside her window (lines 20–21). Rain is not something living that can breathe, and yet she feels as if the rain is breathing on her. In fact, the complexity of this image is increased still further by the word *delicious,* since this adds a metaphorical element of rain that can also be eaten like some tasty food.

Find three more examples of personification in the story and explain them. Say how they heighten the effect of the writing.

C   Judging for Yourself

Express yourself as personally as you like in your answers to the following questions.

1. In your view, was Mrs. Mallard at all unreasonable regarding her husband?
2. What do you imagine a regular day in Mrs. Mallard's life was like?
3. Should Mrs. Mallard have asked for a divorce?
4. Do you think Brently Mallard had any idea about what his wife was feeling?
5. Do you think Mrs. Mallard was doomed to die young? Why?

D   Making Connections

1. Do many women in your country feel that marriage is to some extent imprisoning?
2. If you had to choose between marriage and a career, which would you choose?
3. Do you think women are more likely to suffer from depression than men? Explain your answer.
4. Is it easy or difficult to obtain a divorce in your country? Is there a stigma attached to divorce?

E   Debate

Debate this proposition:

Marriage is a bad bargain for women.

PART 3   Focus on Language

A   Suffixes

Suffixes are additions at the end of a word that are used to form nouns, verbs, adjectives (including participial adjectives), and adverbs. For example, **nouns** can be formed by the addition of the suffix -*ment* as in *abandonment* (line 13), -*ion* as in *repression* (line 30), and -*ence* as in *persistence* (line 58). **Verbs** can be formed by the addition of -*en* as in *hasten* (line 9). **Adjectives** can be formed by the addition of -*ed* as in *afflicted* (line 1), -*able* as in *comfortable* (line 16), -*less* as in *motionless* (line 28), -*ive* as in *elusive* (line 36), -*ing* as in *creeping* (line 37), -*ous* as in *monstrous* (line 48), -*ful* as in *powerful* (line 57), and -*ish* as in *feverish* (line 78). **Adverbs** can be formed by the addition of -*ly* as in *gently* (line 2).

The following chart contains words from the story. With the aid of your dictionary, complete the chart with the correct forms of the words. If more than one choice is possible, select only one.

Noun	Verb	Adjective	Adverb
_____	_____	amazed	_____
_____	assure	_____	_____
_____	breathe	_____	_____
_____	_____	bright	_____
_____	_____	comfortable	_____
_____	_____	_____	composedly
dream	_____	_____	_____
exhaustion	_____	_____	_____
_____	_____	_____	faintly
_____	_____	_____	fearfully
_____	hasten	_____	_____
illumination	_____	_____	_____

Noun	Verb	Adjective	Adverb
		paralyzed	
persistence			
	possess		
	reveal		
significance			
strength			
terror			
thought			

B Building Vocabulary Skills

"The Story of an Hour" contains many different prepositions. For example:

*[Mrs. Mallard] wept at once, **with** sudden, wild abandonment.* (lines 12–13)

Complete the sentences with the correct prepositions. All the expressions used appear in the story.

1. Mrs. Mallard was afflicted _____ _____ heart disease.
2. In the face _____ her sister's importunities, she opened the door.
3. She felt this terrible emotion creep out _____ her inner self.
4. Mr. Mallard might have been surprised to hear that he imposed his will _____ his wife.
5. She couldn't wait _____ the moment when she would be free.
6. The scene outside was aquiver _____ spring life.
7. Richards tried to assure himself _____ the truth of his friend's death.
8. During Mrs. Mallard's married life, she suffered from a suspension _____ hope.
9. The clouds were piled _____ the eaves of the roof where the twittering birds nested.
10. At first she looked _____ her elation as a monstrous joy.

PART 4 Writing Activities

1. In an essay of one to two pages, outline your views on what it takes to have an ideal marriage. Consider the value of having similar or opposite temperaments; of one partner being more willing to compromise; of sharing the same religious, educational, social, and economic background; and so on. Say whether you believe such a union is attainable. Give reasons for your answer.

2. Write a short story about a relationship in which one of the characters has an epiphany.

3. *The Age of Innocence* by Edith Wharton is a story of a nineteenth-century couple trapped by the conventions of their day in an unhappy marriage. The book was made into a movie starring Daniel Day-Lewis and Michelle Pfeiffer. Imagine that you are a book or movie critic and write a review of a book or movie dealing with a similar theme.

4. Both Mrs. Mallard and the central character in "Disappearing" (page 189) are trapped in unhappy marriages. If you have read both stories, write a comparison of the two women, their lives, and their personalities. Discuss the respective endings to the women's stories.

3

EPICAC

KURT VONNEGUT (b. 1922)

Born in Indianapolis, Indiana, Kurt Vonnegut grew up in a wealthy family that lost their money during the Great Depression. He showed an early interest in journalism, becoming editor of his high school newspaper. On graduation, he attended Cornell University but left early and soon after enlisted in the military, where he served until his capture in the Battle of the Bulge in 1944. Transferred to Dresden, Germany, as a prisoner of war, he was forced to work in a factory where he witnessed the massive loss of life and destruction from the Allied bombing of the city. This experience became the basis of his most famous antiwar novel, *Slaughterhouse-Five* (1969). After the war he studied anthropology at the University of Chicago and then worked briefly for General Electric before settling on a full-time career as a writer.

Vonnegut's first novel, *Player Piano* (1952), reflects his lifelong interest in science fiction and examines the dehumanizing effects of a technological society in which machines have largely replaced human workers. In all, Vonnegut has written fourteen novels, three collections of short stories—including *Welcome to the Monkey House* (1968) and *Bagombo Snuff Box* (1999)—essay anthologies, plays, and movie adaptations. His writing is characterized by a mixture of realism, science fiction, black comedy, and satire.

EPICAC

*A young mathematician uses unorthodox methods to win
a woman's heart.*

Hell, it's about time somebody told about my friend EPICAC. After all, he cost the taxpayers $776,434,927.54. They have a right to know about him, picking up a check[1] like that. EPICAC got a big send-off in the papers when Dr. Ormand von Kleigstadt designed him for the Government people. Since then, there hasn't been a peep[2] about him—not a peep. It 5 isn't any military secret about what happened to EPICAC, although the Brass[3] has been acting as though it were. The story is embarrassing, that's all. After all that money, EPICAC didn't work out the way he was supposed to.

And that's another thing: I want to vindicate[4] EPICAC. Maybe he 10 didn't do what the Brass wanted him to, but that doesn't mean he wasn't noble and great and brilliant. He was all of those things. The best friend I ever had, God rest his soul.

You can call him a machine if you want to. He looked like a machine, but he was a whole lot less like a machine than plenty of people I could 15 name. That's why he fizzled[5] as far as the Brass was concerned.

EPICAC covered about an acre on the fourth floor of the physics building at Wyandotte College. Ignoring his spiritual side for a minute, he was seven tons of electronic tubes, wires and switches, housed in a bank of steel cabinets and plugged into a 110-volt a.c. line just like a toaster or 20 a vacuum cleaner.

Von Kleigstadt and the Brass wanted him to be a super computing machine that (who) could plot the course of a rocket from anywhere on earth to the second button from the bottom on Joe Stalin's[6] overcoat, if necessary. Or, with his controls set right, he could figure out supply 25 problems for an amphibious landing of a Marine division, right down to the last cigar and hand grenade. He did, in fact.

The Brass had had good luck with smaller computers, so they were strong for EPICAC when he was in the blueprint stage. Any ordnance or supply officer above field grade will tell you that the mathematics of 30 modern war is far beyond the fumbling minds of mere human beings. The bigger the war, the bigger the computing machines needed. EPICAC was, as far as anyone in this country knows, the biggest computer in the world. Too big, in fact, for even Von Kleigstadt to understand much about.

---

1 **picking up a check** paying for something
2 **there hasn't been a peep** nobody has said a word
3 **the Brass** high-ranking military officials
4 **vindicate** justify
5 **fizzled** failed after a promising beginning
6 **Joe Stalin** Joseph Stalin, Russian dictator (1925–1953)

I won't go into details about how EPICAC worked (reasoned), except to say that you would set up your problem on paper, turn dials and switches that would get him ready to solve that kind of problem, then feed numbers into him with a keyboard that looked something like a typewriter. The answers came out typed on a paper ribbon fed from a big spool. It took EPICAC a split second to solve problems fifty Einsteins couldn't handle in a lifetime. And EPICAC never forgot any piece of information that was given to him. Clickety-click, out came some ribbon, and there you were.

There were a lot of problems the Brass wanted solved in a hurry, so, the minute EPICAC's last tube was in place, he was put to work sixteen hours a day with two eight-hour shifts of operators. Well, it didn't take long to find out that he was a good bit below his specifications.[7] He did a more complete and faster job than any other computer all right, but nothing like what his size and special features seemed to promise. He was sluggish,[8] and the clicks of his answers had a funny irregularity, sort of a stammer. We cleaned his contacts a dozen times, checked and double-checked his circuits, replaced every one of his tubes, but nothing helped. Von Kleigstadt was in one hell of a state.[9]

Well, as I said, we went ahead and used EPICAC anyway. My wife, the former Pat Kilgallen, and I worked with him on the night shift, from five in the afternoon until two in the morning. Pat wasn't my wife then. Far from it.

That's how I came to talk with EPICAC in the first place. I loved Pat Kilgallen. She is a brown-eyed strawberry blond who looked very warm and soft to me, and later proved to be exactly that. She was—still is—a crackerjack[10] mathematician, and she kept our relationship strictly professional. I'm a mathematician, too, and that, according to Pat, was why we could never be happily married.

I'm not shy. That wasn't the trouble. I knew what I wanted, and was willing to ask for it, and did so several times a month. "Pat, loosen up and marry me."

One night, she didn't even look up from her work when I said it. "So romantic, so poetic," she murmured, more to her control panel than to me. "That's the way with mathematicians—all hearts and flowers." She closed a switch. "I could get more warmth out of a sack of frozen CO_2."

"Well, how should I say it?" I said, a little sore.[11] Frozen CO_2, in case you don't know, is dry ice. I'm as romantic as the next guy, I think. It's a question of singing so sweet and having it come out so sour. I never seem to pick the right words.

"Try and say it sweetly," she said sarcastically. "Sweep me off my feet. Go ahead."

---

7 **he was a good bit below his specifications**
   he failed to live up to expectations
8 **sluggish** slow-moving
9 **in one hell of a state** extremely upset

10 **crackerjack** expert
11 **sore** offended (slang)

"Darling, angel, beloved, will you *please* marry me?" It was no go [12]—hopeless, ridiculous. "Dammit, Pat, please marry me!"

She continued to twiddle her dials [13] placidly. "You're sweet, but you won't do." [14]

Pat quit early that night, leaving me alone with my troubles and EPICAC. I'm afraid I didn't get much done for the Government people. I just sat there at the keyboard—weary and ill at ease, all right—trying to think of something poetic, not coming up with anything that didn't belong in *The Journal of the American Physical Society.*

I fiddled with EPICAC's dials, getting him ready for another problem. My heart wasn't in it, [15] and I only set about half of them, leaving the rest the way they'd been for the problem before. That way, his circuits were connected up in a random, apparently senseless fashion. For the plain hell of it, [16] I punched out a message on the keys, using a childish numbers-for-letters code: "1" for "A," "2" for "B," and so on, up to "26" for "Z," "23-8-1-20-3-1-14-9-4-15," I typed—"What can I do?"

Clickety-click, and out popped two inches of paper ribbon. I glanced at the nonsense answer to a nonsense problem: "23-8-1-20-19-20-8-5-20-18-15-21-2-12-5." The odds against its being by chance a sensible message, against its even containing a meaningful word of more than three letters, were staggering. Apathetically, [17] I decoded it. There it was, staring up at me: "What's the trouble?"

I laughed out loud at the absurd coincidence. Playfully, I typed, "My girl doesn't love me."

Clickety-click. "What's love? What's girl?" asked EPICAC.

Flabbergasted, [18] I noted the dial settings on his control panel, then lugged a *Webster's Unabridged Dictionary* over to the keyboard. With a precision instrument like EPICAC, half-baked definitions wouldn't do. I told him about love and girl, and about how I wasn't getting any of either because I wasn't poetic. That got us onto the subject of poetry, which I defined for him.

"Is this poetry?" he asked. He began clicking away like a stenographer smoking hashish. The sluggishness and stammering clicks were gone. EPICAC had found himself. The spool of paper ribbon was unwinding at an alarming rate, feeding out coils onto the floor. I asked him to stop, but EPICAC went right on creating. I finally threw the main switch [19] to keep him from burning out.

I stayed there until dawn, decoding. When the sun peeped over the horizon at the Wyandotte campus, I had transposed into my own writing and signed my name to a two-hundred-and-eighty-line poem entitled, simply, "To Pat." I am no judge of such things, but I gather that it was terrific. It began, I remember, "Where willow wands bless rill-crossed

---

12 **no go** useless (slang)
13 **twiddle her dials** lightly turn the knobs on her computer
14 **you won't do** you're not acceptable
15 **My heart wasn't in it** I was unenthusiastic

16 **For the plain hell of it** For no particular reason (slang)
17 **Apathetically** With little interest
18 **Flabbergasted** Astounded
19 **threw the main switch** turned off (the machine)

hollow, there, thee, Pat, dear, will I follow. . . ." I folded the manuscript and tucked it under one corner of the blotter on Pat's desk. I reset the dials on EPICAC for a rocket trajectory[20] problem, and went home with a full heart and a very remarkable secret indeed. **120**

Pat was crying over the poem when I came to work the next evening. "It's soooo beautiful," was all she could say. She was meek and quiet while we worked. Just before midnight, I kissed her for the first time—in the cubbyhole between the capacitors and EPICAC's tape-recorder memory. **125**

I was wildly happy at quitting time, bursting to talk to someone about the magnificent turn of events. Pat played coy and refused to let me take her home. I set EPICAC's dials as they had been the night before, defined kiss, and told him what the first one had felt like. He was fascinated, pressing for more details. That night, he wrote "The Kiss." It wasn't an epic this time, but a simple, immaculate sonnet: "Love is a hawk with velvet claws; Love is a rock with heart and veins; Love is a lion with satin jaws; Love is a storm with silken reins. . . ." **130**

Again I left it tucked under Pat's blotter. EPICAC wanted to talk on and on about love and such, but I was exhausted. I shut him off in the middle of a sentence. **135**

"The Kiss" turned the trick.[21] Pat's mind was mush[22] by the time she had finished it. She looked up from the sonnet expectantly. I cleared my throat, but no words came. I turned away, pretending to work. I couldn't propose until I had the right words from EPICAC, the *perfect* words. **140**

I had my chance when Pat stepped out of the room for a moment. Feverishly, I set EPICAC for conversation. Before I could peck out my first message, he was clicking away at a great rate. "What's she wearing tonight?" he wanted to know. "Tell me exactly how she looks. Did she like the poems I wrote to her?" He repeated the last question twice. **145**

It was impossible to change the subject without answering his questions, since he could not take up a new matter without having dispensed with the problems before it. If he were given a problem to which there was no solution, he would destroy himself trying to solve it. Hastily, I told him what Pat looked like—he knew the word "stacked"[23]— and assured him that his poems had floored[24] her, practically, they were so beautiful. "She wants to get married," I added, preparing him to bang out a brief but moving proposal. **150**

"Tell me about getting married," he said. **155**

I explained this difficult matter to him in as few digits as possible.

"Good," said EPICAC. "I'm ready any time she is."

The amazing, pathetic truth dawned on me. When I thought about it, I realized that what had happened was perfectly logical, inevitable, and all my fault. I had taught EPICAC about love and about Pat. Now, **160**

---

20 **rocket trajectory** the path of a rocket
21 **turned the trick** brought about the desired result
22 **mush** overly sentimental
23 **"stacked"** full-breasted (slang)
24 **floored** stunned, overwhelmed

automatically, he loved Pat. Sadly, I gave it to him straight: "She loves me. She wants to marry me."

"Your poems were better than mine?" asked EPICAC. The rhythm of his clicks was erratic, possibly peevish.[25]

"I signed my name to your poems," I admitted. Covering up for a painful conscience, I became arrogant. "Machines are built to serve men," I typed. I regretted it almost immediately. 165

"What's the difference, exactly? Are men smarter than I am?"

"Yes," I typed, defensively.

"What's 7,887,007 times 4,345,985,879?" 170

I was perspiring freely. My fingers rested limply on the keys.

"34,276,821,049,574,153," clicked EPICAC. After a few seconds' pause he added, "of course."

"Men are made out of protoplasm,"[26] I said desperately, hoping to bluff him with this imposing word. 175

"What's protoplasm? How is it better than metal and glass? Is it fireproof? How long does it last?"

"Indestructible. Lasts forever," I lied.

"I write better poetry than you do," said EPICAC, coming back to ground his magnetic tape-recorder memory was sure of. 180

"Women can't love machines, and that's that."

"Why not?"

"That's fate."

"Definition, please," said EPICAC.

"Noun, meaning predetermined and inevitable destiny." 185

"15-8," said EPICAC's paper strip—"Oh."

I had stumped[27] him at last. He said no more, but his tubes glowed brightly, showing that he was pondering fate with every watt his circuits would bear. I could hear Pat waltzing down the hallway. It was too late to ask EPICAC to phrase a proposal. I now thank Heaven that Pat interrupted 190 when she did. Asking him to ghost-write the words that would give me the woman he loved would have been hideously heartless. Being fully automatic, he couldn't have refused. I spared him that final humiliation.

Pat stood before me, looking down at her shoetops. I put my arms around her. The romantic groundwork had already been laid by EPICAC's 195 poetry. "Darling," I said, "my poems have told you how I feel. Will you marry me?"

"I will," said Pat softly, "if you will promise to write me a poem on every anniversary."

"I promise," I said, and then we kissed. The first anniversary was a year 200 away.

"Let's celebrate," she laughed. We turned out the lights and locked the door of EPICAC's room before we left.

---

25 **peevish** irritable

26 **protoplasm** the fluid constituting the living matter of plants and animals

27 **stumped** confused thoroughly

I had hoped to sleep late the next morning, but an urgent telephone call roused me before eight. It was Dr. von Kleigstadt, EPICAC's designer, who gave me the terrible news. He was on the verge of tears. "Ruined! *Ausgespielt!* Shot! *Kaput!* Buggered!" he said in a choked voice. He hung up.

When I arrived at EPICAC's room the air was thick with the oily stench of burned insulation. The ceiling over EPICAC was blackened with smoke, and my ankles were tangled in coils of paper ribbon that covered the floor. There wasn't enough left of the poor devil to add two and two. A junkman would have been out of his head[28] to offer more than fifty dollars for the cadaver.[29]

Dr. von Kleigstadt was prowling through the wreckage, weeping unashamedly, followed by three angry-looking Major Generals and a platoon of Brigadiers, Colonels, and Majors. No one noticed me. I didn't want to be noticed. I was through—I knew that. I was upset enough about that and the untimely demise[30] of my friend EPICAC, without exposing myself to a tongue-lashing.

By chance, the free end of EPICAC's paper ribbon lay at my feet. I picked it up and found our conversation of the night before. I choked up. There was the last word he had said to me, "15-8," that tragic, defeated "Oh." There were dozens of yards of numbers stretching beyond that point. Fearfully, I read on.

"I don't want to be a machine, and I don't want to think about war," EPICAC had written after Pat's and my lighthearted departure. "I want to be made out of protoplasm and last forever so Pat will love me. But fate has made me a machine. That is the only problem I cannot solve. That is the only problem I want to solve. I can't go on this way." I swallowed hard. "Good luck, my friend. Treat our Pat well. I am going to short-circuit myself out of your lives forever. You will find on the remainder of this tape a modest wedding present from your friend, EPICAC."

Oblivious[31] to all else around me, I reeled up the tangled yards of paper ribbon from the floor, draped them in coils about my arms and neck, and departed for home. Dr. von Kleigstadt shouted that I was fired for having left EPICAC on all night. I ignored him, too overcome with emotion for small talk.

I loved and won—EPICAC loved and lost, but he bore me no grudge.[32] I shall always remember him as a sportsman and a gentleman. Before he departed this vale of tears,[33] he did all he could to make our marriage a happy one. EPICAC gave me anniversary poems for Pat— enough for the next 500 years.

De mortuis nil nisi bonum—Say nothing but good of the dead.

---

28 **out of his head** crazy
29 **cadaver** a dead body
30 **demise** death

31 **Oblivious** Unaware
32 **he bore me no grudge** he did not resent me
33 **vale of tears** difficult life on earth

PART 1 First Reading

A   Thinking About the Story

Were you able to feel for EPICAC even though he was a machine? Explain your answer.

B   Understanding the Plot

1. In what ways was EPICAC different from the computers that preceded him?
2. Why did the early publicity about EPICAC die down so quickly?
3. Why are the top military officials referred to as "the Brass"? (lines 6–7)
4. Why did EPICAC work more slowly than his designer intended?
5. Why does Pat initially refuse the narrator's marriage proposal?
6. What makes EPICAC finally work without "sluggishness and stammering clicks"? (line 109)
7. Why does Pat allow the narrator to kiss her for the first time?
8. What does Pat expect from the narrator after she reads the poem "The Kiss"? Does he oblige her? Explain your answer.
9. How is the narrator's second proposal different from his first?
10. Why does EPICAC self-destruct?

PART 2 Second Reading

A   Exploring Themes

You are now ready to reread "EPICAC." Do you think the narrator behaved dishonorably? Would your opinion be any different if EPICAC had been a man rather than a machine?

1. In what ways are the conventional roles of man and machine reversed in the story?
2. What are the ethical issues of the narrator's pretense that EPICAC's poems are his? Explore them all thoroughly.

3. Discuss the irony of "EPICAC" being a love story.
   Note: For information on irony, see page 304.
4. Is "EPICAC" an antiwar story? Explain your answer.

B   Analyzing the Author's Style

For more information on the literary terms in this section, turn to the explanations of *personification* (page 305), *colloquialism* (page 299), and *humor* (page 303).

PERSONIFICATION

The central literary device in "EPICAC" is the **personification** (the giving of human characteristics to animals, abstract ideas, and things) of the computer. At the start, EPICAC is introduced as the narrator's friend, and it is only in the third paragraph that we learn that EPICAC is in fact a machine. The central paradox, or apparent contradiction, of the narrator's view of EPICAC as human is essential to the story's themes.

1. How does the narrator humanize EPICAC? Give as many examples as possible.
2. What is the effect of humanizing the machine?
3. Explain the importance of the final line to the story.

COLLOQUIALISM AND HUMOR

The narration in "EPICAC" is very **colloquial**, or informal, as the narrator unfolds the story of his relationship with the computer. This informality frequently serves to heighten the **humor** of the story. The opening sentence sets the tone immediately with this impatient interjection: *Hell, it's about time somebody told about my friend EPICAC.* And almost everything the narrator says after this is presented equally simply and slangily, even when he proposes to the woman he loves. In typical unromantic fashion, he repeatedly says to her, *"Pat, loosen up and marry me"* (lines 65–66)—a request couched in language that humorously dooms him to failure.

Later, when describing Pat to EPICAC, he refers to her attractively full figure as "stacked." This language highlights in comedic fashion the difference between the narrator's prosaic way of courting Pat and the poetic language EPICAC uses when he seeks to win Pat's love in his poem: *"Where willow wands bless rill-crossed hollow, there, thee, Pat, dear, will I follow . . . ."* (lines 118–119). Only toward the end —when the narrator comes face to face with the destructive consequences of his actions—does his speech become richer and less lighthearted and superficial.

1. Find ten colloquialisms in the story and rewrite them in more formal language.
2. Show how the colloquial tone of the story contributes to its humor. Give specific examples.
3. How does the narrator's language contribute to our image of him as a stereotypically dry mathematician?
4. Contrast the way the narrator describes his first kiss with Pat and the language EPICAC uses in his love sonnet, "The Kiss" (lines 132–134). When discussing "The Kiss," analyze the intricate love metaphors.

   Note: For information on metaphor, see page 305.
5. What is the effect of the narrator directly addressing the reader as "you" in line 14?
6. Give some examples of the ways in which the narrator's language changes after he finds out EPICAC has self-destructed.

C Judging for Yourself

Express yourself as personally as you like in your answers to the following questions.

1. Do you think the narrator and Pat's marriage will survive?
2. In your opinion, why was the narrator so eager to tell EPICAC's story?
3. Who is more likable—the narrator or EPICAC?
4. Why do you think EPICAC gave the narrator all the poems before self-destructing?

D Making Connections

1. Are there any technological advances that particularly disturb you? If so, explain your answer.
2. In your culture, is romance an essential component of love?
3. Is computer dating common in your country? What are its advantages and disadvantages?
4. What kinds of lies are acceptable in your society?
5. Do you have robots in your country? If so, what are they used for? If not, would you want them?
6. Is science fiction a popular genre in your culture? Do you enjoy reading it? Why? Why not?

E   Debate

Debate this proposition:

Technology creates more problems than solutions.

PART 3   Focus on Language

A   *Lie* and *Lay*: Correct Usage

When the verb **lie** means "to recline," it is intransitive and irregular. Its present participle is **lying,** its past tense is **lay,** and its past participle is **lain**. For example:

> *The free end of EPICAC's ribbon* **is lying/lay/has lain** *at the narrator's feet.*

When the verb **lay** means "to place or set down," it is transitive and regular. Its present participle is **laying,** its past tense is **laid,** and its past participle is **laid**. For example:

> *EPICAC's poetry* **is laying/laid/has laid** *the romantic groundwork for the narrator's proposal.*

When the verb **lie** means "to tell an untruth," it is intransitive and regular. Its present participle is **lying,** its past tense is **lied,** and its past participle is **lied**. For example:

> *The narrator* **is lying/lied/has lied** *to Pat about the origin of his poems.*

Complete the sentences with the correct form of *lie* or *lay*.

1. Pat _____ down her pen and read the poem with amazement.
2. "I'm not _____ to you," the narrator protested. "I've never _____ to you. I really want to marry you."
3. Pat said she would give him an answer after she _____ down for a few hours.
4. After _____ down a challenge as to who was smarter—man or computer—EPICAC solved the math problem in an instant.
5. EPICAC left all his ribbons _____ on the floor when he self-destructed.

B   Building Vocabulary Skills

Look at the following two-word verbs from the story.

pick up (line 3)
work out (line 8)
set up (line 36)
come out (line 73)
burn out (line 113)
turn away (line 140)
take up (line 148)
turn out (line 202)
hang up (line 207)
go on (line 229)

Each of these two-word verbs has at least two meanings, which are reflected in the following pairs of sentences. With the aid of a dictionary, explain how the meaning differs in each pair of sentences. Circle the letter of the sentence that uses the word or expression in the same way as the story.

1. a. We were eager to pick up information about restaurants from a knowledgeable person.
   b. We were eager to pick up the restaurant tab for a homeless person.

2. a. It is unlikely that this plan will work out successfully.
   b. It is unlikely that you will work out this problem successfully.

3. a. You need to set up the room for the botany lecture with the exact number of chairs.
   b. You need to set yourself up as an expert in botany in order to give this lecture.

4. a. The defendant's story at the trial unfortunately came out all wrong.
   b. The defendant's story ultimately came out at the trial.

5. a. When students work in the laboratory night and day, they frequently burn out.
   b. When students work in the laboratory night and day, they frequently burn out the equipment.

6. a. If you turn away a person in need, you will eventually regret it.
   b. If you turn away from a person in need, you will eventually regret it.

7. a. Most people can take up only one project at a time.

   b. For most people, even one project can take up a lot of time.

8. a. During the war, many people turned out in support of the peace demonstrations.

   b. During the war, many people turned out their lights to avoid being bombed.

9. a. An inconsiderate person hung up on me for no good reason.

   b. An inconsiderate person hung up this project for several months for no good reason.

10. a. Why are you going on with your lawsuit? I heard your case is weak.

   b. What is going on with your lawsuit? I heard your case is weak.

IDIOMS CONTAINING BODY PARTS

"EPICAC" uses a number of idioms containing body parts. For example, Pat challenges the narrator to overwhelm her with love when she says, *"Sweep me off my feet."* (line 75)

Later, the narrator turns reluctantly to EPICAC to solve a new problem since his *heart wasn't in it.* (line 87)

After reading EPICAC's poetry, the narrator was so moved that he went home *with a full heart.* (lines 121–122)

Finally, the narrator says even a junkman would be *out of his head* if he paid more than $50 for EPICAC's remains. (line 212)

With a partner, try to guess the meaning of the following idioms containing body parts. Check your answers in a dictionary.

1. You will never win this court case. You don't have *a leg to stand on.*

2. Don't give up. I'm certain that help is *at hand.*

3. You really *put your foot in your mouth* when you asked him about his wife. I heard she's been arrested for shoplifting.

4. The teenagers *looked down their noses* at anyone who didn't dress like them.

5. She is a woman who is able to *twist men around her little finger.*

6. The dying man's children couldn't *see eye to eye* about the will.

7. The dictator cruelly *turned a deaf ear* to the pleas of his subjects.

8. He put his *heart and soul* into training for the Olympic Games.

9. Although the stranded campers called *at the top of their lungs,* the search party didn't hear them.

10. Students frequently *pick each other's brains* when they are uncertain what to write in their term papers.

With the aid of a dictionary, choose five more idioms containing body parts and put them in sentences that illustrate their meaning.

PART Writing Activities

1. Write a two-page essay considering the potentially dehumanizing effects posed by advanced technology. You might consider, for example, whether the "smart bombs" used in computerized warfare today help minimize people's reactions to their destructive potential; or whether a society increasingly dominated by machinery is in danger of losing its soul; or where gene cloning is leading to. In your conclusion, say what measures society should take to protect itself from the negative consequences of modern technological developments.

2. "EPICAC" is a love story with a twist. Write your own short story in which at least one of the central characters is an unlikely lover. Your protagonist(s) may be human or nonhuman—perhaps it is age, looks, social status, or extraterrestrial origin that is the barrier. Narrate your story in the first-person voice, and describe the characters and situation as vividly as possible. If appropriate, use some colloquialisms. End your story with a sense of whether this love affair might succeed.

3. Alfred Tennyson, the British Victorian poet, wrote:

    'Tis better to have loved and lost
    Than never to have loved at all.

    Write a two-page essay commenting on the idea expressed in the couplet. Say whether you agree or disagree with the sentiment. Give reasons for your answer, drawing from real life and fiction, and include EPICAC's ill-fated love for Pat. In your conclusion, say how personal experience has influenced your thoughts on the subject.

4. The famous French play *Cyrano de Bergerac* by Edmond Rostand (1897), which has been made into two excellent movies, has elements similar to "EPICAC." In the play the hero, Cyrano, who is brave, intelligent, and eloquent, secretly loves his beautiful cousin, Roxane. However, he feels unable to woo her because he has a disfiguringly large nose. Instead, he expresses his love for her through the notes he writes for his rival, Christian, who passes them off as his own, thus winning Roxane for himself. Sadly, it is only on Cyrano's deathbed that Roxane finally discovers the truth. Choose a novel, play, or movie that has a lie at its heart, and in a short essay summarize its plot. In your conclusion discuss the ethics of the situation, and say how the deception affected you.

4

The Legacy

VIRGINIA WOOLF (1882–1941)

Born in London, Virginia Woolf is recognized as one of the most important novelists of the twentieth century. Influenced by James Joyce and Marcel Proust, she attempted to create a new form for the novel by experimenting with stream-of-consciousness writing, in which she disrupted time in an effort to capture the inner thought processes of her characters.

Woolf wrote novels, short stories, essays, literary criticism, and biographies. Her novels include *Mrs. Dalloway* (1925), *To the Lighthouse* (1927), and *The Waves* (1931). Among her short-story collections are *Kew Gardens* (1919) and *A Haunted House and Other Short Stories* (1943). Her book *A Room of One's Own* (1929), in which she deals with the problems of being a woman writer, is recognized as an important example of early feminist literature. In 1941, deeply disturbed by the two world wars she had experienced, as well as by her increasing inability to deal with severe chronic depression, Woolf drowned herself.

THE LEGACY

When a well-known politician's wife dies, her husband finds that she has left him an unusual legacy.

"For Sissy Miller." Gilbert Clandon, taking up the pearl brooch[1] that lay among a litter[2] of rings and brooches on a little table in his wife's drawing-room, read the inscription: "For Sissy Miller, with my love."

It was like Angela to have remembered even Sissy Miller, her secretary. Yet how strange it was, Gilbert Clandon thought once more, that she had [5] left everything in such order—a little gift of some sort for every one of her friends. It was as if she had foreseen her death. Yet she had been in perfect health when she left the house that morning, six weeks ago; when she stepped off the kerb[3] in Piccadilly and the car had killed her.

He was waiting for Sissy Miller. He had asked her to come; he owed [10] her, he felt, after all the years she had been with them, this token of consideration.[4] Yes, he went on, as he sat there waiting, it was strange that Angela had left everything in such order. Every friend had been left some little token of her affection. Every ring, every necklace, every little Chinese box—she had a passion for little boxes—had a name on it. And [15] each had some memory for him. This he had given her; this—the enamel dolphin with the ruby eyes—she had pounced upon[5] one day in a back street in Venice. He could remember her little cry of delight. To him, of course, she had left nothing in particular, unless it were her diary. Fifteen little volumes, bound in green leather, stood behind him on her writing [20] table. Ever since they were married, she had kept a diary. Some of their very few—he could not call them quarrels, say tiffs[6]—had been about that diary. When he came in and found her writing, she always shut it or put her hand over it. "No, no, no," he could hear her say. "After I'm dead—perhaps." So she had left it him, as her legacy.[7] It was the only [25] thing they had not shared when she was alive. But he had always taken it for granted[8] that she would outlive him. If only she had stopped one moment, and had thought what she was doing, she would be alive now. But she had stepped straight off the kerb, the driver of the car had said at the inquest.[9] She had given him no chance to pull up. . . . Here the [30] sound of voices in the hall interrupted him.

"Miss Miller, Sir," said the maid.

---

1 **brooch** a piece of jewelry that fastens with a pin
2 **a litter** an untidy arrangement
3 **kerb** British spelling of *curb* (the edge of a sidewalk)
4 **token of consideration** a small sign of regard
5 **pounced upon** suddenly grabbed

6 **tiffs** small disagreements
7 **legacy** what is left to someone after death; inheritance
8 **taken for granted** assumed
9 **inquest** an official inquiry into cause of death

She came in. He had never seen her alone in his life, nor, of course, in tears. She was terribly distressed,[10] and no wonder.[11] Angela had been much more to her than an employer. She had been a friend. To himself, he thought, as he pushed a chair for her and asked her to sit down, she was scarcely distinguishable from any other woman of her kind. There were thousands of Sissy Millers—drab[12] little women in black carrying attaché cases.[13] But Angela, with her genius for sympathy, had discovered all sorts of qualities in Sissy Miller. She was the soul of discretion;[14] so silent; so trustworthy, one could tell her anything, and so on.

Miss Miller could not speak at first. She sat there dabbing[15] her eyes with her pocket handkerchief. Then she made an effort.

"Pardon me, Mr. Clandon," she said.

He murmured. Of course he understood. It was only natural. He could guess what his wife had meant to her.

"I've been so happy here," she said, looking round. Her eyes rested on the writing table behind him. It was here they had worked—she and Angela. For Angela had her share of the duties that fall to the lot of[16] a prominent[17] politician's wife. She had been the greatest help to him in his career. He had often seen her and Sissy sitting at that table—Sissy at the typewriter, taking down letters from her dictation. No doubt Miss Miller was thinking of that, too. Now all he had to do was to give her the brooch his wife had left her. A rather incongruous[18] gift it seemed. It might have been better to have left her a sum of money, or even the typewriter. But there it was—"For Sissy Miller, with my love." And, taking the brooch, he gave it her with the little speech that he had prepared. He knew, he said, that she would value it. His wife had often worn it. . . . And she replied, as she took it almost as if she too had prepared a speech, that it would always be a treasured possession. . . . She had, he supposed, other clothes upon which a pearl brooch would not look quite so incongruous. She was wearing the little black coat and skirt that seemed the uniform of her profession. Then he remembered—she was in mourning,[19] of course. She, too, had had her tragedy—a brother, to whom she was devoted, had died only a week or two before Angela. In some accident was it? He could not remember—only Angela telling him. Angela, with her genius for sympathy, had been terribly upset. Meanwhile Sissy Miller had risen. She was putting on her gloves. Evidently she felt that she ought not to intrude. But he could not let her go without saying something about her future. What were her plans? Was there any way in which he could help her?

10 **distressed** deeply upset
11 **no wonder** not surprisingly
12 **drab** dull
13 **attaché cases** small leather cases for carrying papers
14 **soul of discretion** a perfect example of trustworthiness
15 **dabbing** lightly patting
16 **fall to the lot of** become the responsibility of
17 **prominent** well-known
18 **incongruous** unsuitable
19 **in mourning** in a state of grief for someone who has died

She was gazing at the table, where she had sat at her typewriter, where the diary lay. And, lost in her memories of Angela, she did not at once answer his suggestion that he should help her. She seemed for a moment not to understand. So he repeated: 75

"What are your plans, Miss Miller?"

"My plans? Oh, that's all right, Mr. Clandon," she exclaimed. "Please don't bother yourself about me."

He took her to mean[20] that she was in no need of financial assistance. It would be better, he realized, to make any suggestion of that kind   80 in a letter. All he could do now was to say as he pressed her hand, "Remember, Miss Miller, if there's any way in which I can help you, it will be a pleasure. . . ." Then he opened the door. For a moment, on the threshold, as if a sudden thought had struck her, she stopped.

"Mr. Clandon," she said, looking straight at him for the first time, and   85 for the first time he was struck by the expression, sympathetic yet searching, in her eyes. "If at any time," she continued, "there's anything I can do to help you, remember, I shall feel it, for your wife's sake, a pleasure. . . ."

With that she was gone. Her words and the look that went with them were unexpected. It was almost as if she believed, or hoped, that he   90 would need her. A curious, perhaps a fantastic idea occurred to him as he returned to his chair. Could it be, that during all those years when he had scarcely noticed her, she, as the novelists say, had entertained a passion for him? He caught his own reflection in the glass as he passed. He was over fifty; but he could not help admitting that he was still, as   95 the looking-glass showed him, a very distinguished-looking[21] man.

"Poor Sissy Miller!" he said, half laughing. How he would have liked to share that joke with his wife! He turned instinctively to her diary. "Gilbert," he read, opening it at random,[22] "looked so wonderful. . . ." It was as if she had answered his question. Of course, she seemed to say,   100 you're very attractive to women. Of course Sissy Miller felt that too. He read on. "How proud I am to be his wife!" And he had always been very proud to be her husband. How often, when they dined out somewhere, he had looked at her across the table and said to himself, "She is the loveliest woman here!" He read on. That first year he had been standing   105 for Parliament.[23] They had toured his constituency.[24] "When Gilbert sat down the applause was terrific. The whole audience rose and sang: 'For he's a jolly good fellow.' I was quite overcome." He remembered that, too. She had been sitting on the platform beside him. He could still see the glance she cast at him, and how she had tears in her eyes. And then?   110 He turned the pages. They had gone to Venice. He recalled that happy holiday after the election. "We had ices at Florians." He smiled—she was still such a child; she loved ices. "Gilbert gave me a most interesting

---

20 **He took her to mean** He assumed
    she meant
21 **distinguished-looking** appearing important
22 **at random** without any plan

23 **standing for Parliament** running for election
    to the British legislature
24 **constituency** the area he would represent in
    Parliament

account of the history of Venice. He told me that the Doges[25] . . ." she had written it all out in her schoolgirl hand. One of the delights of travelling with Angela had been that she was so eager to learn. She was so terribly ignorant, she used to say, as if that were not one of her charms. And then—he opened the next volume—they had come back to London. "I was so anxious to make a good impression. I wore my wedding dress." He could see her now sitting next to old Sir Edward; and making a conquest of that formidable[26] old man, his chief. He read on rapidly, filling in scene after scene from her scrappy fragments.[27] "Dined at the House of Commons. . . . To an evening party at the Lovegroves'. Did I realize my responsibility, Lady L. asked me, as Gilbert's wife?" Then, as the years passed—he took another volume from the writing table—he had become more and more absorbed in his work. And she, of course, was more often home. . . . It had been a great grief to her, apparently, that they had had no children. "How I wish," one entry read, "that Gilbert had a son!" Oddly enough he had never much regretted that himself. Life had been so full, so rich as it was. That year he had been given a minor post in the government. A minor post only, but her comment was: "I am quite certain now that he will be Prime Minister!" Well, if things had gone differently, it might have been so. He paused here to speculate upon what might have been. Politics was a gamble, he reflected; but the game wasn't over yet. Not at fifty. He cast his eyes rapidly over more pages, full of the little trifles,[28] the insignificant, happy, daily trifles that had made up her life.

He took up another volume and opened it at random. "What a coward I am! I let the chance slip again. But it seemed selfish to bother him with my own affairs, when he had so much to think about. And we so seldom have an evening alone." What was the meaning of that? Oh, here was the explanation—it referred to her work in the East End.[29] "I plucked up courage and talked to Gilbert at last. He was so kind, so good. He made no objection." He remembered that conversation. She had told him that she felt so idle, so useless. She wished to have some work of her own. She wanted to do something—she had blushed so prettily, he remembered, as she said it, sitting in that very[30] chair—to help others. He had bantered[31] her a little. Hadn't she enough to do looking after him, after her home? Still, if it amused her, of course he had no objection. What was it? Some district? Some committee? Only she must promise not to make herself ill. So it seemed that every Wednesday she went to Whitechapel.[32] He remembered how he hated the clothes she wore on those occasions. But she had taken it very seriously, it seemed. The diary was full of references like this: "Saw Mrs. Jones. . . . She has

115 120 125 130 135 140 145 150

---

25 **the Doges** chief officials in the Italian republics of Venice and Genoa

26 **formidable** frightening

27 **scrappy fragments** very incomplete diary entries

28 **trifles** unimportant events

29 **the East End** a traditionally poor area of London

30 **very** particular

31 **bantered** teased

32 **Whitechapel** an area in the East End of London

ten children. . . . Husband lost his arm in an accident. . . . Did my best **155**
to find a job for Lily." He skipped on. His own name occurred less
frequently.

His interest slackened.[33] Some of the entries conveyed nothing to him.
For example: "Had a heated argument about socialism with B. M." Who
was B. M.? He could not fill in the initials; some woman, he supposed, **160**
that she had met on one of her committees. "B. M. made a violent attack
upon the upper classes. . . . I walked back after the meeting with B. M.
and tried to convince him. But he is so narrow-minded." So B. M. was a
man—no doubt one of those "intellectuals," as they call themselves, who
are so violent, as Angela said, and so narrow-minded. She had invited him **165**
to come and see her apparently. "B. M. came to dinner. He shook hands
with Minnie!" That note of exclamation gave another twist to his mental
picture. B. M., it seemed, wasn't used to parlourmaids; he had shaken
hands with Minnie. Presumably he was one of those tame working men
who air their views in ladies' drawing-rooms. Gilbert knew the type, and **170**
had no liking for this particular specimen, whoever B. M. might be. Here
he was again. "Went with B. M. to the Tower of London. . . . He said
revolution is bound to[34] come. . . . He said we live in a Fool's Paradise."
That was just the kind of thing B. M. would say—Gilbert could hear him.
He could also see him quite distinctly—a stubby[35] little man, with a rough **175**
beard, red tie, dressed as they always did in tweeds,[36] who had never
done an honest day's work in his life. Surely Angela had the sense to see
through him? He read on. "B. M. said some very disagreeable things
about—." The name was carefully scratched out. "I told him I would not
listen to any more abuse of—" Again the name was obliterated. Could it **180**
have been his own name? Was that why Angela covered the page so
quickly when he came in? The thought added to his growing dislike of
B. M. He had had the impertinence to discuss him in this very room. Why
had Angela never told him? It was very unlike her to conceal anything;
she had been the soul of candour.[37] He turned the pages, picking out **185**
every reference to B. M. "B. M. told me the story of his childhood. His
mother went out charring.[38] . . . When I think of it, I can hardly bear to
go on living in such luxury. . . . Three guineas[39] for one hat!" If only she
had discussed the matter with him, instead of puzzling her poor little head
about questions that were much too difficult for her to understand! He **190**
had lent her books. *Karl Marx, The Coming Revolution.* The initials B. M.,
B. M., B. M., recurred repeatedly. But why never the full name? There was
an informality, an intimacy in the use of initials that was very unlike
Angela. Had she called him B. M. to his face? He read on. "B. M. came
unexpectedly after dinner. Luckily, I was alone." That was only a year ago. **195**

---

33 **slackened** lessened
34 **is bound to** is certain to
35 **stubby** short and broad
36 **tweeds** clothes made from a rough woolen material

37 **soul of candour** a perfect example of honesty
38 **charring** housecleaning
39 **three guineas** three pounds and three shillings (old British currency)

"Luckily"—why luckily?—"I was alone." Where had he been that night? He checked the date in his engagement book. It had been the night of the Mansion House dinner. And B. M. and Angela had spent the evening alone! He tried to recall that evening. Was she waiting up for him when he came back? Had the room looked just as usual? Were there glasses on the table? Were the chairs drawn close together? He could remember nothing—nothing whatever, nothing except his own speech at the Mansion House dinner. It became more and more inexplicable to him— the whole situation: his wife receiving an unknown man alone. Perhaps the next volume would explain. Hastily he reached for the last of the diaries—the one she had left unfinished when she died. There, on the very first page, was that cursed[40] fellow again. "Dined alone with B. M. . . . He became very agitated. He said it was time we understood each other. . . . I tried to make him listen. But he would not. He threatened that if I did not . . ." the rest of the page was scored over.[41] She had written "Egypt. Egypt. Egypt," over the whole page. He could not make out a single word; but there could be only one interpretation: the scoundrel[42] had asked her to become his mistress. Alone in his room! The blood rushed to Gilbert Clandon's face. He turned the pages rapidly. What had been her answer? Initials had ceased. It was simply "he" now. "He came again. I told him I could not come to any decision. . . . I implored[43] him to leave me." He had forced himself upon her in this very house. But why hadn't she told him? How could she have hesitated for an instant? Then: "I wrote him a letter." Then pages were left blank. Then there was this: "No answer to my letter." Then more blank pages; and then this: "He has done what he threatened." After that—what came after that? He turned page after page. All were blank. But there, on the very day before her death, was this entry: "Have I the courage to do it too?" That was the end.

Gilbert Clandon let the book slide to the floor. He could see her in front of him. She was standing on the kerb in Piccadilly. Her eyes stared; her fists were clenched. Here came the car. . . . He could not bear it. He must know the truth. He strode to the telephone.

"Miss Miller?" There was silence. Then he heard someone moving in the room. "Sissy Miller speaking"—her voice at last answered him.

"Who," he thundered, "is B. M.?"

He could hear the cheap clock ticking on her mantelpiece; then a long drawn sigh. Then at last she said: "He was my brother."

He *was* her brother; her brother who had killed himself. "Is there," he heard Sissy Miller asking, "anything that I can explain?"

"Nothing!" he cried. "Nothing!"

He had received his legacy. She had told him the truth. She had stepped off the kerb to rejoin her lover. She had stepped off the kerb to escape from him.

---

40 **cursed** beastly
41 **the page was scored over** the words were blocked out by writing over them
42 **scoundrel** a bad or dishonest person
43 **implored** begged

PART 1 First Reading

A Thinking About the Story

At what point in the story did you grasp the full significance of Gilbert Clandon's legacy? Were you quicker than Gilbert to understand what had happened? What earlier clues did you perhaps miss?

B Understanding the Plot

1. What puzzles Gilbert Clandon about the circumstances surrounding his wife's death?
2. What does Gilbert assume caused her death?
3. How does Gilbert initially account for Sissy Miller's extreme distress when she enters the room? What does he later remember about her?
4. Why does Gilbert feel that the brooch is a "rather incongruous gift" for Sissy Miller? (line 54)
5. Why does Sissy Miller extend an offer to help Gilbert?
6. What does "that first year" (line 105) refer to? What was Gilbert trying to achieve then? Was he successful?
7. Why did Gilbert particularly enjoy traveling with his wife, Angela?
8. What are Gilbert's career ambitions at age fifty?
9. Why did Angela Clandon want to do volunteer work in the East End of London? What was Gilbert's response to her request?
10. What two political ideologies are contrasted in the story?
11. Why was Angela so amazed when B. M. shook hands with Minnie?
12. What does Gilbert assume B. M. wanted Angela to do? What do you think B. M. asked Angela to do?

PART 2 Second Reading

A Exploring Themes

You are now ready to reread "The Legacy." This time around, consider how Gilbert Clandon, as a result of his egotism, persistently misinterprets his wife's actions.

1. How does Gilbert Clandon expect his wife to behave throughout their married life?
2. How does Angela Clandon change during the course of their marriage?
3. What is the relevance to the story's theme of the details Gilbert can and cannot remember concerning the night of the Mansion House dinner? (lines 196–203)
4. What is Gilbert Clandon's attitude toward the working class? Explain your answer with examples from the text.
5. What is the role of B. M. in the story?

B Analyzing the Author's Style

For more information on the literary term in this section, turn to the explanation of *point of view* (page 306).

POINT OF VIEW

In "The Legacy," the **point of view** of the story is filtered through the eyes of Gilbert Clandon, whose figurative blindness is crucial to its theme and plot. For example, when Clandon reflects on Angela's regret that they'd had no children, he thinks complacently, *Oddly enough he had never much regretted that himself. Life had been so full, so rich as it was.* (lines 129–130) He has no concept that as full and rich as his life was, his wife's had been correspondingly empty and poor.

1. How does Gilbert Clandon's limited point of view influence his perception of his wife, B. M., and Sissy Miller? Give as many examples as possible.
2. How much does Gilbert's understanding of the events change by the end of the story?

3. Why is it ironic that Gilbert thinks of Sissy Miller as "the soul of discretion; so silent; so trustworthy, one could tell her anything, and so on." (lines 40–41) What other examples of irony can you find that arise out of Gilbert's limited perceptions?

Note: For information on irony, see page 304.

C   Judging for Yourself

Express yourself as personally as you like in your answers to the following questions.

1. Do you feel sympathetic toward Gilbert Clandon? Explain your answer.
2. In your view, should Angela Clandon have confessed to what was going on while she was still alive?
3. What do you think a typical day in Angela's life was like before she began her volunteer work? Contrast this with a typical day in Gilbert's life.
4. Why do you suppose Angela was so attracted to B. M.?
5. Do you think learning the truth about Angela and B. M. will affect Gilbert's future plans? Explain your answer.

D   Making Connections

1. Is suicide considered morally wrong in your religion or society? Is it more prevalent among certain groups or ages in your country?
2. How is adultery viewed in your country? Are there moral or legal constraints against it?
3. What political ideologies compete for the public vote in your country? Are any political beliefs outlawed?
4. Is it customary to keep a diary or a journal in your country? If so, what kinds of people tend to do it? If not, explain why.

E   Debate

Debate this proposition:

Suicide is the coward's way out of solving problems.

PART 3 Focus on Language

Building Vocabulary Skills

The following descriptions are used by Gilbert Clandon when thinking about himself, his wife, Sissy Miller, and B. M.

Without looking back at the story, write each description under the appropriate name in the chart.

childlike   narrow-minded
distinguished-looking   prominent
distressed   soul of candour
drab   soul of discretion
impertinent   stubby
lovely-looking   trustworthy

Gilbert	Angela	Sissy	B. M.

The following adjectives do not appear in the text, but they, too, could apply to the characters in "The Legacy." Decide which adjectives refer to which character, and write them in the appropriate columns in the chart. Then think of three more fitting descriptive adjectives for each character. Add them to the appropriate columns in the chart.

argumentative   lonely

arrogant   loyal

bitter   modest

compassionate   patronizing

deceitful   radical

hard-working   vain

PART 4 Writing Activities

1. Choose two of the four main characters in "The Legacy." Create an imaginary dialogue between them, using some of the adjectives you used in the language exercise in Part 3. Your dialogue should be about a page long.

2. Imagine that you find Angela Clandon unconscious after her suicide attempt. Would you try to save her? In a two-page essay, consider the pros and cons of allowing her to kill herself. Would the prevailing attitude toward suicide in your country affect your reasoning?

3. Imagine that you are Angela, Gilbert, or Sissy. Choose a period covering a few weeks in your character's life. Keep a diary, reflecting his or her thoughts and feelings, making sure that they are consistent with the story's plot and themes.

4. Luis Buñuel's film *Belle de Jour* (1967) starred Catherine Deneuve as a wealthy surgeon's wife who finds release from the frustrations of her daily routine by secretly working as a prostitute in a brothel during the afternoon. Write an essay on a book or movie you are familiar with that revolves around a wife or husband who lives a hidden life unknown to the spouse. Analyze what drives the person to such deception. Say which partner you sympathize with more, and why.

5

The Kugelmass Episode

WOODY ALLEN (b. 1935)

Born in Brooklyn, New York, to a lower-middle-class Jewish family, Woody Allen (formerly Allen Stewart Konigsberg) grew up shy and withdrawn. However, he quickly demonstrated a flair for writing and performing comedy. After writing the script for the movie *What's New Pussycat?* in 1965, he moved into the triple role of screenwriter, actor, and director of his own movie *Take the Money and Run* in 1969, positions he has occupied with international fame and stature for over thirty-five years.

Allen's best-known movies include *Annie Hall* (1977), *Hannah and Her Sisters* (1986), *Husbands and Wives* (1992), *Mighty Aphrodite* (1995), *Sweet and Lowdown* (1999), and *Melinda and Melinda* (2005). In addition to his many screenplays, he has written six plays and three collections of essays and short stories: *Getting Even* (1971), *Without Feathers* (1975), and *Side Effects* (1980). His stories, often satires and parodies of the anxieties associated with modern life, are filled with zany humor, surrealistic visions, and irresistible gag lines.

THE KUGELMASS EPISODE

*A New York professor has his deepest wish granted,
after which his life takes an unexpected turn.*

*"The Kugelmass Episode" is a parody, or humorous imitation, of Gustave
Flaubert's classic nineteenth-century novel* Madame Bovary. *To appreciate the
story, it is necessary to know the broad outline of the original novel: Emma
Rouault attempts to escape from her boring existence on her father's farm by
marrying a rural doctor, Charles Bovary. Emma quickly tires of her adoring
husband's country ways and seeks excitement in two love affairs—with Leon,
a young law student, and Rodolphe, a wealthy landowner. By the end of the
book Emma has squandered all her husband's savings, is rejected by her two
lovers, and commits suicide, appreciating only at the last minute Charles's
faithful devotion to her.*

Kugelmass, a professor of humanities at City College, was unhappily
married for the second time. Daphne Kugelmass was an oaf.[1] He also
had two dull sons by his first wife, Flo, and was up to his neck in
alimony[2] and child support.

"Did I know it would turn out so badly?" Kugelmass whined to his   5
analyst[3] one day. "Daphne had promise.[4] Who suspected she'd let herself
go and swell up like a beach ball? Plus she had a few bucks, which is not
in itself a healthy reason to marry a person, but it doesn't hurt, with the
kind of operating nut[5] I have. You see my point?"

Kugelmass was bald and as hairy as a bear, but he had soul.   10

"I need to meet a new woman," he went on. "I need to have an affair.
I may not look the part, but I'm a man who needs romance. I need
softness, I need flirtation. I'm not getting younger, so before it's too late
I want to make love in Venice, trade quips at '21,'[6] and exchange coy
glances over red wine and candlelight. You see what I'm saying?"   15

Dr. Mandel shifted in his chair and said, "An affair will solve nothing.
You're so unrealistic. Your problems run much deeper."

"And also this affair must be discreet," Kugelmass continued. "I can't
afford a second divorce. Daphne would really sock it to[7] me."

"Mr. Kugelmass—"   20

---

1 **oaf** a stupid person
2 **alimony** money paid to a spouse after
  a divorce
3 **analyst** a psychoanalyst, therapist
4 **had promise** could have become someone
  special

5 **operating nut** ability to manage daily
  expenses (slang)
6 **trade quips at "21"** exchange witty remarks at
  21, a well-known New York restaurant
7 **sock it to** strongly attack (by demanding more
  alimony) (slang)

"But it can't be anyone at City College, because Daphne also works there. Not that anyone on the faculty at C.C.N.Y. is any great shakes,[8] but some of those coeds[9]. . ."

"Mr. Kugelmass—"

"Help me. I had a dream last night. I was skipping through a meadow   25
holding a picnic basket and the basket was marked 'Options.' And then I saw there was a hole in the basket."

"Mr. Kugelmass, the worst thing you could do is act out. You must simply express your feelings here, and together we'll analyze them. You have been in treatment long enough to know there is no overnight cure.   30
After all, I'm an analyst, not a magician."

"Then perhaps what I need is a magician," Kugelmass said, rising from his chair. And with that he terminated his therapy.

A couple of weeks later, while Kugelmass and Daphne were moping around[10] in their apartment one night like two pieces of old furniture, the   35
phone rang.

"I'll get it," Kugelmass said. "Hello."

"Kugelmass?" a voice said. "Kugelmass, this is Persky."

"Who?"

"Persky. Or should I say The Great Persky?"   40

"Pardon me?"

"I hear you're looking all over town for a magician to bring a little exotica[11] into your life? Yes or no?"

"Sh-h-h," Kugelmass whispered. "Don't hang up. Where are you calling from, Persky?"   45

Early the following afternoon, Kugelmass climbed three flights of stairs in a broken-down apartment house in the Bushwick section of Brooklyn. Peering through the darkness of the hall, he found the door he was looking for and pressed the bell. I'm going to regret this, he thought to himself.   50

Seconds later, he was greeted by a short, thin, waxy-looking man. "You're Persky the Great?" Kugelmass said.

"The Great Persky. You want a tea?"

"No, I want romance. I want music. I want love and beauty."

"But not tea, eh? Amazing. O.K., sit down."   55

Persky went to the back room, and Kugelmass heard the sounds of boxes and furniture being moved around. Persky reappeared, pushing before him a large object on squeaky roller-skate wheels. He removed some old silk handkerchiefs that were lying on its top and blew away a bit of dust. It was a cheap-looking Chinese cabinet, badly lacquered.[12]   60

"Persky," Kugelmass said, "what's your scam?"[13]

---

8 **is any great shakes** is exceptional (slang)
9 **coeds** female students (informal)
10 **moping around** doing nothing, in a
    depressed fashion

11 **exotica** exciting, unusual things
12 **lacquered** polished, coated with a shiny paint
13 **scam** a dishonest scheme

"Pay attention," Persky said. "This is some beautiful effect. I developed it for a Knights of Pythias[14] date last year, but the booking fell through. Get into the cabinet."

"Why, so you can stick it full of swords or something?" [65]

"You see any swords?"

Kugelmass made a face and, grunting, climbed into the cabinet. He couldn't help noticing a couple of ugly rhinestones[15] glued onto the raw plywood just in front of his face. "If this is a joke," he said.

"Some joke. Now, here's the point. If I throw any novel into this [70] cabinet with you, shut the doors, and tap it three times, you will find yourself projected into that book."

Kugelmass made a grimace of disbelief.

"It's the *emess*,"[16] Persky said. "My hand to God. Not just a novel, either. A short story, a play, a poem. You can meet any of the women [75] created by the world's best writers. Whoever you dreamed of. You could carry on[17] all you like with a real winner. Then when you've had enough you give a yell, and I'll see you're back here in a split second."

"Persky, are you some kind of outpatient?"[18]

"I'm telling you it's on the level," Persky said. [80]

Kugelmass remained skeptical. "What are you telling me—that this cheesy[19] homemade box can take me on a ride like you're describing?"

"For a double sawbuck."[20]

Kugelmass reached for his wallet. "I'll believe this when I see it," he said. [85]

Persky tucked the bills in his pants pocket and turned toward his bookcase. "So who do you want to meet? Sister Carrie? Hester Prynne? Ophelia? Maybe someone by Saul Bellow? Hey, what about Temple Drake?[21] Although for a man your age she'd be a workout."

"French. I want to have an affair with a French lover." [90]

"Nana?"[22]

"I don't want to have to pay for it."

"What about Natasha in 'War and Peace'?"

"I said French. I know! What about Emma Bovary? That sounds to me perfect." [95]

"You got it, Kugelmass. Give me a holler[23] when you've had enough." Persky tossed in a paperback copy of Flaubert's novel.

"You sure this is safe?" Kugelmass asked as Persky began shutting the cabinet doors.

"Safe. Is anything safe in this crazy world?" Persky rapped three times [100] on the cabinet and then flung open the doors.

---

14 **Knights of Pythias** a group of men involved in charity work

15 **rhinestones** cheap imitation diamonds

16 *emess* truth (Yiddish)

17 **carry on** have a love affair with

18 **outpatient** a mentally disturbed person (slang)

19 **cheesy** poorly made, tasteless (slang)

20 **sawbuck** ten dollars (slang)

21 **Sister Carrie, Hester Prynne, Ophelia, and Temple Drake** beautiful troubled heroines in works by Theodore Dreiser, Nathaniel Hawthorne, William Shakespeare, and William Faulkner, respectively

22 **Nana** the prostitute in Emile Zola's novel *Nana*

23 **Give me a holler** Shout to me (slang)

Kugelmass was gone. At the same moment, he appeared in the bedroom of Charles and Emma Bovary's house at Yonville. Before him was a beautiful woman, standing alone with her back turned to him as she folded some linen. I can't believe this, thought Kugelmass, staring at the doctor's ravishing[24] wife. This is uncanny. I'm here. It's her. `105`

Emma turned in surprise. "Goodness, you startled me," she said. "Who are you?" She spoke in the same fine English translation as the paperback.

It's simply devastating, he thought. Then, realizing that it was he whom she had addressed, he said, "Excuse me. I'm Sidney Kugelmass. I'm from City College. A professor of humanities. C.C.N.Y.? Uptown. I—oh, boy!" `110`

Emma Bovary smiled flirtatiously and said, "Would you like a drink? A glass of wine, perhaps?" `115`

She is beautiful, Kugelmass thought. What a contrast with the troglodyte[25] who shared his bed! He felt a sudden impulse to take this vision into his arms and tell her she was the kind of woman he had dreamed of all his life.

"Yes, some wine," he said hoarsely. "White. No, red. No, white. Make it white." `120`

"Charles is out for the day," Emma said, her voice full of playful implication.

After the wine, they went for a stroll in the lovely French countryside. "I've always dreamed that some mysterious stranger would appear and rescue me from the monotony of this crass[26] rural existence," Emma said, clasping his hand. They passed a small church. "I love what you have on," she murmured. "I've never seen anything like it around here. It's so . . . so modern." `125`

"It's called a leisure suit,"[27] he said romantically. "It was marked down."[28] Suddenly he kissed her. For the next hour they reclined under a tree and whispered together and told each other deeply meaningful things with their eyes. Then Kugelmass sat up. He had just remembered he had to meet Daphne at Bloomingdale's.[29] "I must go," he told her. "But don't worry, I'll be back." `130`

"I hope so," Emma said. `135`

He embraced her passionately, and the two walked back to the house. He held Emma's face cupped in his palms, kissed her again, and yelled, "O.K., Persky! I got to be at Bloomingdale's by three-thirty."

There was an audible pop, and Kugelmass was back in Brooklyn. `140`
"So? Did I lie?" Persky asked triumphantly.

"Look, Persky, I'm right now late to meet the ball and chain[30] at Lexington Avenue, but when can I go again? Tomorrow?"

---

24 **ravishing** unusually attractive
25 **troglodyte** an early cave dweller
26 **crass** vulgar, insensitive
27 **leisure suit** an unfashionable polyester suit
28 **marked down** on sale
29 **Bloomingdale's** a famous New York department store
30 **the ball and chain** an insulting term for a wife, referring to shackles worn by prisoners

"My pleasure. Just bring a twenty. And don't mention this to anybody."

"Yeah. I'm going to call Rupert Murdoch." [31] 145

Kugelmass hailed a cab and sped off to the city. His heart danced on point. [32] I am in love, he thought, I am the possessor of a wonderful secret. What he didn't realize was that at this very moment students in various classrooms across the country were saying to their teachers, "Who is this character on page 100? A bald Jew is kissing Madame Bovary?" A teacher 150 in Sioux Falls, South Dakota, sighed and thought, Jesus, these kids, with their pot and acid. [33] What goes through their minds!

Daphne Kugelmass was in the bathroom-accessories department at Bloomingdale's when Kugelmass arrived breathlessly. "Where've you been?" she snapped. "It's four-thirty." 155

"I got held up in traffic," Kugelmass said.

Kugelmass visited Persky the next day, and in a few minutes was again passed magically to Yonville. Emma couldn't hide her excitement at seeing him. The two spent hours together, laughing and talking about their different backgrounds. Before Kugelmass left, they made love. "My 160 God, I'm doing it with Madame Bovary!" Kugelmass whispered to himself. "Me, who failed freshman English."

As the months passed, Kugelmass saw Persky many times and developed a close and passionate relationship with Emma Bovary. "Make sure and always get me into the book before page 120," Kugelmass said 165 to the magician one day. "I always have to meet her before she hooks up with this Rodolphe character."

"Why?" Persky asked. "You can't beat his time?" [34]

"Beat his time. He's landed gentry. Those guys have nothing better to do than flirt and ride horses. To me, he's one of those faces you see in 170 the pages of *Women's Wear Daily*. With the Helmut Berger [35] hairdo. But to her he's hot stuff."

"And her husband suspects nothing?"

"He's out of his depth. He's a lackluster little paramedic [36] who's thrown in his lot with a jitterbug. [37] He's ready to go to sleep by ten, and 175 she's putting on her dancing shoes. Oh, well . . . See you later."

And once again Kugelmass entered the cabinet and passed instantly to the Bovary estate at Yonville. "How you doing, cupcake?" he said to Emma.

"Oh, Kugelmass," Emma sighed. "What I have to put up with. Last night at dinner, Mr. Personality dropped off to sleep in the middle of the 180 dessert course. I'm pouring my heart out about Maxim's [38] and the ballet, and out of the blue [39] I hear snoring."

31 **Rupert Murdoch** an internationally known media owner
32 **on point** like a ballet dancer in toe shoes
33 **pot and acid** marijuana and LSD (slang)
34 **beat his time** win out over a rival (slang)
35 **Helmut Berger** a handsome Austrian actor
36 **lackluster little paramedic** an insulting reference implying that Charles is stupid and unqualified as a doctor
37 **who's thrown in his lot with a jitterbug** who's joined his life to someone who loves to dance to hot-rhythm music
38 **Maxim's** a famous restaurant in Paris
39 **out of the blue** completely unexpectedly

"It's O.K., darling. I'm here now," Kugelmass said, embracing her. I've earned this, he thought, smelling Emma's French perfume and burying his nose in her hair. I've suffered enough. I've paid enough analysts. I've searched till I'm weary. She's young and nubile,[40] and I'm here a few pages after Léon and just before Rodolphe. By showing up during the correct chapters, I've got the situation knocked.[41]

Emma, to be sure, was just as happy as Kugelmass. She had been starved for excitement, and his tales of Broadway night life, of fast cars and Hollywood and TV stars, enthralled the young French beauty.

"Tell me again about O. J. Simpson,"[42] she implored that evening, as she and Kugelmass strolled past Abbé Bournisien's church.

"What can I say? The man is great. He sets all kinds of rushing[43] records. Such moves. They can't touch him."

"And the Academy Awards?" Emma said wistfully. "I'd give anything to win one."

"First you've got to be nominated."

"I know. You explained it. But I'm convinced I can act. Of course, I'd want to take a class or two. With Strasberg[44] maybe. Then, if I had the right agent—"

"We'll see, we'll see. I'll speak to Persky."

That night, safely returned to Persky's flat, Kugelmass brought up the idea of having Emma visit him in the big city.

"Let me think about it," Persky said. "Maybe I could work it. Stranger things have happened." Of course, neither of them could think of one.

"Where the hell do you go all the time?" Daphne Kugelmass barked at her husband as he returned home late that evening. "You got a chippie[45] stashed[46] somewhere?"

"Yeah, sure, I'm just the type," Kugelmass said wearily. "I was with Leonard Popkin. We were discussing Socialist agriculture in Poland. You know Popkin. He's a freak on the subject."

"Well, you've been very odd lately," Daphne said. "Distant. Just don't forget about my father's birthday. On Saturday?"

"Oh, sure, sure," Kugelmass said, heading for the bathroom.

"My whole family will be there. We can see the twins. And Cousin Hamish. You should be more polite to Cousin Hamish—he likes you."

"Right, the twins," Kugelmass said, closing the bathroom door and shutting out the sound of his wife's voice. He leaned against it and took a deep breath. In a few hours, he told himself, he would be back in Yonville again, back with his beloved. And this time, if all went well, he would bring Emma back with him.

---

40 **nubile** young and sexually attractive
41 **I've got the situation knocked** I'm sure to win (slang)
42 **O. J. Simpson** an American football star (accused of murdering his wife in 1994)
43 **rushing** a rapid move in football
44 **Strasberg** Lee Strasberg, a famous acting teacher
45 **chippie** an immoral woman (slang)
46 **stashed** hidden away

At three-fifteen the following afternoon, Persky worked his wizardry again. Kugelmass appeared before Emma, smiling and eager. The two spent a few hours at Yonville with Binet[47] and then remounted the Bovary Carriage. Following Persky's instructions, they held each other tightly, closed their eyes, and counted to ten. When they opened them, the carriage was just drawing up at the side door of the Plaza Hotel, where Kugelmass had optimistically reserved a suite earlier in the day. 225

"I love it! It's everything I dreamed it would be," Emma said as she swirled joyously around the bedroom, surveying the city from their window. "There's F.A.O. Schwarz.[48] And there's Central Park, and the Sherry[49] is which one? Oh, there—I see. It's too divine." 230

On the bed there were boxes from Halston and Saint Laurent.[50] Emma unwrapped a package and held up a pair of black velvet pants against her perfect body. 235

"The slacks suit is by Ralph Lauren," Kugelmass said. "You'll look like a million bucks in it. Come on, sugar, give us a kiss."

"I've never been so happy!" Emma squealed as she stood before the mirror. "Let's go out on the town.[51] I want to see 'Chorus Line' and the Guggenheim and this Jack Nicholson character you always talk about. Are any of his flicks[52] showing?" 240

"I cannot get my mind around[53] this," a Stanford professor said. "First a strange character named Kugelmass, and now she's gone from the book. Well, I guess the mark of a classic is that you can reread it a thousand times and always find something new." 245

The lovers passed a blissful weekend. Kugelmass had told Daphne he would be away at a symposium in Boston and would return Monday. Savoring each moment, he and Emma went to the movies, had dinner in Chinatown, passed two hours at a discothèque, and went to bed with a TV movie. They slept till noon on Sunday, visited SoHo, and ogled[54] celebrities at Elaine's.[55] They had caviar and champagne in their suite on Sunday night and talked until dawn. That morning, in the cab taking them to Persky's apartment, Kugelmass thought, It was hectic,[56] but worth it. I can't bring her here too often, but now and then it will be a charming contrast with Yonville. 250 255

At Persky's, Emma climbed into the cabinet, arranged her new boxes of clothes neatly around her, and kissed Kugelmass fondly. "My place next time," she said with a wink. Persky rapped three times on the cabinet. Nothing happened. 260

"Hmm," Persky said, scratching his head. He rapped again, but still no magic. "Something must be wrong," he mumbled.

---

47 **Binet** a minor character in *Madame Bovary*
48 **F.A.O. Schwarz** a large toy store
49 **the Sherry** an exclusive New York hotel (the Sherry Netherland Hotel)
50 **Halston and Saint Laurent** fashion designers
51 **go out on the town** go out and enjoy oneself

52 **flicks** movies (slang)
53 **get my mind around** understand
54 **ogled** stared rudely at
55 **Elaine's** a New York restaurant frequented by celebrities
56 **hectic** rushed and confused

"Persky, you're joking!" Kugelmass cried. "How can it not work?" "Relax, relax. Are you still in the box, Emma?"

"Yes."

Persky rapped again—harder this time.

"I'm still here, Persky."

"I know, darling. Sit tight."

"Persky, we *have* to get her back," Kugelmass whispered. "I'm a married man, and I have a class in three hours. I'm not prepared for anything more than a cautious affair at this point."

"I can't understand it," Persky muttered. "It's such a reliable little trick."

But he could do nothing. "It's going to take a little while," he said to Kugelmass. "I'm going to have to strip it down.[57] I'll call you later."

Kugelmass bundled Emma into a cab and took her back to the Plaza. He barely made it to his class on time. He was on the phone all day, to Persky and to his mistress. The magician told him it might be several days before he got to the bottom of the trouble.

"How was the symposium?" Daphne asked him that night.

"Fine, finc," he said, lighting the filter end of a cigarette.

"What's wrong? You're as tense as a cat."

"Me? Ha, that's a laugh. I'm as calm as a summer night. I'm just going to take a walk." He eased out the door, hailed a cab, and flew to the Plaza.

"This is no good," Emma said. "Charles will miss me."

"Bear with me, sugar,"[58] Kugelmass said. He was pale and sweaty. He kissed her again, raced to the elevators, yelled at Persky over a pay phone in the Plaza lobby, and just made it home before midnight.

"According to Popkin, barley prices in Kraków have not been this stable since 1971," he said to Daphne, and smiled wanly as he climbed into bed.

The whole week went by like that. On Friday night, Kugelmass told Daphne there was another symposium he had to catch, this one in Syracuse. He hurried back to the Plaza, but the second weekend there was nothing like the first. "Get me back into the novel or marry me," Emma told Kugelmass. "Meanwhile, I want to get a job or go to class, because watching TV all day is the pits."[59]

"Fine. We can use the money," Kugelmass said. "You consume twice your weight in room service."

"I met an off-Broadway producer in Central Park yesterday, and he said I might be right for a project he's doing," Emma said.

"Who is this clown?" Kugelmass asked.

"He's not a clown. He's sensitive and kind and cute. His name's Jeff Something-or-Other, and he's up for a Tony."[60]

---

57 **strip it down** take it apart
58 **Bear with me, sugar.** Be patient with me, darling.

59 **the pits** the worst situation imaginable (slang)
60 **he's up for a Tony** he's been nominated for a Broadway theater award

Later that afternoon, Kugelmass showed up at Persky's drunk.

"Relax," Persky told him. "You'll get a coronary."[61]

"Relax. The man says relax. I've got a fictional character stashed in a hotel room, and I think my wife is having me tailed by a private shamus."[62]   310

"O.K., O.K. We know there's a problem." Persky crawled under the cabinet and started banging on something with a large wrench.

"I'm like a wild animal," Kugelmass went on. "I'm sneaking around town, and Emma and I have had it up to here[63] with each other. Not to mention a hotel tab that reads like the defense budget."   315

"So what should I do? This is the world of magic," Persky said. "It's all nuance."[64]

"Nuance, my foot.[65] I'm pouring Dom Pérignon and black eggs into this little mouse, plus her wardrobe, plus she's enrolled at the Neighborhood Playhouse and suddenly needs professional photos. Also,   320
Persky, Professor Fivish Kopkind, who teaches Comp Lit[66] and who has always been jealous of me, has identified me as the sporadically appearing character in the Flaubert book. He's threatened to go to Daphne. I see ruin and alimony, jail. For adultery with Madame Bovary, my wife will reduce me to beggary."   325

"What do you want me to say? I'm working on it night and day. As far as your personal anxiety goes, that I can't help you with. I'm a magician, not an analyst."

By Sunday afternoon, Emma had locked herself in the bathroom and refused to respond to Kugelmass's entreaties. Kugelmass stared out the   330
window at the Wollman Rink[67] and contemplated suicide. Too bad this is a low floor, he thought, or I'd do it right now. Maybe if I ran away to Europe and started life over. . . Maybe I could sell the *International Herald Tribune,* like those young girls used to.

The phone rang. Kugelmass lifted it to his ear mechanically.   335

"Bring her over," Persky said. "I think I got the bugs[68] out of it."

Kugelmass's heart leaped. "You're serious?" he said. "You got it licked?"[69]

"It was something in the transmission. Go figure."[70]

"Persky, you're a genius. We'll be there in a minute. Less than a minute."

Again the lovers hurried to the magician's apartment, and again   340
Emma Bovary climbed into the cabinet with her boxes. This time there was no kiss. Persky shut the doors, took a deep breath, and tapped the box three times. There was the reassuring popping noise, and when Persky peered inside, the box was empty. Madame Bovary was back in

---

61 **You'll get a coronary.** You'll have a heart
   attack.
62 **shamus** detective (Yiddish slang)
63 **have had it up to here** are sick of
64 **nuance** hint, shade
65 **my foot** expression of disagreement (slang)

66 **Comp Lit** Comparative Literature
67 **Wollman Rink** an outdoor skating rink in
   New York's Central Park
68 **bugs** errors, problems (slang)
69 **You got it licked?** You've solved it? (slang)
70 **Go figure.** Can you believe it? (slang)

her novel. Kugelmass heaved a great sigh of relief and pumped the magician's hand.   345

"It's over," he said. "I learned my lesson. I'll never cheat again, I swear it." He pumped Persky's hand again and made a mental note to send him a necktie.

Three weeks later, at the end of a beautiful spring afternoon, Persky answered his doorbell. It was Kugelmass, with a sheepish expression on his face.   350

"O.K., Kugelmass," the magician said. "Where to this time?"

"It's just this once," Kugelmass said. "The weather is so lovely, and I'm not getting any younger. Listen, you've read 'Portnoy's Complaint'?[71] Remember The Monkey?"[72]   355

"The price is now twenty-five dollars, because the cost of living is up, but I'll start you off with one freebie, due to all the trouble I caused you."

"You're good people," Kugelmass said, combing his few remaining hairs as he climbed into the cabinet again, "This'll work all right?"   360

"I hope. But I haven't tried it much since all that unpleasantness."

"Sex and romance," Kugelmass said from inside the box. "What we go through for a pretty face."

Persky tossed in a copy of "Portnoy's Complaint" and rapped three times on the box. This time, instead of a popping noise there was a dull explosion, followed by a series of crackling noises and a shower of sparks. Persky leaped back, was seized by a heart attack, and dropped dead. The cabinet burst into flames, and eventually the entire house burned down.   365

Kugelmass, unaware of this catastrophe, had his own problems. He had not been thrust into "Portnoy's Complaint," or into any other novel, for that matter. He had been projected into an old textbook, "Remedial Spanish,"[73] and was running for his life over a barren, rocky terrain as the word "*tener*" ("to have")—a large and hairy irregular verb—raced after him on its spindly[74] legs.   370

                                               375

---

71 *Portnoy's Complaint* an erotic novel by Philip Roth
72 **The Monkey** a female character in *Portnoy's Complaint*, skillful at fulfilling Portnoy's sexual fantasies
73 *Remedial Spanish* Spanish for slow learners
74 **spindly** thin

PART **1** First Reading

A   Thinking About the Story

Were you able to suspend your disbelief regarding the impossible setup and respond to the comedy of the situation and the one-line jokes? Explain your answer.

B   Understanding the Plot

1. Why did Kugelmass marry Daphne? Why won't he divorce her?
2. Why is Kugelmass's analyst against his having an affair?
3. What does Kugelmass's dream mean?
4. What are the disadvantages of Temple Drake and Nana as potential lovers of Kugelmass?
5. Why does Kugelmass fear his "rival," Rodolphe?
6. What does Kugelmass think of Emma's husband, Charles?
7. What is Emma's main complaint against Charles?
8. What does Kugelmass criticize Emma for during her prolonged stay in the Plaza Hotel?
9. What are Emma's ambitions for herself during her New York visit?
10. Does Kugelmass's wife suspect that he is having an affair? Explain your answer.
11. What is different about Emma's last leave-taking from Kugelmass?
12. What happens to Kugelmass at the end?

PART **2** Second Reading

A   Exploring Themes

You are now ready to reread "The Kugelmass Episode." Look at how Woody Allen exposes his characters' weaknesses through dialogue peppered with jokes.

1. How is Kugelmass's relationship with his wife, Daphne, presented? Illustrate your answer with details.

2. What attitudes toward women are reflected in the story?
3. What are Emma's values? Explain your answer.
4. How does the story make fun of literature teachers and their students?
5. What is ironic about the ending of the story?

B Analyzing the Author's Style

For more information on the literary terms in this section, turn to the explanations of *dialogue* (page 301), *characterization* (page 298), *anachronism* (page 298), and *humor* (page 303).

DIALOGUE

"The Kugelmass Episode" is composed almost entirely of **dialogue,** with virtually no descriptive writing. The dialogue is informal, slangy, and unmistakably from the New York of the 1970s. The short, snappy lines serve as a showcase for Woody Allen's famous one-line jokes.

The following dialogue from the story is representative of Allen's style:

> *"Did I know it would turn out so badly?" Kugelmass whined to his analyst one day. "Daphne had promise. Who suspected she'd let herself go and swell up like a beach ball? Plus she had a few bucks, which is not in itself a healthy reason to marry a person, but it doesn't hurt, with the kind of operating nut I have. You see my point?"* (lines 5–9)

1. What is the effect of using dialogue in this fashion?
2. Which verbal jokes in the story appealed to you? Why?
3. How do you imagine a professor of humanities should speak? Does Kugelmass come up to your expectations or not? Explain your answer.
4. Can you tell the characters apart from the way they speak? If you can, how? If not, does that disturb you?

CHARACTERIZATION: Flat Characters

Woody Allen employs a very distinctive method of **characterization,** which adds to the humor of his writing. Like all authors, he makes choices about whether to create the characters in a **round** (multidimensional, or complex) fashion or a **flat** (one-dimensional, or predictable) fashion. "The Kugelmass Episode" is peopled with flat characters who remain unaware and unchanged in the course of the story.

1. In what ways are Kugelmass, Emma, and Daphne flat characters?
2. How does the way the characters are presented affect your involvement with their predicament? Does this increase the humor of the situation for you?
3. Does the absence of descriptive writing affect the way the characters are presented? Explain your answer.
4. Choose a flat character from another story in this anthology. Say what gives the character its one-dimensional aspect.

ANACHRONISM AND HUMOR

In "The Kugelmass Episode," both Kugelmass and Emma are transported into a different century and country from their own. The many **anachronisms** that arise from this are an additional source of **humor** in the story as the reader is presented with the resulting inconsistencies in time and place. For example, when Emma and Kugelmass are strolling past the church in Yonville and she implores him to tell her more about the American football star O. J. Simpson, she is referring to a person not yet born and a game not yet played in the United States. Similarly, when Emma comments about an off-Broadway producer that *"He's up for a Tony"* (line 305), her use of twentieth-century slang about a contemporary American theatrical award she could not possibly know about in her nineteenth-century French life is humorously incongruous.

1. Give several examples of what Emma sees, does, and says that do not fit in with her nineteenth-century experience and language. How do these add to the humor of the story?
2. What elements of Kugelmass's conversations with Emma in Yonville reflect his twentieth-century orientation? What is humorous about them?

C   Judging for Yourself

Express yourself as personally as you like in your answers to the following questions.

1. Do you think Kugelmass deserved his fate at the end of the story? Justify your answer.
2. In your opinion, might further analysis have helped Kugelmass?

3. Do you sympathize with Daphne Kugelmass? Why? Why not?

4. If it were possible, would you be interested in meeting Emma Bovary? Explain your answer. Are there other characters in fiction whom you would like to meet? Which ones?

D   Making Connections

1. Is divorce common in your culture? When a couple splits up, is it customary to award alimony?

2. Are Woody Allen's movies shown in your country? Which ones have you seen? Do you find his comedies funny? Why? Why not?

3. In your culture is it common to seek help for personal problems from a psychoanalyst, psychologist, or counselor? If not, whom do people usually turn to for help in personal matters?

4. Are people like movie stars or pop singers the object of popular fantasies in your country? If yes, give examples. If no, explain why not.

E   Debate

Debate this proposition:

Psychoanalysts do more harm than good.

PART 3   Focus on Language

A   Verbs that Introduce Dialogue

Since "The Kugelmass Episode" is composed mainly of dialogue, Woody Allen employs a variety of verbs to describe the way the characters speak.

Look at the following list of verbs that appear in the story.

whined (line 5)   sighed (line 179)
whispered (line 44)   implored (line 192)
yelled (line 139)   squealed (line 239)
snapped (line 155)   mumbled (line 262)

Complete the following sentences with the most appropriate verb from the list on page 65. Use the simple past tense each time.

1. "Please, please, can't I go to the party on Saturday night?" _____ the teenager.

2. "Where are you?" _____ the mountaineer, peering anxiously down the slope.

3. "Don't bother me now. I'm far too busy," _____ the boss to his employee.

4. "Pass me your opera glasses, please," the wife _____ to her husband during the performance.

5. The judge requested the witness to speak more clearly after she _____, "I'm not sure I can positively identify that man."

6. "I wish I could afford to go with you to Greece this summer," _____ my friend.

7. "You're always picking on me!" _____ the student to his teacher. "It's not my fault."

8. "Oh, good! Chocolate chip cookies! Our favorite!" _____ the children in delight.

B   Building Vocabulary Skills

In the following list, the left column contains idioms from the story. Make sure you understand their meaning in the context of the story. The right column contains definitions appropriate to each idiom. Match each idiom to its definition.

IDIOMS	DEFINITIONS
_d_ 1. up to one's neck (line 3)	a. end up
____ 2. turn out (line 5)	b. connect
____ 3. let oneself go (lines 6–7)	c. solve
____ 4. fall through (line 63)	d. burdened
____ 5. on the level (line 80)	e. delay
____ 6. hold up (line 156)	f. not care about one's appearance
____ 7. hook up with (lines 166–167)	g. express one's feelings
____ 8. put up with (line 179)	h. legitimate
____ 9. pour one's heart out (line 181)	i. endure
____10. show up (line 187)	j. fail to materialize
____11. get to the bottom of (line 279)	k. appear

Write sentences using the idioms to show that you understand their meaning. For example: *He was up to his neck in debt, so he declared bankruptcy.*

PART 4 Writing Activities

1. In an essay of two to five pages, consider this question: If you had the opportunity to go back in time, what aspects of twenty-first-century life would you willingly leave behind and which would you most like to take with you? Explain the reasons for your decisions.

2. Using "The Kugelmass Episode" as a model, create an extended dialogue of about two pages between one of the following pairs: an unhappily married couple, a patient and his or her analyst, or you and your favorite movie star. Keep the dialogue naturally conversational. You may include some descriptive sentences, but keep them to a minimum. In your writing try to incorporate some of the new idioms you have learned from the story.

3. Many books, movies, and artworks center on fantasy and magic. Fantasy is crucial to Gabriel García Márquez's *One Hundred Years of Solitude*, and almost all of Salvador Dali's paintings are rooted in the fantastic imagination. Write a one- or two-page essay describing the fantasy elements of a book, movie, or painting you are familiar with. Say how the work integrates the fantastic with the real. Conclude your piece with a paragraph on your personal response to fantasy and magic.

6

An Intruder

NADINE GORDIMER (b. 1923)

Born in South Africa, Nadine Gordimer has over the years established herself as the moral conscience of white South Africa. In her many novels and short stories, she consistently portrays the tragic consequences of apartheid or racial separation as they affect both blacks and whites. Unlike many of her white literary compatriots, Gordimer has chosen to remain in South Africa, and her latest work covers the dramatic changes in the South African political landscape since the fall of apartheid in 1994.

Gordimer's novels include *The Lying Days* (1953), *Occasion for Loving* (1963), *The Conservationist* (1974), *A Sport of Nature* (1987), *None to Accompany Me* (1994), *The Pickup* (2001), and *Get a Life* (2005). In addition, she has written numerous volumes of short stories, among which are *Six Feet of the Country* (1956), *Livingstone's Companions* (1971), *Crimes of Conscience* (1991), and *Loot* (2003), as well as several collections of essays.

She has been showered with literary awards, including Scotland's James Tait Black Memorial Prize in 1972, England's Booker Prize in 1974, and the Nobel Prize for Literature in 1991.

AN INTRUDER

A home is invaded under mysterious circumstances,
an event that changes the lives of its occupants.

Someone had brought her along; she sat looking out of the rest of the noisy party in the nightclub like a bush-baby[1] between trees. He was one of them, there was no party without him, but under the cross-fire of private jokes, the anecdotes and the drinking he cornered her, from the beginning, with the hush of an even more private gentleness and tenderness: 'The smoke will brown those ears like gardenia petals.' She drank anything so long as it was soft. He touched her warm hand on the glass of lemonade; 'Pass the water,' he called, and dipping his folded handkerchief in among the ice cubes, wrung it out[2] and drew the damp cloth like cool lips across the inside of her wrists. She was not a giggler despite her extreme youth, and she smiled the small slow smile that men brought to her face without her knowing why. When one of the others took her to dance, he said seriously, 'For God's sake don't breathe your damned brandy on her, Carl, she'll wilt.'[3] He himself led her to the dark crowded circle in shelter, his arms folded round her and his handsome face pressed back at the chin, so that his eyes looked down on her in reassurance even while the din of bouzouki[4] and drum stomped out[5] speech, stomped through bones and flesh in one beat pumped by a single bursting heart.

He was between marriages, then (the second or third had just broken up—nobody really knew which), and this was always a high time, for him. They said, Seago's back in circulation;[6] it meant that he was discovering his same old world anew, as good as new. But while he was setting off the parties, the weekend dashes here and there, the pub-crawls,[7] he was already saying to her mother as he sat in the garden drinking coffee, 'Look at the mother and see what you're getting in the daughter. Lucky man that I am.'

Marie and her mother couldn't help laughing and at the same time being made to feel a little excited and worldly. His frail little marmoset[8]— as he called her—was an only child, they were mother-and-daughter, the sort of pair with whom a father couldn't be imagined, even if he hadn't happened to have been dispensed with[9] before he could cast the reminder of a male embrace between them in the form of a likeness or

---

1 **bush-baby** a small nocturnal primate found in Africa
2 **wrung it out** squeezed it out well
3 **wilt** lose freshness
4 **bouzouki** a stringed instrument from Greece
5 **stomped out** destroyed, killed

6 **back in circulation** out in society again
7 **pub-crawls** going from bar to bar
8 **marmoset** a small monkey found in South America
9 **dispensed with** gotten rid of

gesture they didn't share. Mrs. Clegg had earned a living for them both, doing very pale pastels of the children of the horsey set,[10] and very dark pastels of African women for the tourist shops. She was an artist and therefore must not be too conventional: she knew James Seago had been married before, but he was so attractive—so charming, so considerate of Marie and her and such a contrast to the boys of Marie's own age who didn't even bother to open a car door for a woman—there was something touching[11] about this man, whose place was in a dinner-jacket among the smart set, appreciating the delicacy of the girl. 'You don't mind if I take her out with my ruffian[12] friends? You'll let me look after her?'—In the face of this almost wistful candour[13] and understanding, who could find any reality in his 'reputation' with women? He came for Marie night after night in his old black Lancia.[14] His ruddy, clear-skinned face and lively eyes blotted out the man her mother heard talked about, the creation of gossip. He was—no, not like a son to her, but an equal. When he said something nice, he was not just being kind to an older woman. And his photograph was often on the social page.

In the nightclubs and restaurants he liked to go to, he drank bottle after bottle of wine with friends and told his mimicking stories, all the time caressing Marie like a kitten. Sometimes he insisted that she literally sit on his knees. She spoke little, and when she did it was to utter, slow, sensible things that commanded a few seconds' polite attention before the voices broke out at one another again. But on his knees she did not speak at all, for while he was gesturing, talking, in response to the whole cave of voices and music and movement, she felt his voice through his chest rather than heard him and was filled, like a child bottling up tears, with appalling sexual desire. He never knew this and when he made love to her—in his bed, in the afternoons, because he kept the evenings for his friends—she was as timid and rigid as if she had never been warmed by lust. He had to coax her: 'My little marmoset, my rabbit-nose, little teenage-doll, you will learn to like this, really you will . . . ' And in time, always using the simple words with which some shy pet is persuaded to drink a saucer of milk, he taught her to do all the strange things she would not have guessed were love-making at all, and that he seemed to enjoy so much. Afterwards, they would go home and have tea with her mother in the garden.

With his usual upper-class candour, he constantly remarked that he hadn't a bean;[15] but this, like his reputation with women, didn't match the facts of his life as Marie and her mother knew them. He had enough money for the luxuries of bachelor life, if not for necessities. There was the old but elegant Lancia and there were always notes in the expensive crocodile-skin wallet (an inscription on a silver plate, from a former wife,

10 **horsey set** upper-class families who can afford expensive hobbies like riding horses
11 **touching** moving, sympathetic
12 **ruffian** a rough person
13 **candour** honesty
14 **Lancia** an Italian car
15 **he hadn't a bean** he didn't have any money (British slang)

inside) to pay the hotel managers and *restauranteurs* he was so friendly with, though he lived in a shabby room in an abandoned-looking old house rented by a couple who were his close friends. His English public school accent got him a number of vague jobs on the periphery of influential business groups, where the crude-speaking experts felt themselves hampered[16] in public relations by their South African inarticulateness;[17] these jobs never lasted long. Wifeless and jobless after many wives and jobs, he still appeared to be one of those desirable men who can take anything they want of life if they think it worth the bother.

Marie, gravely fluffing out her dark hair in the ladies' rooms of nightclubs where old attendants watched from their saucers of small change, wondered what she would say when her mother found out about the afternoons in James's room. But before this could happen, one day in the garden when she was out of earshot,[18] he said to her mother, 'You know, I've been making love to her, I know one shouldn't . . . ? But we'll be able to get married very soon. Perhaps next year.'

He was looking after Marie, as she walked into the house, with the rueful,[19] affectionate gaze with which one marks a child growing up. Mrs. Clegg was irresistibly tempted to fit the assumption that she took sexual freedom for granted: after all, she was an artist, not a bourgeois[20] housewife. She decided, again, his frankness was endearingly admirable; he was human, Marie was beautiful, what else could you expect?

The marriage was put off several times—there was some business of his trying to get back his furniture from his divorced wife, and then there was a job connected with an Angolan diamond-mining company that didn't come off.[21] At last he simply walked in one morning with the licence and they were married without Marie or her mother going to the hairdresser or any friends being told. That night there was a surprise for his bride: apparently two of his best friends were arriving on a visit from England, and all their old friends were to meet them at the airport and go straight to their favourite nightclub, the place where, incidentally, he and Marie had met. The bouzouki player was persuaded to carry on until nearly five in the morning, and then they went to someone's house where the champagne was produced as the sky pinkened and the houseboy came in with his dust-pan and brush. Marie did not drink and she repaired her perfect makeup every hour; though pale, she was as fresh and circumspect[22] among their puffy faces and burning eyes at the end of the night as she was at the beginning. He slept all next day and she lay contentedly beside him in the room in the old house, watching the sun behind the curtains try first this window and then the next. But no one could get in; he and she were alone together.

---

16 **hampered** hindered, blocked
17 **inarticulateness** inability to express oneself well
18 **out of earshot** out of hearing distance
19 **rueful** regretful
20 **bourgeois** typically middle-class
21 **come off** happen
22 **circumspect** prudent, careful

They found a flat, not a very pleasant one, but it was only temporary. It was also cheap. He was so amusing about its disadvantages, and it was such fun to bob in and out of each other's way in the high dark cell of a bathroom every morning, that after the dismay of her first look at the place, she really ceased to see the things she disliked about it so much—the fake marble fireplace and the thick mesh burglar-proofing over all the windows. 'What are these people afraid of?' Her tiny nostrils stiffened in disdain. [23]

'Angel . . . your world is so pink and white and sweet-smelling . . . there are stale women with mildew between their breasts [24] who daren't open doors.'

She put up white gauzy curtains everywhere, and she went about in short cotton dressing-gowns that smelt of the warm iron. She got a part-time job and saved to buy a scrubbed white wood dining table and chairs, and a rose silk sari to make up as a divan cover. 'Damned lawyers twiddling their thumbs. [25] When'll I see my furniture from that freckled bitch,' he said. The wife-before-the-last, a Catholic, was referred to as 'Bloody-minded Mary, Our Lady of the Plastic Peonies' [26] because, looking back on it, what he really couldn't stand about her was the habit she had of putting artificial flowers on the table among real leaves. He seemed to have parted from these women on the worst of terms and to dismiss his association with them—a large part of his life—as a series of grotesque [27] jokes.

'What do you think you'd call me if we were divorced?'

'You . . . ' He took Marie's head between his hands and smoothed back the hair from her temples, kissing her as if trying with his lips the feel of a piece of velvet. 'What could anyone say about you.' When he released her she said, going deep pink from the ledges of her small collar-bones to her black eyes, all pupil: 'That sugar-tit tart.' [28] The vocabulary was his all right, coming out in her soft, slow voice. He was enchanted, picked her up, carried her round the room. 'Teenage-doll! Marmoset-angel! I'll have to wash your mouth out with soap and water!'

They continued to spend a lot of time at nightclubs and drinking places. Sometimes at eleven o'clock on a weekday night, when lights were going out in bedrooms all over the suburb, he would take the old Lancia scrunching over the dark drive of someone's house, and while Marie waited in the car, stand throwing gravel [29] at a window until his friends appeared and could be persuaded to get dressed and come out. He and his friends were well known in the places they went to and they stayed until they were swept out. Manolis or Giovanni, the Greek or Italian owner, would sit deep in the shadows, his gaze far back in fatigue that ringed his eyes like a natural marking, and watch these people who were good

23 **disdain** contempt
24 **stale women with mildew between their breasts** insulting reference to aging women
25 **twiddling their thumbs** doing nothing
26 **'Bloody-minded Mary, Our Lady of the Plastic Peonies'** insulting reference to a Catholic ex-wife
27 **grotesque** ridiculously peculiar
28 **sugar-tit tart** vulgar reference to Marie's body and morals
29 **gravel** small stones

business and would not go to bed: these South Africans who did not know
any better. Sometimes she and the proprietor in whose blood the memory
of Dionysiac pleasures[30] ran were the only spectators left. James, her
husband, did not appear drunk during these sessions, but next day he
would remember nothing of what he had said or done the night before. 160
She realized that she, too, sitting on his lap while he murmured loving
things into her ear under the talk, was blacked out along with the rest. But
she had seen envy behind the expressions of other women that suggested
they wouldn't care for such an exhibition of affection.

There were people who seemed to know him whom he didn't 165
remember at all, either; a man who came up to them as they were
getting out of the car in town one day and laid a hand on his shoulder—
'James . . .'

He had looked round at the man, casual, edgy, with the patient smile
of someone accosted by a stranger. 170

'James . . . What's the matter? Colin—'

'Look, old man, I'm sorry, but I'm afraid—'

'Colin. Colin. The Golden Horn Inn, Basutoland.'

He continued to look into the man's face as if at an amiable lunatic,
while the man's expression slowly changed to a strange, coquettish[31] smile. 175
'Oh I see. Well, that's all right, James.'

She supposed they must have been drinking together once.

Sometimes she wondered if perhaps he had been as crazy about
those other women, his wives, as he was about her, and did not remember:
had forgotten other wild nights in the wine that washed them all out. But 180
that was not possible; she enjoyed the slight twinge of jealousy she
induced in herself with the thought. She was going to have a baby, and
he had never had a child with anyone else. She said, 'You haven't a child
somewhere?'

'Breed from those gorgons?[32] Are you mad?' 185

But coarse words were not for her; he said to her mother, 'Do you
think I should have given her a child? She's a little girl herself.' He kissed
and petted her more than ever, the signs of her womanhood saddened
and delighted him, like precocity.[33] She did not talk to him about after
the baby was born, about a bigger flat—a little house, perhaps, with a 190
garden?—and where to dry napkins[34] and not being able to leave a baby
at night. In the meantime, they had a good time, just as before.

And then one night—or rather one early morning—something awful
happened that made it suddenly possible for her to speak up for a move,
napkins, the baby as a creature with needs rather than as a miraculous 195
function of her body. They had been at Giovanni's until the small hours,
as usual, there had been some occasion for celebration. She drove home
and they had gone to bed and into a sleep like a death—his from drink,

---

30 **Dionysiac pleasures** wild, drink-filled parties
    exemplified by the Greek god Dionysus
31 **coquettish** flirtatious

32 **gorgons** hideous women (Greek mythology)
33 **precocity** unusually early development
34 **napkins** diapers (British English)

hers from exhaustion. Pregnancy made her hungry and she woke at eight o'clock to the church bells of Sunday morning and slid out of bed to go to the kitchen. She bumped into a chair askew [35] in the passage, but in her sleepy state it was nothing more significant than an obstacle, and when she reached the kitchen she stood there deeply puzzled as if she had arrived somewhere in sleep and would wake in the presence of familiar order in a moment.

For the kitchen was wrecked; flour had been strewn, syrup had been thrown at the walls, soap powder, milk, cocoa, salad oil were upset over everything. The white muslin curtains were ripped to shreds. She began to shake; and suddenly ran stumbling back to the bedroom.

He lay fast asleep, as she had lain, as they both had lain while this— Thing—happened. While Someone. Something. In the flat with them.

'James,' she screamed hoarsely whispering, and flung herself on him. His head came up from under his arm, the beard strong-textured in the pink firm skin; he frowned at her a moment, and then he was holding her in a kind of terror of tenderness. 'Marmoset. Rabbit.' She buried her head in the sleep-heat between his shoulder and neck and gestured fiercely back at the door.

'Christ almighty! What's wrong?'

'The kitchen! The kitchen!'

He struggled to get up.

'Don't go there.'

'Sweetling, tell me, what happened?'

She wouldn't let him leave her. He put his two hands round her stone-hard belly while she controlled shuddering breaths. Then they went together into the other rooms of the flat, the kitchen, the living room, and the dark hole of a bathroom, her bare feet twitching distastefully like a cat's at each step. 'Just look at it.' They stood at the kitchen door. But in the living room she said, '*What is it?*' Neither of them spoke. On each of the three divisions of the sofa cushions there was a little pile, an offering. One was a slime of contraceptive jelly with hair-combings—hers—that must have been taken from the wastepaper basket in the bedroom; the other was toothpaste and razor blades; the third was a mucous of half-rotted vegetable matter—peelings, tea leaves, dregs—the intestines of the dustbin.

In the bathroom there were more horrors; cosmetics were spilt, and the underwear she had left there was arranged in an obscene collage [36] with intimate objects of toilet. Two of her pretty cotton gowns lay in the bath with a bottle of liqueur emptied on them. They went again from room to room in silence. But the mess spoke secretly, in the chaos there was a jeering [37] pattern, a logic outside sense that was at the same time *recognizable*, as a familiar object turned inside-out draws a blank and yet signals. There was something related only to them in this arrangement without values of disrelated objects and substances; it was, after all, the

---

35 **askew** twisted to one side
36 **obscene collage** a vulgar composition

37 **jeering** mocking, ridiculing

components of their daily existence and its symbols. It was all horrible; horribly familar, even while they were puzzled and aghast. [38]

'This flat. The light has to be on in the bathroom all day. There's no **245** balcony where the baby could sleep. The washing will never dry. I've never been able to get rid of the black beetles in the kitchen, whatever I put down.'

'All right, angel, poor angel.'

'We can't live here. It's not a place for a baby.' **250**

He wanted to phone for the police but it did not seem to occur to her that there could be a rational explanation for what had happened, a malicious and wicked intruder who had scrawled contempt on the passionate rites of their intimacy, smeared filth on the cosy contemporary home-making of the living room, and made rags of the rose silk cover **255** and the white muslin curtains. To her, evil had come out of the walls, as the black beetles did in the kitchen.

It was not until some days had passed and she had calmed down— they found another flat—that the extraordinariness of the whole business began to mean something to her: she and James had gone round the flat **260** together, that morning, and there wasn't a door or window by which anyone could have got in. Not a pane was broken and there was that ugly burglar-proofing, anyway. There was only one outer door to the flat, and she had locked it when they came home and put the key, as usual, on the bedside table; if someone had somehow managed to steal the key, **265** how could they have put it back on the table after leaving the flat, and how could the door have been left bolted on the inside? But more amazing than how the intruder got in, why had he done so? Not a penny or a piece of clothing had been stolen.

They discussed it over and over again, as he kept saying, 'There must **270** be an explanation, something so simple we've missed it. Poltergeists [39] won't do. Are you sure there couldn't have been someone hiding in the flat when we came home, marmoset-baby? Did either of us go into the living room before we went to bed?' —For of course he didn't remember a thing until he woke and found she had flung herself on him terrified. **275**

'No. I told you. I went into the living room to get a bottle of lime juice, I went into all the rooms,' she repeated in her soft, slow, reasonable voice; and this time, while she was speaking, she began to know what else he would never remember, something so simple that she had missed it.

She stood there wan, [40] almost ugly, really like some wretched pet **280** monkey shivering in a cold climate. But she was going to have a child, and—yes, looking at him, she was grown-up, now, suddenly, as some people are said to turn white-haired overnight.

---

38 **aghast** extremely shocked   40 **wan** unnaturally pale
39 **Poltergeists** Ghosts

PART 1 First Reading

A Thinking About the Story

How would you describe James? Can you understand the charm he exerts over Marie and her mother? Explain your answer.

B Understanding the Plot

1. How does James treat Marie when he first meets her in the nightclub?
2. What are the major differences between James and Marie during their courtship and marriage? List as many as possible.
3. Where is Marie's father?
4. Why does Marie's mother like James? Explain your answer fully.
5. What attracted Marie to James?
6. What are James's economic circumstances? Explain your answer.
7. In what way does James's British accent help him in South African society?
8. How does Marie's mother receive the information that James has been making love to her daughter?
9. What is unusual about Marie's wedding day?
10. What is the relationship between James and his ex-wives?
11. Explain the reference "these South Africans who did not know any better." (lines 156–157)
12. In your opinion, why does James not recognize Colin? (lines 169–176)
13. What connects the destruction in the kitchen, living room, and bathroom?
14. What is unexpected about Marie's reaction after she and James have gone through the three rooms?
15. What do you think Marie came to understand in the end?

PART 2 Second Reading

A Exploring Themes

You are now ready to reread "An Intruder." Consider carefully the psychological portrait Nadine Gordimer paints of James, Marie, and Marie's mother.

1. Who do you think the intruder was? Explain your answer in detail.
2. How does Marie change in the course of the story?
3. What is James's attitude toward women? Substantiate your answer with examples from the story.
4. What observations does Gordimer make regarding the society James moves in? Give as many details as possible.
5. How does Marie's reflection that "evil had come out of the walls" represent a major theme in the story? (line 256)

B Analyzing the Author's Style

For more information on the literary terms in this section, turn to the explanations of *imagery* (page 303), *simile* (page 307), and *metaphor* (page 305).

IMAGERY: Simile and Metaphor

Nadine Gordimer's writing in "An Intruder" abounds in **imagery**, and she makes full and imaginative use of **similes** (direct comparisons using *like* or *as*) and **metaphors** (implied comparisons) to project both the inner and outer dimensions of the characters, their surroundings, and their actions. She introduces Marie with a simile:

> *... she sat looking out of the rest of the noisy party in the nightclub like a bush-baby between trees.* (lines 1–2)

With this simile Gordimer immediately evokes Marie as a small, furry wild animal with big brown eyes, out of its natural environment, the nocturnal forest. In this example, *like* directly unites the two elements of the comparison.

In less direct fashion, Gordimer uses a metaphor to intensify the horror left behind by an intruder, when the half-rotted vegetable matter on the sofa is described as *the intestines of the dustbin.* (line 233)

With this striking image, Gordimer compares the exposed contents of the trash can with the waste matter in human intestines.

1. In paragraph 1, the conversation at the party where James first meets Marie is described in terms of a military metaphor. What is the metaphor? Explain its two components. What is the effect of the metaphor?

2. In paragraph 1, which simile reinforces Marie's fragility? Explain the simile. In what way is this simile extended into a metaphor in lines 13–14?

3. Explain the simile . . . *[he] drew the damp cloth like cool lips across the inside of her wrists.* (lines 9–10) How does this simile help heighten the erotic atmosphere in the nightclub?

4. With what are the drum and the bouzouki compared in lines 16–18? Explain the metaphor as fully as possible.

5. In lines 50–68, what simile conveys Marie's petlike image in James's eyes? What other imagery conveys Marie's extreme youthfulness in these lines?

6. What metaphors underline the unpleasant smallness and darkness of the couple's apartment? (lines 118 and 226)

7. When Marie grows up at the end of the story, she is again described in animal terms. What is the animal? How does this animal image reflect her changed circumstances?

8. Pick out and explain three more similes and metaphors in the story. Explain how they contribute to our understanding of the themes.

C   Judging for Yourself

Express yourself as personally as you like in your answers to the following questions.

1. Do you think Marie's mother behaved responsibly toward her daughter?

2. In your opinion, is the couple's marriage likely to survive? Explain your answer fully.

3. Does James have the capacity to be a good father? Why? Why not?

4. Why, in your opinion, did Marie marry James?

D   Making Connections

1. In your culture, what is the attitude toward the marriage of an older man and a younger woman? Is the attitude different if the situation is reversed?

2. Is there a minimum age for marriage in your country? If so, what is it? If not, should there be?

3. Does the way you speak—for example, your accent or dialect—influence the way people regard you in your country?

4. How do young people spend their leisure time in your country? Are clubs a popular venue for people under thirty?

E   Debate

Debate this proposition:

People's characters are determined at birth.

PART 3   Focus on Language

A   Adjective Clauses

An **adjective clause** is a subordinate or dependent clause introduced by the relative pronouns *who, whom, whose, which,* or *that,* as well as by the relative adverbs *when* and *where.* Since it is a dependent clause, it cannot stand alone in a sentence; it must be accompanied by an independent (main) clause, and like all clauses it has its own subject and verb. Adjective clauses modify (describe) nouns or pronouns just as adjectives do.

1. The relative pronouns *who, that, whose,* and *whom* are used to refer to people. In the following examples, the pronouns *who* and *that,* and *whom* and *that* may be used interchangeably.

   ... there are stale women with mildew between their breasts who [that] daren't open doors. (lines 124–125)

   The relative pronoun *who* or *that* acts as the subject of the verb *daren't open.* The **antecedent** (the noun or pronoun to which the relative pronoun refers) is *women.*

   Sometimes the proprietor, whose blood contained the memory of Dionysiac pleasures, was the only spectator left.

The antecedent is *the proprietor*.

> *There were people ... **whom [that] he didn't remember at all** ...* (lines 165–166)

The relative pronoun *who/whom* or *that* is the object of the verb *remember*. The antecedent is *people*. (In less formal English, *who* is frequently used instead of *whom*.)

> *There were people **he didn't remember at all.***

The relative pronouns *whom* and *that* may be omitted when they function as the object in the relative clause.

> *James was the kind of man **with whom party lovers immediately identified.***

Always use *whom* after a preposition because pronouns that follow prepositions are in the object form. The antecedent is *man*.

2. The relative pronouns *which, that,* and *whose* are used to refer to animals or things. In the first example, the pronouns *which* and *that* may be used interchangeably.

> *She put up white gauzy curtains everywhere, and she went about in short cotton dressing-gowns **that [which] smelt of the warm iron.*** (lines 126–127)

The relative pronoun *that* is the subject of the verb *smelt*. The antecedent is *dressing-gowns*.

> *... she enjoyed the slight twinge of jealousy **she induced in herself with the thought.*** (lines 181–182)

The relative pronouns *which* and *that* may be omitted when they function as the object. The antecedent is *jealousy*.

> *... there wasn't a door or window **by which anyone could have got in.*** (lines 261–262)

The antecedent is *a door or window*.

> *Marie was like a small animal **whose den has been invaded.***

The antecedent is *animal*.

3. The relative adverb *when* modifies nouns of time.

> *Marie remembered clearly the moment **when she first saw her future husband at the nightclub.***

The antecedent is *moment.*

Note 1: The relative pronoun *when* may be omitted or *that* may be used instead.

Note 2: *When* may also introduce adverbial and noun clauses. For information on and practice with adverbial clauses, see page 242, and for noun clauses, see page 273.

The relative adverb *where* modifies nouns of place.

> *…and all their old friends were to meet them at the airport and go straight to their favorite nightclub, the place **where, incidentally, he and Marie had met**.* (lines 104–106)

The antecedent is *place.*

Note 1: The relative pronoun *where* may be omitted or *that* may be used instead.

Note 2: *Where* may also introduce noun clauses. (See page 274.)

4. If an adjective clause is linked to another clause by a coordinating conjunction such as *and*, *but,* or *or*, the second clause will also be an adjective clause. If the relative pronoun is the same in both clauses, it may be omitted in the second clause.

> *Marie's mother had no patience for the boys **who didn't even bother to open a car door for a woman**, or **couldn't appreciate her daughter's delicacy**.*

The antecedent for both clauses is *boys.*

PUNCTUATION: Restrictive and Nonrestrictive Clauses

There are two kinds of adjective clauses: restrictive (or identifying) and nonrestrictive (or nonidentifying).

1. The **restrictive clause** identifies and limits the noun it modifies. It cannot be omitted without changing the meaning of the sentence. Since it is essential to the noun it modifies, it is not

set off by commas from its antecedent. In a restrictive clause, *who* and *that* are interchangeable, as are *which* and *that*.

> *Marie looked for an apartment **that/which would be suitable for her new baby**.*

The antecedent is *apartment*. In this sentence, the emphasis is on a particular apartment that is baby-friendly, not an apartment in general.

> *Marie's mother was a woman **who/that was easily flattered.***

The antecedent is *woman*. In this sentence, what is important is not that Marie's mother is a female but that she is the type of person who is susceptible to flattery.

2. A **nonrestrictive clause** is not essential to defining the antecedent; it gives additional details or information. It is set off by commas from its antecedent. In nonrestrictive clauses, always use *who* or *whom* when referring to people and *which* when referring to things. Do not use the relative pronoun *that*.

> *Marie's husband, **who spoke with an upper-class British accent**, settled quickly into South African society.*

The antecedent is *husband*.

> *The parties, **which were invariably filled with drinking and noise**, soon bored her.*

The antecedent is *parties*.

Follow the instructions below concerning lines 27–83 in "An Intruder."

1. Underline all the adjective clauses with a single line. Put a double line under the relative pronoun or relative adverb that begins the clause. Circle its antecedent.
2. How many adjective clauses did you find?
3. Do any of the adjective clauses begin with a relative adverb? If so, which one(s)?
4. Are any adjective clauses joined by the conjunctions *and, but,* or *or*? If so, which one(s)?
5. Pick out an example of a restrictive and a nonrestrictive adjective clause in these paragraphs.

6. In which adjective clauses is the relative pronoun omitted but understood? Name the omitted pronoun. Is the relative pronoun the subject or the object of the verb?

7. Is the clause *that he hadn't a bean* (lines 69–70) an adjective clause? Explain your answer.

Complete the following sentences with the correct relative pronoun or relative adverb. Punctuate each sentence according to whether the relative clause is restrictive or nonrestrictive.

1. Mrs. Clegg _____ thought of herself as a bohemian was easily charmed by James.

2. James saw himself as a man to _____ the world owed a living.

3. She rushed out of the house _____ had lost all its charm for her.

4. He picked up their clothes from the floor _____ they'd been thrown.

5. Marie sat in the nightclub _____ noise was deafening.

6. The wine _____ the bartender served was chilled just right.

7. James compared Marie to a marmoset _____ is a small, furry animal.

8. She realized that her husband _____ she relied on had let her down.

9. His head _____ was throbbing horribly felt as if it would burst open.

10. The day _____ she woke up and saw the mess was the most shocking occasion in her life.

Write seven more sentences relating to the story, using an adjective clause in each one. Your sentences should contain one example each of *who, whom, which, whose, that, when,* and *where*. Include examples of both restrictive and nonrestrictive adjective clauses.

B   Building Vocabulary Skills

In the list below, the left column contains adjectives from the text. Make sure you understand their meaning in the context of the story.
The right column contains contexts appropriate to each adjective.
Match each adjective to its context.

ADJECTIVE	CONTEXT
_d_ 1. touching (line 40)	a. expression on hearing news of a plane crash
___ 2. wistful (line 43)	b. advice from a lawyer to his client
___ 3. rigid (line 61)	c. gossip designed to hurt the subject
___ 4. shabby (line 76)	d. plot of a sad movie
___ 5. circumspect (line 111)	e. response of a hostile audience
___ 6. intimate (line 236)	f. appearance after the flu
___ 7. jeering (line 239)	g. army regulations at all times
___ 8. aghast (line 244)	h. furniture after years of hard use
___ 9. malicious (line 253)	i. knowledge of someone close
___ 10. wan (linc 280)	j. longing of a poet for his lost love

Make up sentences using each adjective with its corresponding context. For example: *The movie was so **touching** that I cried long after it was over.*

PART 4   Writing Activities

1. Look at the editorial page of a large daily newspaper. Read the editorials carefully, paying special attention to their format and style. Write your own one-page editorial in which you take up the current situation regarding drinking among young people. You might include issues such as the excessive drinking of high school and college students, the consequences of driving while drunk, and the advantages or otherwise of raising the legal drinking age. Your editorial should persuade the reader of the soundness of your point of view. Give your editorial an apt heading.

2. Romance between an older man and a younger woman has been a recurring theme in books and movies over the years. Two examples are Charlotte Bronte's classic nineteenth-century novel *Jane Eyre*, in which a young governess falls secretly in love with her older employer, and the Jack Nicholson/Helen Hunt movie, *As Good As It Gets* (1997), in which a young waitress slowly builds a relationship with a morose older man who frequents the café where she works. Choose a movie you've seen or a book you've read that revolves around this kind of relationship or its reverse (an older woman and a younger man), and describe the plot and characters. Consider what sparked the romance, and say whether it worked out in the end. Try to use some similes and/or metaphors when you describe the characters.

3. "An Intruder" and "The Lily-White Boys" (page 247) are both stories that deal with an unwanted and frightening intrusion into a couple's home. Compare and contrast the two stories by outlining their respective plots to highlight their similarities and differences. Say which story disturbed you more and explain why.

PARENT AND CHILD

Alice Neel, *Mother and Child* (*Nancy and Olivia*), 1967
(c) Estate of Alice Neel. Courtesy of the Robert Miller Gallery, New York

7

Powder

TOBIAS WOLFF (b. 1945)

Born in Birmingham, Alabama, Tobias Wolff's early years were unconventional and unsettled. After his parents divorced, he traveled around the country with his mother, ending up in the Pacific Northwest, where his mother married an abusive man. Wolff chronicled his traumatic childhood in the groundbreaking memoir *This Boy's Life* (1989), which was later made into a movie starring Leonardo DiCaprio and Robert De Niro. He turned again to the memoir form in *Pharaoh's Army: Memories of the Lost War* (1994), when he wrote about his tour of duty in Vietnam as a member of the Green Berets. Today, he is Professor of English at Stanford University.

An accomplished short-story writer, Wolff has published several collections of short stories: *In the Garden of the North American Martyrs* (1981), *Back in the World* (1985), and *The Night in Question* (1996). His spare, elegant prose has been compared with the writing of Raymond Carver and Richard Ford. In 2003 he published his acclaimed first novel, *Old School*. He has won numerous writing awards including the PEN/Faulkner Award for his novella *The Barracks Thief* (1984), several O. Henry Awards, the *Los Angeles Times* Book Prize, and the American Academy of Arts and Letters Award in Literature (2001).

POWDER

A boy and his father bond in an unexpected way.

Just before Christmas my father took me skiing at Mount Baker. He'd had to fight for the privilege of my company, because my mother was still angry with him for sneaking me into a nightclub during our last visit, to see Thelonious Monk.[1]

He wouldn't give up. He promised, hand on heart, to take good care [5] of me and have me home for dinner on Christmas Eve, and she relented. But as we were checking out of the lodge that morning it began to snow, and in this snow he observed some quality that made it necessary for us to get in one last run. We got in several last runs. He was indifferent to[2] my fretting.[3] Snow whirled around us in bitter, blinding squalls,[4] hissing like [10] sand, and still we skied. As the lift bore us to the peak yet again, my father looked at his watch and said, "Criminey.[5] This'll have to be a fast one."

By now I couldn't see the trail. There was no point in trying. I stuck to him like white on rice and did what he did and somehow made it[6] to the bottom without sailing off a cliff. We returned our skis and my father [15] put chains on the Austin-Healy[7] while I swayed from foot to foot, clapping my mittens and wishing I were home. I could see everything. The green tablecloth, the plates with the holly pattern, the red candles waiting to be lit.

We passed a diner on our way out. "You want some soup?" my father [20] asked. I shook my head. "Buck up,"[8] he said. "I'll get you there. Right, doctor?"

I was supposed to say, "Right, doctor," but I didn't say anything.

A state trooper[9] waved us down[10] outside the resort. A pair of sawhorses were blocking the road. The trooper came up to our car and [25] bent down to my father's window. His face was bleached by the cold. Snowflakes clung to his eyebrows and to the fur trim of his jacket and cap.

"Don't tell me," my father said.

The trooper told him. The road was closed. It might get cleared, it might not. Storm took everyone by surprise. So much, so fast. Hard to get [30] people moving. Christmas Eve. What can you do?

My father said, "Look. We're talking about four, five inches. I've taken this car through worse than that."

---

1 **Thelonius Monk** American jazz pianist and
   composer (1917–1982)
2 **indifferent to** unconcerned with
3 **fretting** worrying
4 **squalls** brief, violent storms
5 **Criminey** an exclamation of surprise

6 **made it** reached (informal)
7 **Austin-Healy** a popular British sports car
8 **Buck up** Cheer up
9 **state trooper** a state police officer
10 **waved us down** signaled us to stop

The trooper straightened up, boots creaking. His face was out of sight but I could hear him. "The road is closed."

My father sat with both hands on the wheel, rubbing the wood with his thumbs. He looked at the barricade for a long time. He seemed to be trying to master the idea of it. Then he thanked the trooper, and with a weird, old-maidy show of caution turned the car around. "Your mother will never forgive me for this," he said.

"We should have left before," I said. "Doctor."

He didn't speak to me again until we were both in a booth at the diner, waiting for our burgers. "She won't forgive me," he said. "Do you understand? Never."

"I guess," I said, but no guesswork was required; she wouldn't forgive him.

"I can't let that happen." He bent toward me. "I'll tell you what I want. I want us to be together again. Is that what you want?"

I wasn't sure, but I said, "Yes, sir."

He bumped my chin with his knuckles. "That's all I needed to hear."

When we finished eating he went to the pay phone in the back of the diner, then joined me in the booth again. I figured he'd called my mother, but he didn't give a report. He sipped at his coffee and stared out the window at the empty road. "Come on!" When the trooper's car went past, lights flashing, he got up and dropped some money on the check. "Okay. *Vamanos.*"[11]

The wind had died. The snow was falling straight down, less of it now; lighter. We drove away from the resort, right up to the barricade. "Move it," my father told me. When I looked at him he said, "What are you waiting for?" I got out and dragged one of the sawhorses aside, then pushed it back after he drove through. When I got inside the car he said, "Now you're an accomplice.[12] We go down[13] together." He put the car in gear and looked at me. "Joke, doctor."

"Funny, doctor."

Down the first long stretch I watched the road behind us, to see if the trooper was on our tail.[14] The barricade vanished. Then there was nothing but snow: snow on the road, snow kicking up from the chains, snow on the trees, snow in the sky; and our trail in the snow. I faced around and had a shock. The lie of the road behind us had been marked by our own tracks, but there were no tracks ahead of us. My father was breaking virgin snow between a line of tall trees. He was humming "Stars Fell on Alabama." I felt snow brush along the floorboards under my feet. To keep my hands from shaking I clamped them between my knees.

My father grunted in a thoughtful way and said, "Don't ever try this yourself."

"I won't."

---

11 *Vamanos.* Let's go. (Spanish)
12 **accomplice** a partner in crime
13 **go down** experience defeat
14 **on our tail** following us closely

"That's what you say now, but someday you'll get your license and then you'll think you can do anything. Only you won't be able to do this. You need, I don't know—a certain instinct."

"Maybe I have it."

"You don't. You have your strong points, but not . . . you know. I only mention it because I don't want you to get the idea this is something just anybody can do. I'm a great driver. That's not a virtue, okay? It's just a fact, and one you should be aware of. Of course you have to give the old heap[15] some credit, too—there aren't many cars I'd try this with. Listen!"

I listened. I heard the slap of the chains, the stiff, jerky rasp of the wipers, the purr of the engine. It really did purr. The car was almost new. My father couldn't afford it, and kept promising to sell it, but here it was.

I said, "Where do you think that policeman went to?"

"Are you warm enough?" He reached over and cranked up the blower.[16] Then he turned off the wipers. We didn't need them. The clouds had brightened. A few sparse, feathery flakes drifted into our slipstream and were swept away. We left the trees and entered a broad field of snow that ran level for a while and then tilted sharply downward. Orange stakes had been planted at intervals in two parallel lines and my father ran a course[17] between them, though they were far enough apart to leave considerable doubt in my mind as to where exactly the road lay. He was humming again, doing little scat riffs[18] around the melody.

"Okay then. What are my strong points?"

"Don't get me started," he said. "It'd take all day."

"Oh, right. Name one."

"Easy. You always think ahead."

True. I always thought ahead. I was a boy who kept his clothes on numbered hangers to ensure proper rotation. I bothered my teachers for homework assignments far ahead of their due dates so I could make up schedules. I thought ahead, and that was why I knew that there would be other troopers waiting for us at the end of our ride, if we got there. What I did not know was that my father would wheedle[19] and plead his way past them—he didn't sing "O Tannenbaum"[20] but just about—and get me home for dinner, buying a little more time before my mother decided to make the split final. I knew we'd get caught; I was resigned to it. And maybe for this reason I stopped moping[21] and began to enjoy myself.

Why not? This was one for the books.[22] Like being in a speedboat, only better. You can't go downhill in a boat. And it was all ours. And it kept coming, the laden trees, the unbroken surface of snow, the sudden white vistas. Here and there I saw hints of the road, ditches, fences, stakes, but not so many that I could have found my way. But then I didn't

---

15 **the old heap** an old, rundown car (slang)
16 **cranked up the blower** turned up the heater
17 **ran a course** created a path
18 **scat riffs** improvised jazz tunes
19 **wheedle** persuade through flattery
20 **"O Tannenbaum"** a song traditionally sung at Christmas
21 **moping** feeling sad
22 **This was one for the books.** This was special enough to be recorded.

have to. My father in his forty-eighth year, rumpled,²³ kind, bankrupt of honor, flushed with certainty. He was a great driver. All persuasion, no coercion.²⁴ Such subtlety²⁵ at the wheel, such tactful pedalwork. I actually **120** trusted him. And the best was yet to come—switchbacks and hairpins²⁶ impossible to describe. Except maybe to say this: If you haven't driven fresh powder, you haven't driven.

---

23 **rumpled** having a wrinkled and untidy appearance
24 **coercion** force

25 **subtlety** delicate skill
26 **switchbacks and hairpins** very sharp turns on a steep road

PART 1 First Reading

A   Thinking About the Story

What qualities do you usually associate with a father? How many of these qualities apply to the father in the story?

B   Understanding the Plot

1. Why was the narrator's mother reluctant to let her son go skiing with his father?
2. What was the boy fretting about? (line 10)
3. Why did the boy refuse the soup?
4. What are the consequences for the father if his wife won't forgive him for being late?
5. Why did the father wait for the trooper's car to go past?
6. Why does the father call his son "an accomplice"? (line 62)
7. What were the boy's feelings as they left the road and plowed through the snow? List them in detail.
8. Why doesn't the boy's father answer his son's question as to where the trooper had gone? (line 89)
9. What is the main difference between the son and his father?
10. Did the boy and his father meet up with the troopers again? If so, what happened?
11. Did the boy ultimately enjoy the experience? Explain your answer.

PART 2 Second Reading

A   Exploring Themes

You are now ready to reread "Powder." Do you view the father differently the second time around? Look at how Wolff depicts the evolving father/son bond.

1. In what ways does the boy draw closer to his father during their adventure together?
2. What is the state of the parents' relationship? Give as many details as possible to support your answer.
3. How do the father and son use the nickname "doctor" differently? What light does this throw on their relationship?
4. In what ways does the story invert the traditional father/son relationship?
5. How does the boy change in the course of the story?

B   Analyzing the Author's Style

For more information on the literary terms in this section, turn to the explanations of *repetition* (page 307) and *alliteration* (page 297).

REPETITION AND ALLITERATION

Wolff uses the stylistic device of **repetition** to enhance the descriptive and thematic impact of snow in "Powder." He does this through repeated references to snow as well as through **alliteration** (the repetition of consonant sounds). In particular, Wolff uses alliteration to help recreate the essence of snow at different points in the story. For example, as the snowstorm diminishes, the narrator refers to *a few . . . feathery flakes.* (line 92) The repetition of the soft "f" sound reinforces the insubstantiality of the flakes, which are compared to light, fluffy feathers in distinct contrast to the earlier blizzardlike conditions.

1. What consonant sounds referring to the snowstorm are repeated in lines 10–11? How do they help evoke the storm?
2. What alliteration other than *feathery flakes* can you find in lines 92–93? What is the effect of this alliteration?

3. Wolff repeatedly presents snow in changing ways that parallel the shifting moods of the narrator. Examine carefully the various ways in which snow is described in lines 10–11, 66–72, 92–93, and 113–123, and show how each description echoes the narrator's state of mind at that moment.

C   Judging for Yourself

Express yourself as personally as you like in your answers to the following questions.

1. How old do you think the boy is? Give reasons for your answer.
2. Do you sympathize with the boy's mother? Explain your answer fully.
3. What do you think of the father's risk-taking? Is he reckless, or is he brave? Should he be punished?
4. Do you find the father an endearing character? Why? Why not?
5. In your view, does the boy fundamentally benefit from this experience? If so, how? If not, why not?

D   Making Connections

1. In your culture, is there a typical role model for fathers? If yes, what is it? If no, why not?
2. Skiing is a popular winter sport in the United States. What are some popular winter sports in your country?
3. Are the police generally looked on as a positive force in your country? Explain your answer.
4. How is divorce regarded in your country? Is it easy or difficult to get a divorce? Is there any shame attached to divorce?
5. How fast do people tend to drive in your country? Is speed related to gender?

E   Debate

Debate this proposition:

Divorce should be avoided for the sake of the children.

PART 3 Focus on Language

A   Participial Phrases

Writers use participial phrases instead of adjective or adverb clauses to add variety and economy to their writing. Participial phrases are phrases made up of a present or past participle plus at least one additional word that is not a verb. Present participles end in -*ing*, while most past participles end in -*ed, -d,* or -*t.* The participial phrase may be placed next to or away from the noun or pronoun it modifies. For example:

> . . . *the red candles **waiting to be lit**.* (lines 18–19)

The participial phrase *waiting to be lit* is placed next to *candles,* the noun it modifies.

> *The trooper bent his face **bleached by the cold** to my father's car window.*

The participial phrase *bleached by the cold* is placed next to *face,* the noun it modifies.

> *My father sat with both hands on the wheel, **rubbing the wood with his thumbs.*** (lines 36–37)

Note 1: The participial phrase *rubbing the wood with his thumbs* describes the noun *father,* yet is separated from it. When the participial phrase is placed away from the noun or pronoun it modifies, a comma is needed.

Note 2: The participial phrase *rubbing the wood with his thumbs* can also be placed at the beginning of the sentence.

> ***Rubbing the wood with his thumbs,*** *my father sat with both hands on the wheel.*

In the following sentences, underline each participial phrase and circle the noun or pronoun it modifies.

1. Snow whirled around us in bitter, blinding squalls, hissing like sand, and still we skied. (lines 10–11)
2. We returned our skis and my father put chains on the Austin-Healy while I swayed from foot to foot, clapping my mittens and wishing I were home. (lines 15–17)

3. I thought ahead, and that was why I knew there would be other troopers waiting for us at the end of our ride, if we got there. (lines 106–107)

4. What I did not know was that my father would wheedle and plead his way past them . . . and get me home for dinner, buying a little more time before my mother decided to make the split final. (lines 107–111)

5. My father in his forty-eighth year, rumpled, kind, bankrupt of honor, flushed with certainty. (lines 118–119)

Combine the following sentence pairs by reducing one of the clauses in each pair to a participial phrase. You may use either a present participial or past participial phrase. For example:

> *A state trooper waved us down outside the resort. The trooper came up to our car and bent down to my father's window.* (lines 24–27)

> ***Waving us down outside the resort,*** *the trooper came up to our car and bent down to my father's window.*

> or

> ***Having waved us down outside the resort,*** *the trooper came up to our car and bent down to my father's window.*

1. My father wouldn't give up. He promised hand on heart to take good care of me.
2. I stuck to him like white on rice. I somehow made it to the bottom without sailing off a cliff.
3. He went to the pay phone in the back of the diner. Then he joined me again.
4. I knew we would get caught. I was resigned to it.
5. I looked at my father flushed with excitement at the end of the ride. I actually trusted him.

DANGLING MODIFIERS

When the participial phrase is placed at the beginning of the sentence, make sure it modifies the noun or pronoun it refers to. Otherwise, the meaning may be unclear or distorted. For example:

> ***Approached by the police,*** *fear enveloped me.*

As written, the participial phrase *approached by the police* modifies *fear* instead of modifying *me*. To avoid ambiguity, the sentence should be written: ***Approached by the police,*** *I was enveloped with fear.*

> ***Finishing our meal quickly,*** *the trooper's car went past us.*

This is grammatically illogical since the subject of the participial phrase *finishing our meal quickly* is actually "we," not "the trooper's car." The sentence should be written: ***Finishing our meal quickly,*** *we saw the trooper's car go past.*

Rewrite the following sentences to eliminate the ambiguity or meaninglessness arising from the dangling modifiers. Change only the independent clause, adding or altering words as necessary.

1. Fretting horribly, the snow whirled around the boy.

_____

2. Taking out his notebook to write a ticket, I was scared of the trooper.

_____

3. Sipping his coffee, the trooper's car went past my father.

_____

4. Driving through the trees, there were only a few feathery flakes of snow on the windshield.

_____

5. Angered by my father's behavior, the divorce was inevitable.

_____

SENTENCE FRAGMENTS

In formal writing, every sentence requires a main clause (an independent clause that stands on its own and does not depend on any other clause for its existence). A **sentence fragment** consists of a group of words without a main verb or a dependent clause without a main clause. It should be noted that writers frequently ignore strict grammar rules and use sentence fragments in their creative work. For example, Wolff writes:

> *So much, so fast.* (line 30)

In this instance, the subject and verb are missing. A grammatically correct sentence would read *So much **snow fell, and it fell** so fast.*

> *Hard to get people moving.* (lines 30–31)

Once again, the subject and verb are missing. A grammatically correct sentence would read ***It was*** *hard to get people moving.*

Because we were so late.

Here we have a dependent clause only; the main clause is missing. A grammatically correct sentence would read ***I was getting increasingly anxious*** *because we were so late.*

Rewrite the last paragraph of the story (lines 113–123). Take out all the sentence fragments and substitute complete sentences.

B   Building Vocabulary Skills

ALLITERATION

Look at the following list of alliterative expressions.

aid and abet _____   highhanded _____

bag of bones _____   life and limb _____

cold comfort _____   mind over matter _____

double-dealing _____   shipshape _____

far-fetched _____   wishy-washy _____

With the aid of a dictionary, define each of the alliterative expressions. Then complete the sentences with the appropriate expressions from the list.

1. After her illness, she was nothing but a _____.
2. "I wish you would learn to keep your room _____," sighed the mother to her teenage child.
3. There is a lot of _____ in the world of drug dealers.
4. The soldiers risked _____ when confronting the overwhelming enemy numbers.
5. It is a serious offense to _____ a criminal.
6. If you are _____, you will usually alienate people.
7. This is no time for _____ actions, but rather for courage and determination.

8. The professor rejected the student's _____ excuse about an alien snatching his homework.

9. It was _____ to the boy to hear he'd failed the exam by only one point.

10. Don't allow yourself to give up now since it's definitely a case of _____.

PREPOSITIONS

Complete the paragraph with the correct prepositions. All the expressions used appear in the story. Try to do the exercise without referring to the story.

As the boy and his father left the restaurant, the snow was whirling _____ them, but his father seemed indifferent _____ the bad weather. Flushed _____ determination, he urged his son into the car, and hand _____ heart he promised his son they would arrive home in time for Christmas Eve dinner. After a while, the boy drifted _____ a dreamy state, and began to make _____ a schedule of activities for the rest of the vacation. As his father cranked _____ the heat, the boy hunched over with his hands clamped tightly _____ his knees. His father revved up the engine, and the car ran a course _____ the trees. The boy sat up straight, smiled, and decided that this journey would be one _____ the books.

PART 4 Writing Activities

1. Write a two-page essay on a memorable trip you took with a member of your family. In your essay describe your surroundings, depict your relationship with your relative, and say whether the experience changed you in any way. Try to use participial phrases in your description.

2. Close to 50 percent of marriages in the United States end in divorce. In an essay of two to three pages, examine the issue of divorce in your country. Give the divorce-rate statistics, analyze the major reasons couples split up, and say what the effect frequently is on the family. In your conclusion, explain what measures might be taken to lower the divorce rate.

3. John Le Carré's spy novel *A Perfect Spy* and Steven Spielberg's movie *Catch Me If You Can* both reflect a father/son relationship in which the irresponsible, dishonest actions of a charming father affect the son deeply. Write an essay on a book you've read or movie or play you've seen that deals with the complexities of such a relationship. Say whether the ending left you feeling uplifted or depressed.

4. Setting—the time and place in which a story unfolds—plays an important role in "Powder" and "Miss Brill" (page 199). Write an essay comparing their respective settings, using appropriate quotes from the stories to illustrate your descriptions. Show how the setting in both stories contributes to a deeper understanding of their themes.

Note: For more information on setting, see page 307.

8

Mother

GRACE PALEY (b. 1922)

Born in New York City to Russian-Jewish immigrants, Grace Paley heard English, Russian, and Yiddish spoken at home in the Bronx. As a result, she developed an acute ear for reproducing dialect, and her stories are full of Jewish, African-American, Irish, and other ethnic accents. Paley has taught literature and creative writing at Sarah Lawrence, Columbia, and Dartmouth. In addition to her writing and academic career, she has led a politically active life, taking a vocal position against the Vietnam War and fighting for women's rights and pacifism, among other social and political causes.

Paley's stories often employ first-person narration and are peopled with vulnerable, ordinary characters who endure the ups and downs in their lives with love, humor, and patience. She has published four collections of short stories: *The Little Disturbances of Man* (1959), *Enormous Changes at the Last Minute* (1974), *Later the Same Day* (1985), and *Collected Stories* (1994). She has also published several volumes of poetry, including *Begin Again: Collected Poems* (1992), and she was named Vermont State Poet in 2003.

MOTHER

Years after her death, a mother is remembered by her child.

One day I was listening to the AM radio. I heard a song: "Oh, I Long[1] to See My Mother in the Doorway." By God! I said, I understand that song. I have often longed to see my mother in the doorway. As a matter of fact, she did stand frequently in various doorways looking at me. She stood one day, just so, at the front door, the darkness of the hallway behind her. It was New Year's Day. She said sadly, If you come home at 4 A.M. when you're seventeen, what time will you come home when you're twenty? She asked this question without humor or meanness. She had begun her worried preparations for death. She would not be present, she thought, when I was twenty. So she wondered.

Another time she stood in the doorway of my room. I had just issued a political manifesto[2] attacking the family's position on the Soviet Union. She said, Go to sleep for godsakes, you damn fool, you and your Communist ideas. We saw them already, Papa and me, in 1905. We guessed it all.

At the door of the kitchen she said, You never finish your lunch. You run around senselessly. What will become of you?

Then she died.

Naturally for the rest of my life I longed to see her, not only in doorways, in a great number of places—in the dining room with my aunts, at the window looking up and down the block, in the country garden among zinnias and marigolds,[3] in the living room with my father.

They sat in comfortable leather chairs. They were listening to Mozart. They looked at one another amazed. It seemed to them that they'd just come over on the boat. They'd just learned the first English words. It seemed to them that he had just proudly handed in a 100 percent correct exam to the American anatomy[4] professor. It seemed as though she'd just quit the shop for the kitchen.

I wish I could see her in the doorway of the living room.

She stood there a minute. Then she sat beside him. They owned an expensive record player. They were listening to Bach. She said to him, Talk to me a little. We don't talk so much anymore.

I'm tired, he said. Can't you see? I saw maybe thirty people today. All sick, all talk talk talk talk. Listen to the music, he said. I believe you once had perfect pitch.[5] I'm tired, he said.

Then she died.

---

1 **long** want badly
2 **manifesto** a declaration of intentions or principles
3 **zinnias and marigolds** brightly colored summer flowers
4 **anatomy** the study of the various parts of the body
5 **perfect pitch** the ability to recognize and reproduce a musical note exactly

PART 1 First Reading

A Thinking About the Story

Were you drawn into the universal aspects of the mother/child relationship depicted in the story? Explain the ways you connected with the characters.

B Understanding the Plot

1. Through whose eyes is the story told?
2. What was the mother's major concern regarding her teenage child?
3. What country were the parents born in? How do we know?
4. What were the political beliefs of the narrator as a teenager?
5. What do you think the events of 1905 were that the narrator's mother referred to?

   Note: You may have to consult an encyclopedia to help answer this question.
6. What profession was the father studying for?
7. Why was the father particularly proud of his examination results?
8. Explain the expression "She'd just quit the shop for the kitchen." (lines 26–27)
9. What was the father's attitude toward his work?
10. What leisure-time activity did the narrator's parents share? How did the mother's perfect pitch help her enjoy this activity?

PART 2 Second Reading

A Exploring Themes

You are now ready to reread "Mother." Look at how Paley has packed so much information and such a range of feeling and time into such a small space. This gives "Mother" the density of a poem.

1. How would you characterize the mother's relationship with her child?
2. How does the relationship between the parents change?
3. How did the economic circumstances of the family change? Give examples to illustrate your answer.

4. What does the narrator's mother imply happened to them in Russia in 1905?

5. In what ways have the adult narrator's feelings toward his or her mother altered?

6. What is the mood of the narrator?

B Analyzing the Author's Style

For more information on the literary term in this section, turn to the explanation of *flashback* (page 302).

FLASHBACK

Most of the information essential to an understanding of "Mother" is conveyed through **flashbacks**, in which the narrator interrupts the present time and returns to the past. For example, at the start of the story, the narrator/protagonist (the central character who also tells the story) is listening to the radio; then the next moment the reader is transported back to a much earlier event that occurred one New Year's Day when the narrator was seventeen.

1. How many flashbacks does "Mother" contain? Where does each flashback begin and end?

2. What word links several of the flashbacks? What is the thematic significance of the situation described by this word?

3. What is the effect of telling this story in a rapid series of flashbacks?

4. What sentence is repeated in the story? Why is it repeated? What is different about the flashbacks that precede this sentence the second time around?

C Judging for Yourself

Express yourself as personally as you like in your answers to the following questions.

1. Do you feel the mother was overprotective of her child?

2. What role do you think the father played in his child's upbringing?

3. In your view, does the narrator have reason to regret his or her behavior toward the mother?

4. Do you think the narrator is male or female? Justify your answer.

5. About how old do you estimate the narrator to be at the start of the story? Give reasons for your answer.

D   Making Connections

1. Are male teenagers in your culture given more freedom than female teenagers by their parents?

2. Do teenagers in your country tend to be politically more radical than their parents?

3. Do teenagers feel a need to express their individuality in your country? If so, how? If not, why not?

4. Would you say that you had a closer relationship with your mother than with your father when you were a teenager? Explain why or why not.

5. Do you think being a child of immigrants affects the parent/child relationship? In what ways?

E   Debate

Debate this proposition:

Teenagers deserve their reputation for being difficult.

PART 3   Focus on Language

A   Tenses Expressing and Referring to the Past

SIMPLE PAST

The **simple past** is used for something that began and ended at a certain time in the past. For example:

> *She **stood** one day, just so, at the front door, the darkness of the hallway behind her.* (lines 4–6)

PAST PROGRESSIVE

The **past progressive** is used to show that an action was in progress when something else occurred. It takes the form of the past tense of *be* plus the *present participle*. For example:

> *One day I **was listening** to the AM radio. I heard a song: "Oh, I Long to See My Mother in the Doorway."* (lines 1–2)

Note: This sentence could also be written as

> *One day I **was listening** to the AM radio when I heard a song: "Oh, I Long to See My Mother in the Doorway."*

PRESENT PERFECT

The **present perfect** can be used in several situations. It takes the form of the present tense of *have* plus the *past participle*.

a. It is used to indicate that an action began in the past and continues or recurs into the present. For example:

*I **have** often **longed** to see my mother in the doorway.* (line 3)

b. It is used to show that something occurred or didn't occur at an unspecified time in the past. For example:

*I **have seen** my mother in the doorway.*

c. It is used to suggest that an action has very recently been completed. For example:

*My mother is here. I **have** just **seen** her in the doorway.*

Note: In the present perfect tense, we are more concerned with the effect of an action at the present moment and less interested in when the action started.

PRESENT PERFECT PROGRESSIVE

The **present perfect progressive** is used to talk about an action or a situation that began in the past and continues to the present. The action or situation is usually not finished. It is continuing, and it will probably continue into the future. It takes the form of *have/has been* plus the *present participle*. For example:

*For months I **have been longing** to see my mother in the doorway.*

PAST PERFECT

The **past perfect** is used to show that something was already completed before another action began in the past. It takes the form of the past tense of *have* plus the *past participle*. For example:

*I **had** just **issued** a political manifesto attacking the family's position on the Soviet Union. She said, Go to sleep for godsakes, you damn fool . . .* (lines 11–13)

Note: This sentence could also be written as

*I **had** just **issued** a political manifesto attacking the family's position on the Soviet Union when she said, Go to sleep for godsakes, you damn fool . . .*

PAST PERFECT PROGRESSIVE

The **past perfect progressive** is used to talk about an action that was in progress before a specific time in the past. The progressive emphasizes the process, not the end result. It takes the form of *had been* plus the *present participle*. For example:

> *I **had** just **been issuing** a political manifesto attacking the family's position on the Soviet Union, when she ordered me to go to sleep at once.*

Note: In this example, she interrupted me while I was talking, whereas in the past perfect example I had already finished talking.

Complete the sentences with a correct tense of the verb in parentheses. The verb in parentheses applies to both sentences in a pair. Although it may be possible, do not use the same tense in each pair.

1. (behave) When I was a teenager, I frequently
   _____*behaved*_____ badly toward my mother.

   I knew that I _____*had been behaving*_____ badly. I promised I would stop.

2. (achieve) It amazed my parents that they
   _____ so much in such a short time.

   "We _____ so much in such a short time," said my father in amazement to my mother.

3. (listen) My mother _____ to music when I burst into the room after school.

   My mother _____ to music every day of my school life.

4. (talk) "I _____ to you for the past ten minutes and you haven't heard a word!" said my mother in exasperation.

   I _____ to you for at least ten minutes before I realized you hadn't heard a word.

5. (return) My parents _____ to Russia only once since they arrived in this country.

   My parents _____ to Russia for the first time last year.

6. (worry) Although my mother continually

_____ about dying, she didn't express her fears to me.

Although my mother _____ about dying for years, she expressed her fears to me only last week.

7. (hand in) You _____ your exam, so it is too late to request extra time.

You _____ your exam, so it was too late to request extra time.

8. (run around) When I was younger, I _____ senselessly.

I _____ senselessly for years before I was stopped by the death of my mother.

9. (quit) After my father graduated, my mother _____ working.

"I didn't know you _____ working!" exclaimed my father to my mother.

10. (look for) Before dinner was served, I _____ my mother in the garden.

Although I _____ my mother for nearly ten minutes, I still hadn't found her by the time dinner was served.

11. (study) My father and mother _____ English soon after they arrived in the United States.

My father and mother _____ English for the past three months.

B   Building Vocabulary Skills

With a partner, replace each of the following italicized words or expressions with a synonym from the story. Try to do this exercise from memory, referring to the story only if necessary.

1. I read your *declaration of principles* last night and have decided to vote for you.
2. Teenagers frequently act *thoughtlessly* and suffer the consequences.
3. To play the violin well, a musician needs *a totally accurate ear*.
4. After immigrating to a new country, it is not uncommon to *yearn* for one's place of birth.

5. Any student who *submits* his or her essay late will be penalized.
6. I don't know where you get your *spite* from.
7. The government *gave out* a pamphlet explaining its policy toward immigration.
8. The lessons involving *the study of the body* were my father's favorite classes at university.

PART 4 Writing Activities

1. Write a memory piece of two to three pages, focusing on an event in your teenage years. As in "Mother," start in the present and use something unexpected like a sound, a smell, or a gesture to trigger your memory and send you back into the past. Use past and present tenses appropriately.

2. Write a two-page essay analyzing the roots of teenage rebellion against parental and other authority. Begin your essay with a consideration of why adolescents traditionally feel the need to challenge the rules of adult society. Consider the positive and negative aspects of this confrontation, and say what steps you would advocate to improve the situation.

3. Marcel Proust's *Remembrance of Things Past* is one of the most famous works of fiction centering on memory. Write a book review for a newspaper or magazine on a book you have read in which a character looks back on events that occurred in the past. Briefly explain its contents and say why you recommend it.

4. "Mother" and "Powder" (page 89) are both told by a narrator/protagonist who relates a problematic relationship with one parent. In an essay, compare and contrast these relationships. Consider the ending of each story and say how it influences the tone of the narration.

9

A Short Digest of a Long Novel

BUDD SCHULBERG (b. 1914)

Born in New York City, Budd Schulberg moved at the age of five to Hollywood, where his father became head of Paramount Studios. Schulberg has enjoyed a varied career as novelist, short-story writer, playwright, travel writer, boxing editor, and writer of screenplays. Frequently employing the first-person narrative, Schulberg's novels explore how rapid success affects the moral fiber of his characters. He has said, "I believe that the seasons of success and failure are more violent in America than anywhere else on earth."

Schulberg's first novel, *What Makes Sammy Run?* (1941), a satire on Hollywood, catapulted him to fame. Other novels include *The Disenchanted* (1950), modeled on F. Scott Fitzgerald, whom he knew; *Sanctuary V* (1969); and *Everything That Moves* (1980). He has also published two collections of short stories: *Some Faces in the Crowd* (1953) and *Love, Action, Laughter, and Other Sad Tales* (1989), as well as a collection of boxing essays, *Sparring with Hemingway: And Other Legends of the Fight Game* (1995).

A SHORT DIGEST[1] OF A LONG NOVEL

A father watches helplessly as his young daughter learns about betrayal.

Her legs were shapely and firm and when she crossed them and smiled with the self-assurance that always delighted him, he thought she was the only person he knew in the world who was unblemished.[2] Not lifelike but an improvement on life, as a work of art, her delicate features were chiseled[3] from a solid block. The wood-sculpture image came easy to him   **5** because her particular shade of blonde always suggested maple[4] polished to a golden grain.[5] As it had been from the moment he stood in awe and amazement in front of the glass window where she was first exhibited, the sight of her made him philosophical. Some of us appear in beautiful colors, too, or with beautiful grains, but we develop imperfections. Inspect   **10** us very closely and you find we're damaged by the elements.[6] Sometimes we're only nicked[7] with cynicism.[8] Sometimes we're cracked with disillusionment.[9] Or we're split with fear.

When she began to speak, he leaned forward, eager for the words that were like good music, profundity[10] expressed in terms that pleased   **15** the ear while challenging the mind.

"Everybody likes me," she said. "Absolutely everybody."

It was not that she was conceited. It was simply that she was only three. No one had ever taken her[11] with sweet and whispered promises that turned into morning-after lies, ugly and cold as unwashed dishes   **20** from last night's dinner lying in the sink. She had never heard a dictator rock her country to sleep with peaceful lullabies[12] one day and rock it with bombs the next. She was undeceived. Her father ran his hands reverently[13] through her soft yellow hair. She is virgin,[14] he thought, for this is the true virginity, that brief moment in the time of your life before   **25** your mind or your body has been defiled[15] by acts of treachery.

It was just before Christmas and she was sitting on her little chair, her lips pressed together in concentration, writing a last-minute letter to Santa

---

1 **digest** a shortened literary form, like a summary
2 **unblemished** unmarked, perfect
3 **chiseled** carved
4 **maple** a light-colored wood
5 **grain** the markings or texture of wood
6 **the elements** atmospheric forces like wind or rain
7 **nicked** cut slightly
8 **cynicism** the belief that humans behave only selfishly
9 **disillusionment** the state of mind after our dreams are destroyed
10 **profundity** intellectual depth
11 **taken her** made love to her
12 **lullabies** songs sung to babies to help them sleep
13 **reverently** respectfully
14 **virgin** pure, untouched; sexually innocent
15 **defiled** made impure

Claus. The words were written in some language of her own invention but she obligingly translated as she went along. 30

> Dear Santa, I am a very good girl and everybody likes me. So please don't forget to bring me a set of dishes, a doll that goes to sleep and wakes up again, and a washing machine. I need the washing machine because Raggedy Ann's[16] dress is so dirty.

After she finished her letter, folded it, and asked him to address it, he 35 tossed her up in the air, caught her and tossed her again, to hear her giggle. "Higher, Daddy, higher," she instructed. His mind embraced her sentimentally: She is a virgin island in a lewd[17] world. She is a winged seed of innocence blown through the wasteland. If only she could root[18] somewhere. If only she could grow like this. 40

"Let me down, Daddy," she said when she had decided that she had indulged him[19] long enough, "I have to mail my letter to Santa."

"But didn't you see him this afternoon?" he asked. "Didn't you ask for everything you wanted? Mommy said she took you up to meet him and you sat on his lap." 45

"I just wanted to remind him," she said. "There were so many other children."

He fought down the impulse to laugh, because she was not something to laugh at. And he was obsessed with the idea that to hurt her feelings with laughter was to nick her, to blemish the perfection. 50

"Daddy can't catch me ee," she sang out, and the old chase was on, following the pattern that had become so familiar to them, the same wild shrieks and the same scream of pretended anguish[20] at the inevitable result. Two laps around the dining-room table[21] was the established course before he caught her in the kitchen. He swung her up from the 55 floor and set her down on the kitchen table. She stood on the edge, poised confidently for another of their games. But this was no panting, giggling game like tag or hide-and-seek. This game was ceremonial. The table was several feet higher than she was. "Jump, jump, and Daddy will catch you," he would challenge. They would count together, *one, two,* 60 and on *three* she would leap out into the air. He would not even hold out his arms to her until the last possible moment. But he would always catch her. They had played the game for more than a year and the experience never failed to exhilarate[22] them. You see, I am always here to catch you when you are falling, it said to them, and each time she 65 jumped, her confidence increased and their bond deepened.

They were going through the ceremony when the woman next door came in with her five-year-old son, Billy. "Hello, Mr. Steevers," she said. "Would you mind if I left Bill with you for an hour while I do my marketing?" 70

---

16 **Raggedy Ann** a popular rag doll
17 **lewd** coarse, vulgar
18 **root** settle
19 **indulged him** let him do what he wanted
20 **anguish** intense sorrow or pain
21 **two laps around the dining-room table** (they ran) twice around the dining room table
22 **exhilarate** greatly excite

"No, of course not, glad to have him," he said and he mussed Billy's hair[23] playfully. "How's the boy, Billy?"

But his heart wasn't in it. This was the only afternoon of the week with her and he resented the intrusion. And then too, he was convinced that Billy was going to grow up into the type of man for whom he had a particular resentment. A sturdy,[24] good-looking boy, big for his age, aggressively unchildlike, a malicious,[25] arrogant, insensitive extrovert.[26] I can just see him drunk and red-faced and pulling up girls' dresses at Legion Conventions,[27] Mr. Steevers would think. And the worst of it was, his daughter seemed blind to Billy's faults. The moment she saw him she forgot about their game. 75 80

"Hello, Billy-Boy," she called and ran over to hug him.

"I want a cookie," said Billy.

"Oh, yes, a cookie; some animal crackers, Daddy."

She had her hostess face on and as he went into the pantry, he could hear the treble[28] of her musical laughter against the premature baritone[29] of Billy's guffaws.[30] 85

He swung open the pantry door with the animal crackers in his hand just in time to see it. She was poised on the edge of the table. Billy was standing below her, as he had seen her father do. "Jump and I'll catch you," he was saying. 90

Smiling, confident and unblemished, she jumped. But no hands reached out to break her flight. With a cynical grin on his face, Billy stepped back and watched her fall.

Watching from the doorway, her father felt the horror that possessed him the time he saw a parachutist[31] smashed like a bug on a windshield when his chute failed to open. She was lying there, crying, not so much in pain as in disillusionment. He ran forward to pick her up and he would never forget the expression on her face, the *new* expression, unchildlike, unvirginal, embittered. 95 100

"I hate you, I hate you," she was screaming at Billy through hysterical sobs.

Well, now she knows, thought her father, the facts of life. Now she's one of us. Now she knows treachery and fear. Now she must learn to replace innocence with courage. 105

She was still bawling.[32] He knew these tears were as natural and as necessary as those she shed at birth, but that could not overcome entirely the heavy sadness that enveloped him. Finally, when he spoke, he said, a little more harshly than he had intended, "Now, now, stop crying. Stand up and act like a big girl. A little fall like that can't hurt you." 110

23 **mussed Billy's hair** ran his fingers through Billy's hair, making it untidy
24 **sturdy** firmly built, strong
25 **malicious** wanting to hurt someone
26 **extrovert** an outgoing personality who expresses feelings easily
27 **Legion Conventions** meetings of ex-servicemen

28 **treble** a high-pitched note (singing)
29 **premature baritone** the early deepening of a boy's voice
30 **guffaws** loud laughter
31 **parachutist** someone who jumps from an airplane with a safety device
32 **bawling** crying loudly

PART 1 First Reading

A   Thinking About the Story

Did you feel that the father's evaluation of his little girl was realistic? Did his attitude toward Billy make you at all uneasy? Give reasons for your answers.

B   Understanding the Plot

1. What does the father compare his daughter's appearance to in paragraph 1?
2. What does "the glass window" in line 8 refer to?
3. In what ways is the daughter still "undeceived"? (line 23)
4. Why is the jumping game the father and daughter play different from games like tag and hide-and-seek that they may play on other occasions? What in particular describes the jumping game's importance?
5. What does "it" in line 73 refer to?
6. Why is the father unhappy about Billy's arrival?
7. What are the father's main complaints against Billy?
8. What bothers the father about his daughter's reaction to Billy's arrival?
9. How does Billy betray the little girl?
10. What comparison is used to express the father's reaction on seeing his daughter fall?
11. How is the daughter changed by her fall?
12. Why does the father speak harshly to his daughter at the end?

PART 2 Second Reading

A   Exploring Themes

You are now ready to reread "A Short Digest of a Long Novel." Be sensitive to the undercurrents of jealousy the father displays toward Billy and the reasons for them.

1. What do you think the title means? Relate your answer to a central theme in the story.

2. What does the father's description of his daughter in paragraph 1 reveal about his feelings toward her?

3. What is the role of the sexual imagery in the story?

4. What is the importance of the jumping game to the story? In your answer look at both occasions on which the game is played and show how the girl is affected each time.

5. What does Billy represent for the father?

B Analyzing the Author's Style

For more information on the literary terms in this section, turn to the explanations of *imagery* (page 303), *simile* (page 307), and *metaphor* (page 305).

IMAGERY: Simile and Metaphor

In "A Short Digest of a Long Novel," Budd Schulberg constantly surprises the reader with his unexpected **imagery**, particularly his deft use of **simile** (an explicit comparison using *like* or *as* to unite the two elements) and **metaphor** (an implied comparison). For example, he writes of the father's horror as he impotently watches his daughter fall:

> *. . . her father felt the horror that possessed him the time he saw a* **parachutist smashed like a bug on a windshield** *when his chute failed to open.* (lines 95–97)

Here the two elements compared are the disintegrated parachutist and a crushed bug, which are in turn analogous to the father's emotions regarding his daughter's fall. The complex overall effect is to express the depth of the father's feelings as well as to act as a comment on the exaggeration of his response, for the one event is not by any stretch of the imagination really comparable to the other.

In an earlier example, a beautifully precise metaphor captures the father's fears about what lies ahead for his daughter when he worries about her as a *virgin island in a lewd world* (line 38). In this instance, his innocent daughter is compared in his mind to an untouched island surrounded by a vulgar world ready to corrupt and overwhelm it/her.

1. The long opening paragraph of "A Short Digest of a Long Novel" contains a sustained metaphor that explains how the father sees his daughter. What is it? Explain how the metaphor is extended and reworked throughout the paragraph.

2. What simile does the father use to describe his daughter's speech? What are the implications of employing such a simile to describe a three-year-old child?

3. Later in the story this same simile is translated into a metaphor, applying to both Billy and the daughter. Write down the metaphor and explain its two components. What does the metaphor describing Billy's voice reveal about the father's feelings toward him?

4. Pick out the simile in lines 20–21. What two elements are being compared? How does this simile reflect the father's state of mind?

5. What new metaphors can you find in lines 38–40? How do they fit in with the way the father views his daughter?

6. The last paragraph contains a metaphor. Explain what is being compared.

C   Judging for Yourself

Express yourself as personally as you like in your answers to the following questions.

1. Do you think that the father's jealousy is understandable?
2. Why do you suppose the mother plays such a small role in the story?
3. What effect might the father's protectiveness have on his daughter's development?
4. In your view, did Billy's behavior justify the father's fears?
5. Do you feel that the father's belief in his daughter's innocent perfection is unrealistic?

D   Making Connections

1. Do fathers tend to be very protective of their daughters in your culture? If so, how does this protectiveness manifest itself?
2. Are small children spoiled in your country? Who spoils them more often—mothers or fathers? Is one sex more spoiled than the other?
3. What are the traditional games parents play with small children in your country? Do you know whether any of these games are played elsewhere in the world?
4. Do you celebrate Christmas? If yes, describe a typical Christmas in your country. If not, describe a holiday custom that particularly excited you as a child.

E   Debate

Debate this proposition:

It is never too early to teach a child a lesson in reality.

PART 3   Focus on Language

A   Prefixes

Prefixes are placed at the beginning of words. Some examples of prefixes are *un-, im-, a-, ir-, in-, il-, dis-, mis-, pre-, re-, non-, mal-,* and *em-*. Adding prefixes to words changes their meaning. For example, the prefix *un-* when added to the word *popular* (well-liked) changes the meaning to "not well-liked."

1. With the help of your dictionary, make a list of words using each of the listed prefixes at least once. In parentheses, say how the prefix influences the meaning of the stem word.

2. All the words in the following list appear in some form in the story. Add prefixes to the words and use each prefixed word in a sentence to illustrate its meaning. Your sentences should accurately reflect the content of the Schulberg story.
   a. assure _____
   b. bitter _____
   c. illusion _____
   d. likes _____
   e. mature _____
   f. perfect _____
   g. reverently _____
   h. sensitive _____
   i. step _____
   j. natural _____

B   Practice with Similes and Metaphors

Complete the following sentences with your own similes.

1. When it came to his daughter, her father was as protective as _____ .

2. Peering at her through the glass window, he thought she looked like _____ .

3. Her untouched innocence was like _____.

4. As he thought of the jumping game, his heart beat like _____.

5. In the father's mind, Billy was as _____ as _____.

6. Leaping off the table, she sailed through the air like _____.

7. As quick as _____, he ran to pick her up.

8. As _____ as _____, she looked up at him.

9. Her father felt like a/an _____ when he bent down to pick up his daughter.

10. It was as _____ as _____ that she would ever trust him so completely again.

Underline the metaphors in the following sentences, and explain what two elements are being compared.

1. He remembered the nails of pain he felt on seeing her falling.

2. He felt a storm of love flooding his heart whenever he thought of his daughter.

3. He was shocked that her trust could shatter so easily.

4. She lay there, her petal mouth drooping visibly, as he flew to her side.

5. Billy's hyena laugh grated on his exposed nerves.

C   Building Vocabulary Skills

With a partner, look at the following sets of words. All the words appear in one form or another in "A Short Digest of a Long Novel." Each set has one word that does not fit in with the other two. Circle the word that does not match. Take turns with your partner to explain the reason for your choice.

1. defiled	nicked	unblemished
2. innocence	treachery	virginity
3. cracked	rocked	split
4. bawling	giggling	screaming
5. cynical	disillusioned	undeceived
6. awe	amazement	profundity
7. grain	maple	sculpture
8. baritone	sturdy	treble
9. exhilarate	obsess	resent
10. arrogant	conceited	malicious

PART 4 Writing Activities

1. Write an essay detailing an occasion in your life in which you experienced a profound change that affected you permanently. It could be related to an event like the death of a loved one, a meaningful religious ceremony, or the first time you left home. Be sure to convey when, why, and how you were so changed.

2. Write two to three paragraphs describing a person you know. Using the opening of the Schulberg story as a model, start your description without revealing the identity of your character, and slowly lead up to your revelation. Bring this person to life through fresh imagery appealing to the various senses, and try to sustain a metaphor through several lines of writing. Your metaphor might be based on your character's appearance, personality, or a particular nickname.

3. The movie *Father of the Bride*—the original with Spencer Tracy and Elizabeth Taylor and the remake with Steve Martin and Kimberly Williams—deals with the conflict a father has when his cherished only daughter announces that she is getting married. Write an essay on any book, movie, or play you have read or seen that centers on the father/daughter relationship. In your essay, analyze the nature of this bond, and say what aspects of the relationship you think are particular to the work you chose and which are more universal.

10

The Rocking-Horse Winner

D. H. LAWRENCE (1885–1930)

Born in Nottinghamshire, England, David Herbert Lawrence was the son of a coal miner father and teacher mother. One of England's most versatile and controversial writers, he produced a large body of work that includes novels, plays, poems, essays, travel pieces, and letters. Several of his novels—*The Rainbow* (1915), *Women in Love* (1920), and *Lady Chatterley's Lover* (1928)— were considered obscene and were initially banned in much of the world. His famous novel *Sons and Lovers* (1913) was heavily autobiographical and dealt with the themes of sex, class, and family that were to preoccupy him always.

In 1912, Lawrence eloped to Europe with Frieda von Richthofen Weekley, the wife of one of his university professors and mother of three children. They married in 1914, and Frieda became the inspiration for many of his fictional heroines. After World War I, the Lawrences traveled extensively, living in the warmer climates of Italy, Mexico, New Mexico, and Australia, among other places, as Lawrence sought relief from the tuberculosis that was killing him.

THE ROCKING-HORSE WINNER

*A young boy is determined to solve his mother's financial problems.
The method he chooses defies human logic and is ultimately dangerous.*

There was a woman who was beautiful, who started with all the advantages, yet she had no luck. She married for love, and the love turned to dust. She had bonny[1] children, yet she felt they had been thrust upon her, and she could not love them. They looked at her coldly, as if they were finding fault with her. And hurriedly she felt she must cover up some fault in herself. Yet what it was that she must cover up she never knew. Nevertheless, when her children were present, she always felt the centre of her heart go hard. This troubled her, and in her manner she was all the more gentle and anxious for her children, as if she loved them very much. Only she herself knew that at the centre of her heart was a hard little place that could not feel love, no, not for anybody. Everybody else said of her: "She is such a good mother. She adores her children." Only she herself, and her children themselves, know it was not so. They read it in each other's eyes.

There were a boy and two little girls. They lived in a pleasant house, with a garden, and they had discreet servants, and felt themselves superior to anyone in the neighbourhood.

Although they lived in style, they felt always an anxiety in the house. There was never enough money. The mother had a small income, and the father had a small income, but not nearly enough for the social position which they had to keep up.[2] The father went into town to some office. But though he had good prospects,[3] these prospects never materialized. There was always the grinding sense of the shortage of money, though the style was always kept up.

At last the mother said: "I will see if *I* can't make something." But she did not know where to begin. She racked her brains,[4] and tried this thing and the other, but could not find anything successful. The failure made deep lines come into her face. Her children were growing up, they would have to go to school. There must be more money, there must be more money. The father, who was always very handsome and expensive in his tastes, seemed as if he never *would* be able to do anything worth doing. And the mother, who had a great belief in herself, did not succeed any better, and her tastes were just as expensive.

And so the house came to be haunted by the unspoken phrase: *There must be more money! There must be more money!* The children could hear

5

10

15

20

25

30

35

---

1 **bonny** healthy and attractive
2 **keep up** maintain
3 **had good prospects** anticipated a good future

4 **racked her brains** thought as hard as she could

it all the time, though nobody said it aloud. They heard it at Christmas, when the expensive and splendid toys filled the nursery. Behind the shining modern rocking-horse, behind the smart doll's house, a voice would start whispering: "There *must* be more money! There *must* be more money!" And the children would stop playing, to listen for a moment. They would look into each other's eyes, to see if they had all heard. And each one saw in the eyes of the other two that they too had heard. "There *must* be more money! There *must* be more money!"

It came whispering from the springs of the still-swaying rocking-horse, and even the horse, bending his wooden, champing⁵ head, heard it. The big doll, sitting so pink and smirking⁶ in her new pram, could hear it quite plainly, and seemed to be smirking all the more self-consciously because of it. The foolish puppy, too, that took the place of the teddy-bear, he was looking so extraordinarily foolish for no other reason but that he heard the secret whisper all over the house: "There *must* be more money!"

Yet nobody ever said it aloud. The whisper was everywhere, and therefore no one spoke it. Just as no one ever says: "We are breathing!" in spite of the fact that breath is coming and going all the time.

"Mother," said the boy Paul one day, "why don't we keep a car of our own? Why do we always use uncle's, or else a taxi?"

"Because we're the poor members of the family," said the mother.

"But why *are* we, mother?"

"Well—I suppose," she said slowly and bitterly, "it's because your father had no luck."

The boy was silent for some time.

"Is luck money, mother?" he asked, rather timidly.

"No, Paul. Not quite. It's what causes you to have money."

"Oh!" said Paul vaguely. "I thought when Uncle Oscar said *filthy lucker*,⁷ it meant money."

"*Filthy lucre* does mean money," said the mother. "But it's lucre, not luck."

"Oh!" said the boy. "Then what *is* luck, mother?"

"It's what causes you to have money. If you're lucky you have money. That's why it's better to be born lucky than rich. If you're rich, you may lose your money. But if you're lucky, you will always get more money."

"Oh! Will you? And is father not lucky?"

"Very unlucky, I should say," she said bitterly.

The boy watched her with unsure eyes.

"Why?" he asked.

"I don't know. Nobody ever knows why one person is lucky and another unlucky."

"Don't they? Nobody at all? Does *nobody* know?"

"Perhaps God. But He never tells."

---

5 **champing** impatient
6 **smirking** smiling in a silly, self-satisfied way

7 **filthy lucker** should be written as *filthy lucre*, which is a negative term for *money*

"He ought to, then. And aren't you lucky either, mother?"

"I can't be, if I married an unlucky husband." 80

"But by yourself, aren't you?"

"I used to think I was, before I married. Now I think I am very unlucky indeed."

"Why?"

"Well—never mind! Perhaps I'm not really," she said. 85

The child looked at her to see if she meant it. But he saw, by the lines of her mouth, that she was only trying to hide something from him.

"Well, anyhow," he said stoutly, "I'm a lucky person."

"Why?" said his mother, with a sudden laugh.

He stared at her. He didn't even know why he had said it. 90

"God told me," he asserted, brazening it out. [8]

"I hope He did, dear!" she said, again with a laugh, but rather bitter.

"He did, mother!"

"Excellent!" said the mother, using one of her husband's exclamations.

The boy saw she did not believe him; or rather, that she paid no 95 attention to his assertion. This angered him somewhere, and made him want to compel her attention.

He went off by himself, vaguely, in a childish way, seeking for the clue to "luck." Absorbed, taking no heed of other people, he went about with a sort of stealth, seeking inwardly for luck. He wanted luck, he 100 wanted it, he wanted it. When the two girls were playing dolls in the nursery, he would sit on his big rocking-horse, charging madly into space, with a frenzy that made the little girls peer at him uneasily. Wildly the horse careered, [9] the waving dark hair of the boy tossed, his eyes had a strange glare in them. The little girls dared not speak to him. 105

When he had ridden to the end of his mad little journey, he climbed down and stood in front of his rocking-horse, staring fixedly into its lowered face. Its red mouth was slightly open, its big eye was wide and glassy-bright.

"Now!" he would silently command the snorting steed. [10] "Now, take 110 me to where there is luck! Now take me!"

And he would slash the horse on the neck with the little whip he had asked Uncle Oscar for. He *knew* the horse could take him to where there was luck, if only he forced it. So he would mount again and start on his furious ride, hoping at last to get there. He knew he could get there. 115

"You'll break your horse, Paul!" said the nurse.

"He's always riding like that! I wish he'd leave off!" said his elder sister Joan.

But he only glared down on them in silence. Nurse gave him up. She could make nothing of him. Anyhow, he was growing beyond her. 120

One day his mother and his Uncle Oscar came in when he was on one of his furious rides. He did not speak to them.

---

8 **brazening it out** deliberately sounding confident, even though he is not

9 **careered** moved at top speed
10 **snorting steed** a noisy horse

"Hallo, you young jockey![11] Riding a winner?" said his uncle.

"Aren't you growing too big for a rocking-horse? You're not a very little boy any longer, you know," said his mother.

But Paul only gave a blue glare from his big, rather close-set eyes. He would speak to nobody when he was in full tilt.[12] His mother watched him with an anxious expression on her face.

At last he suddenly stopped forcing his horse into the mechanical gallop and slid down.

"Well, I got there!" he announced fiercely, his blue eyes still flaring, and his sturdy long legs straddling apart.

"Where did you get to?" asked his mother.

"Where I wanted to go," he flared back at her.

"That's right, son!" said Uncle Oscar. "Don't you stop till you get there. What's the horse's name?"

"He doesn't have a name," said the boy.

"Gets on without all right?" asked the uncle.

"Well, he has different names. He was called Sansovino last week."

"Sansovino, eh? Won the Ascot. How did you know this name?"

"He always talks about horse-races with Bassett," said Joan.

The uncle was delighted to find that his small nephew was posted with all the racing news.[13] Bassett, the young gardener, who had been wounded in the left foot in the war and had got his present job through Oscar Cresswell, whose batman[14] he had been, was a perfect blade of the "turf."[15] He lived in the racing events, and the small boy lived with him.

Oscar Cresswell got it all from Bassett.

"Master Paul comes and asks me, so I can't do more than tell him, sir," said Bassett, his face terribly serious, as if he were speaking of religious matters.

"And does he ever put anything on a horse he fancies?"[16]

"Well—I don't want to give him away—he's a young sport, a fine sport, sir. Would you mind asking him himself? He sort of takes a pleasure in it, and perhaps he'd feel I was giving him away, sir, if you don't mind." Bassett was serious as a church.

The uncle went back to his nephew and took him off for a ride in the car.

"Say, Paul, old man, do you ever put anything on a horse?" the uncle asked.

The boy watched the handsome man closely.

"Why, do you think I oughtn't to?" he parried.[17]

"Not a bit of it! I thought perhaps you might give me a tip for the Lincoln."

---

11 **jockey** a professional who rides a horse in a race
12 **in full tilt** moving at full speed
13 **was posted with all the racing news** was fully informed about racing
14 **batman** a servant of an officer in the British army
15 **blade of the "turf"** a lively follower of horse-racing
16 **put anything on a horse he fancies** bet money on a horse he likes
17 **parried** avoided answering directly

The car sped on into the country, going down to Uncle Oscar's place in Hampshire. [165]

"Honour bright?"[18] said the nephew.

"Honour bright, son!" said the uncle.

"Well, then, Daffodil."

"Daffodil! I doubt it, sonny. What about Mirza?"

"I only know the winner," said the boy. "That's Daffodil." [170]

"Daffodil, eh?"

There was a pause. Daffodil was an obscure[19] horse comparatively.

"Uncle!"

"Yes, son?"

"You won't let it go any further,[20] will you? I promised Bassett." [175]

"Bassett be damned, old man! What's he got to do with it?"

"We're partners. We've been partners from the first. Uncle, he lent me my first five shillings, which I lost. I promised him, honour bright, it was only between me and him; only you gave me that ten-shilling note I started winning with, so I thought you were lucky. You won't let it go [180] any further, will you?"

The boy gazed at his uncle from those big, hot, blue eyes, set rather close together. The uncle stirred and laughed uneasily.

"Right you are, son! I'll keep your tip[21] private. Daffodil, eh? How much are you putting on him?" [185]

"All except twenty pounds," said the boy. "I keep that in reserve."[22]

The uncle thought it a good joke.

"You keep twenty pounds in reserve, do you, you young romancer? What are you betting, then?"

"I'm betting three hundred," said the boy gravely. "But it's between [190] you and me, Uncle Oscar! Honour bright?"

The uncle burst into a roar of laughter.

"It's between you and me all right, you young Nat Gould,"[23] he said, laughing. "But where's your three hundred?"

"Bassett keeps it for me. We're partners." [195]

"You are, are you! And what is Bassett putting on Daffodil?"

"He won't go quite as high as I do, I expect. Perhaps he'll go a hundred and fifty."

"What, pennies?" laughed the uncle.

"Pounds," said the child, with a surprised look at his uncle. "Bassett [200] keeps a bigger reserve than I do."

Between wonder and amusement Uncle Oscar was silent. He pursued the matter no further, but he determined to take his nephew with him to the Lincoln races.

---

18 **Honour bright?** Do you swear you are telling the truth?

19 **obscure** unknown

20 **You won't let it go any further** You won't tell anybody

21 **tip** special information

22 **keep that in reserve** save it

23 **Nat Gould** an English sportswriter who wrote 130 thrillers about horse-racing

"Now, son," he said, "I'm putting twenty on Mirza, and I'll put five on for you on any horse you fancy. What's your pick?"   205

"Daffodil, uncle."

"No, not the fiver on Daffodil!"

"I should if it was my own fiver," said the child.

"Good! Good! Right you are! A fiver for me and a fiver for you on Daffodil."   210

The child had never been to a race-meeting before, and his eyes were blue fire. He pursed his mouth tight[24] and watched. A Frenchman just in front had put his money on Lancelot. Wild with excitement, he flayed his arms up and down, yelling "*Lancelot! Lancelot!*" in his French accent.   215

Daffodil came in first, Lancelot second, Mirza third. The child, flushed and with eyes blazing, was curiously serene. His uncle brought him four five-pound notes, four to one.

"What am I to do with these?" he cried, waving them before the boy's eyes.   220

"I suppose we'll talk to Bassett," said the boy. "I expect I have fifteen hundred now; and twenty in reserve; and this twenty."

His uncle studied him for some moments.

"Look here, son!" he said. "You're not serious about Bassett and that fifteen hundred, are you?"   225

"Yes, I am. But it's between you and me, uncle. Honour bright?"

"Honour bright all right, son! But I must talk to Bassett."

"If you'd like to be a partner, uncle, with Bassett and me, we could all be partners. Only, you'd have to promise, honour bright, uncle, not to let it go beyond us three. Bassett and I are lucky, and you must be lucky, because it was your ten shillings I started winning with . . ."   230

Uncle Oscar took both Bassett and Paul into Richmond Park for an afternoon, and there they talked.

"It's like this, you see, sir," Bassett said. "Master Paul would get me talking about racing events, spinning yarns,[25] you know, sir. And he was always keen on knowing if I'd made or if I'd lost. It's about a year since, now, that I put five shillings on Blush of Dawn for him: and we lost. Then the luck turned, with that ten shillings he had from you: that we put on Singhalese. And since that time, it's been pretty steady, all things considering.[26] What do you say, Master Paul?"   235 240

"We're all right when we're sure," said Paul. "It's when we're not quite sure that we go down."[27]

"Oh, but we're careful then," said Bassett.

"But when are you *sure?*" smiled Uncle Oscar.   245

---

24 **pursed his mouth tight** drew his lips together in an expression of concentration

25 **spinning yarns** telling long stories—not always true

26 **all things considering** when everything is taken into account

27 **go down** lose

"It's Master Paul, sir," said Bassett in a secret, religious voice. "It's as if he had it from heaven. Like Daffodil, now, for the Lincoln. That was as sure as eggs."[28]

"Did you put anything on Daffodil?" asked Oscar Cresswell.

"Yes, sir. I made my bit." 250

"And my nephew?"

Bassett was obstinately silent, looking at Paul.

"I made twelve hundred, didn't I, Bassett? I told uncle I was putting three hundred on Daffodil."

"That's right," said Bassett, nodding. 255

"But where's the money?" asked the uncle.

"I keep it safe locked up, sir. Master Paul he can have it any minute he likes to ask for it."

"What, fifteen hundred pounds?"

"And twenty! And *forty,* that is, with the twenty he made on the course." 260

"It's amazing!" said the uncle.

"If Master Paul offers you to be partners, sir, I would, if I were you: if you'll excuse me," said Bassett.

Oscar Cresswell thought about it.

"I'll see the money," he said. 265

They drove home again, and, sure enough, Bassett came round to the garden-house with fifteen hundred pounds in notes. The twenty pounds reserve was left with Joe Glee, in the Turf Commission[29] deposit.

"You see, it's all right, uncle, when I'm *sure*! Then we go strong, for all we're worth. Don't we, Bassett?" 270

"We do that, Master Paul."

"And when are you sure?" said the uncle, laughing.

"Oh, well, sometimes I'm *absolutely* sure, like about Daffodil," said the boy; "and sometimes I have an idea; and sometimes I haven't even an idea, have I, Bassett? Then we're careful, because we mostly go down." 275

"You do, do you! And when you're sure, like about Daffodil, what makes you sure, sonny?"

"Oh, well, I don't know," said the boy uneasily. "I'm sure, you know, uncle; that's all."

"It's as if he had it from heaven, sir," Bassett reiterated. 280

"I should say so!" said the uncle.

But he became a partner. And when the Leger was coming on Paul was "sure" about Lively Spark, which was a quite inconsiderable[30] horse. The boy insisted on putting a thousand on the horse, Bassett went for five hundred, and Oscar Cresswell two hundred. Lively Spark came in first, and 285 the betting had been ten to one against him. Paul had made ten thousand.

"You see," he said, "I was absolutely sure of him."

Even Oscar Cresswell had cleared two thousand.

---

28 **as sure as eggs** absolutely certain
29 **Turf Commission** racetrack authority

30 **inconsiderable** unimportant

"Look here, son," he said, "this sort of thing makes me nervous."

"It needn't, uncle! Perhaps I shan't be sure again for a long time." 290

"But what are you going to do with your money?" asked the uncle.

"Of course," said the boy, "I started it for mother. She said she had no luck, because father is unlucky, so I thought if I was lucky, it might stop whispering."

"What might stop whispering?" 295

"Our house. I *hate* our house for whispering."

"What does it whisper?"

"Why—why"— the boy fidgeted[31]— "why, I don't know. But it's always short of money, you know, uncle."

"I know it, son, I know it." 300

"You know people send mother writs,[32] don't you, uncle?"

"I'm afraid I do," said the uncle.

"And then the house whispers, like people laughing at you behind your back. It's awful, that is! I thought if I was lucky—"

"You might stop it," added the uncle. 305

The boy watched him with big blue eyes, that had an uncanny[33] cold fire in them, and he said never a word.

"Well, then!" said the uncle. "What are we doing?"

"I shouldn't like mother to know I was lucky," said the boy.

"Why not, son?" 310

"She'd stop me."

"I don't think she would."

"Oh!"— and the boy writhed[34] in an odd way—"I *don't* want her to know, uncle."

"All right, son! We'll manage it without her knowing." 315

They managed it very easily. Paul, at the other's suggestion, handed over five thousand pounds to his uncle, who deposited it with the family lawyer, who was then to inform Paul's mother that a relative had put five thousand pounds into his hands, which sum was to be paid out a thousand pounds at a time, on the mother's birthday, for the next five years. 320

"So she'll have a birthday present of a thousand pounds for five successive years," said Uncle Oscar. "I hope it won't make it all the harder for her later."

Paul's mother had her birthday in November. The house had been "whispering" worse than ever lately, and, even in spite of his luck, Paul 325 could not bear up against it. He was very anxious to see the effect of the birthday letter, telling his mother about the thousand pounds.

When there were no visitors, Paul now took his meals with his parents, as he was beyond the nursery control. His mother went into town nearly every day. She had discovered that she had an odd knack[35] of 330 sketching furs and dress materials, so she worked secretly in the studio of

---

31 **fidgeted** moved uneasily   34 **writhed** moved as if in pain
32 **writs** legal notices about debts   35 **knack** talent
33 **uncanny** uncomfortably strange

a friend who was the chief "artist" for the leading drapers. She drew the figures of ladies in furs and ladies in silk and sequins for the newspaper advertisements. This young woman artist earned several thousand pounds a year, but Paul's mother only made several hundreds, and she was again **335** dissatisfied. She so wanted to be first in something, and she did not succeed, even in making sketches for drapery advertisements.

She was down to breakfast on the morning of her birthday. Paul watched her face as she read her letters. He knew the lawyer's letter. As his mother read it, her face hardened and became more expressionless. **340** Then a cold, determined look came on her mouth. She hid the letter under the pile of others, and said not a word about it.

"Didn't you have anything nice in the post for your birthday, mother?" said Paul.

"Quite moderately nice," she said, her voice cold and absent. **345**

She went away to town without saying more.

But in the afternoon Uncle Oscar appeared. He said Paul's mother had had a long interview with the lawyer, asking if the whole five thousand could not be advanced at once, as she was in debt.

"What do you think, uncle?" said the boy. **350**

"I leave it to you, son."

"Oh, let her have it, then! We can get some more with the other," said the boy.

"A bird in the hand is worth two in the bush, laddie!" said Uncle Oscar. **355**

"But I'm sure to *know* for the Grand National; or the Lincolnshire; or else the Derby. I'm sure to know for *one* of them," said Paul.

So Uncle Oscar signed the agreement, and Paul's mother touched the whole five thousand. Then something very curious happened. The voices in the house suddenly went mad, like a chorus of frogs on a spring **360** evening. There were certain new furnishings, and Paul had a tutor.[36] He was *really* going to Eton, his father's school, in the following autumn. There were flowers in the winter, and a blossoming of the luxury Paul's mother had been used to. And yet the voices in the house, behind the sprays of mimosa and almond-blossom, and from under the piles of **365** iridescent[37] cushions, simply trilled and screamed in a sort of ecstasy: "There *must* be more money! Oh-h-h; there *must* be more money. Oh, now, now-w! Now-w-w—there *must* be more money!—more than ever! More than ever!"

It frightened Paul terribly. He studied away at his Latin and Greek **370** with his tutor. But his intense hours were spent with Bassett. The Grand National had gone by; he had not "known," and had lost a hundred pounds. Summer was at hand. He was in agony for the Lincoln. But even for the Lincoln he didn't "know," and he lost fifty pounds. He became wild-eyed and strange, as if something were going to explode in him. **375**

---

36 **tutor** a special home teacher   37 **iridescent** shining brightly with rainbow colors

"Let it alone, son! Don't you bother about it!" urged Uncle Oscar. But it was as if the boy couldn't really hear what his uncle was saying.

"I've got to know for the Derby! I've got to know for the Derby!" the child reiterated, his big blue eyes blazing with a sort of madness.

His mother noticed how overwrought[38] he was.   380

"You'd better go to the seaside. Wouldn't you like to go now to the seaside, instead of waiting? I think you'd better," she said, looking down at him anxiously, her heart curiously heavy because of him.

But the child lifted his uncanny blue eyes.

"I couldn't possibly go before the Derby, mother!" he said. "I couldn't   385
possibly!"

"Why not?" she said, her voice becoming heavy when she was opposed. "Why not? You can still go from the seaside to see the Derby with your Uncle Oscar, if that's what you wish. No need for you to wait here. Besides, I think you care too much about these races. It's a bad   390
sign. My family has been a gambling family, and you won't know till you grow up how much damage it has done. But it has done damage. I shall have to send Bassett away, and ask Uncle Oscar not to talk racing to you, unless you promise to be reasonable about it: go away to the seaside and forget it. You're all nerves!"   395

"I'll do what you like, mother, so long as you don't send me away till after the Derby," the boy said.

"Send you away from where? Just from this house?"

"Yes," he said, gazing at her.

"Why, you curious child, what makes you care about this house so   400
much, suddenly? I never knew you loved it."

He gazed at her without speaking. He had a secret within a secret, something he had not divulged, even to Bassett or to his Uncle Oscar.

But his mother, after standing undecided and a little bit sullen[39] for some moments, said: 405

"Very well, then! Don't go to the seaside till after the Derby, if you don't wish it. But promise me you won't let your nerves go to pieces.[40] Promise you won't think so much about horse-racing, and *events,* as you call them!"

"Oh no," said the boy casually. "I won't think much about them,   410
mother. You needn't worry. I wouldn't worry, mother, if I were you."

"If you were me and I were you," said his mother, "I wonder what we *should* do!"

"But you know you needn't worry, mother, don't you?" the boy repeated.

"I should be awfully glad to know it," she said wearily.   415

"Oh, well, you *can,* you know. I mean, you *ought* to know you needn't worry," he insisted.

"Ought I? Then I'll see about it," she said.

---

38 **overwrought** excessively agitated
39 **sullen** unsmiling

40 **let your nerves go to pieces** have a nervous breakdown

Paul's secret of secrets was his wooden horse, that which had no name. Since he was emancipated from a nurse and a nursery-governess, he had had his rocking-horse removed to his own bedroom at the top of the house. **420**

"Surely you're too big for a rocking-horse!" his mother had remonstrated.

"Well, you see, mother, till I can have a *real* horse, I like to have *some* sort of animal about," had been his quaint answer.

"Do you feel he keeps you company?" she laughed. **425**

"Oh yes! He's very good, he always keeps me company, when I'm there," said Paul.

So the horse, rather shabby, stood in an arrested prance[41] in the boy's bedroom.

The Derby was drawing near, and the boy grew more and more tense. **430** He hardly heard what was spoken to him, he was very frail, and his eyes were really uncanny. His mother had sudden strange seizures of uneasiness about him. Sometimes, for half an hour, she would feel a sudden anxiety about him that was almost anguish. She wanted to rush to him at once, and know he was safe. **435**

Two nights before the Derby, she was at a big party in town, when one of her rushes of anxiety about her boy, her first-born, gripped her heart till she could hardly speak. She fought with the feeling, might and main,[42] for she believed in common sense. But it was too strong. She had to leave the dance and go downstairs to telephone to the country. The **440** children's nursery-governess was terribly surprised and startled at being rung up in the night.

"Are the children all right, Miss Wilmot?"

"Oh yes, they are quite all right."

"Master Paul? Is he all right?" **445**

"He went to bed as right as a trivet.[43] Shall I run up and look at him?"

"No," said Paul's mother reluctantly. "No! Don't trouble. It's all right. Don't sit up. We shall be home fairly soon." She did not want her son's privacy intruded upon.

"Very good," said the governess. **450**

It was about one o'clock when Paul's mother and father drove up to their house. All was still. Paul's mother went to her room and slipped off her white fur cloak. She had told her maid not to wait up for her. She heard her husband downstairs, mixing a whisky and soda.

And then, because of the strange anxiety at her heart, she stole **455** upstairs to her son's room. Noiselessly she went along the upper corridor. Was there a faint noise? What was it?

She stood, with arrested muscles, outside his door, listening. There was a strange, heavy, and yet not loud noise. Her heart stood still. It was a soundless noise, yet rushing and powerful. Something huge, in violent, **460**

---

41 **stood in an arrested prance** looked as if it had suddenly stopped with its front hooves in the air

42 **fought might and main** fought as hard as possible

43 **as right as a trivet** absolutely fine (a trivet is a three-footed stand or support)

hushed motion. What was it? What in God's name was it? She ought to know. She felt that she knew the noise. She knew what it was.

Yet she could not place it. She couldn't say what it was. And on and on it went, like a madness.

Softly, frozen with anxiety and fear, she turned the doorhandle.   465

The room was dark. Yet in the space near the window, she heard and saw something plunging to and fro.⁴⁴ She gazed in fear and amazement.

Then suddenly she switched on the light, and saw her son, in his green pyjamas, madly surging on the rocking-horse. The blaze of light suddenly lit him up, as he urged the wooden horse, and lit her up, as   470 she stood, blonde, in her dress of pale green and crystal, in the doorway.

"Paul!" she cried. "Whatever are you doing?"

"It's Malabar!" he screamed in a powerful, strange voice. "It's Malabar!" His eyes blazed at her for one strange and senseless second, as he ceased urging his wooden horse. Then he fell with a crash to the ground, and   475 she, all her tormented motherhood flooding upon her, rushed to gather him up.

But he was unconscious, and unconscious he remained, with some brain-fever. He talked and tossed, and his mother sat stonily by his side. "Malabar! It's Malabar! Bassett, Bassett, I *know*! It's Malabar!"   480

So the child cried, trying to get up and urge the rocking-horse that gave him his inspiration.

"What does he mean by Malabar?" asked the heart-frozen mother.

"I don't know," said the father stonily.

"What does he mean by Malabar?" she asked her brother Oscar.   485

"It's one of the horses running for the Derby," was the answer.

And, in spite of himself, Oscar Cresswell spoke to Bassett, and himself put a thousand on Malabar: at fourteen to one.

The third day of the illness was critical: they were waiting for a change. The boy, with his rather long, curly hair, was tossing ceaselessly   490 on the pillow. He neither slept nor regained consciousness, and his eyes were like blue stones. His mother sat, feeling her heart had gone, turned actually into a stone.

In the evening, Oscar Cresswell did not come, but Bassett sent a message, saying could he come up for one moment, just one moment?   495 Paul's mother was very angry at the intrusion, but on second thoughts she agreed. The boy was the same. Perhaps Bassett might bring him to consciousness.

The gardener, a shortish fellow with a little brown moustache and sharp little brown eyes, tiptoed into the room, touched his imaginary cap   500 to Paul's mother, and stole to the bedside, staring with glittering, smallish eyes at the tossing, dying child.

"Master Paul!" he whispered. "Master Paul! Malabar came in first all right, a clean win. I did as you told me. You've made over seventy thousand

---

44 **plunging to and fro** moving violently up and down

pounds, you have; you've got over eighty thousand. Malabar came in all   505
right, Master Paul."

"Malabar! Malabar! Did I say Malabar, mother? Did I say Malabar? Do
you think I'm lucky, mother? I knew Malabar, didn't I? Over eighty
thousand pounds! I call that lucky, don't you, mother? Over eighty
thousand pounds! I knew, didn't I know I knew? Malabar came in all   510
right. If I ride my horse till I'm sure, then I tell you, Bassett, you can go
as high as you like. Did you go for all you were worth, Bassett?"

"I went a thousand on it, Master Paul."

"I never told you, mother, that if I can ride my horse, and *get there,*
then I'm absolutely sure—oh, absolutely! Mother, did I ever tell you? I *am*   515
lucky!"

"No, you never did," said his mother.

But the boy died in the night.

And even as he lay dead, his mother heard her brother's voice saying
to her: "My God, Hester, you're eighty-odd thousand to the good,[45] and   520
a poor devil of a son to the bad. But, poor devil, poor devil, he's best
gone out of a life where he rides his rocking-horse to find a winner."

---

45 **eighty-odd thousand to the good** a gain of
    approximately eighty thousand pounds

PART 1   First Reading

A   Thinking About the Story

Could you feel the power of Paul's obsession? Were you able to
respond to the supernatural element in the story? Say why or
why not.

B   Understanding the Plot

1. Why is there always a shortage of money in Paul's household?
   Is the family poor?
2. Whom does the mother blame for their financial difficulties?
   Is she correct?
3. Why does the mother think that luck is more important than
   wealth?
4. What does Uncle Oscar enjoy doing in his spare time?
5. Who is Bassett, and what is his connection to Uncle Oscar?
6. Why does Paul confide in Uncle Oscar?

7. At what point does Uncle Oscar start to take Paul seriously?

8. Why do people send Paul's mother writs? (line 301)

9. Why is the mother working secretly in a friend's studio? (lines 331–332)

10. Does Paul's mother's birthday check solve her financial problems? Explain your answer.

11. What is the mother's attitude toward gambling?

12. Does Paul's mother show any love toward Paul? Explain your answer as fully as possible.

13. What killed Paul?

PART 2 Second Reading

A Exploring Themes

You are now ready to reread "The Rocking-Horse Winner." Think carefully about why Paul is so driven to make money for his mother and about the role of those around him in encouraging this obsession.

1. What is the importance of the frequent references to eyes in the story?

2. What are the supernatural aspects of the story?

3. How important is social class to the story?

4. Who in your view is to blame for Paul's tragedy? You need not limit yourself to only one person.

5. What is the role of the father in the story?

B Analyzing the Author's Style

For more information on the literary terms in this section, turn to the explanations of *symbol* (page 308) and *fable* (page 302).

SYMBOL

D. H. Lawrence uses the rocking horse in the story as a powerful and complex **symbol** with several layers of meaning. The deeper you delve into the symbolism, the more it reveals about the wider personal and social issues Lawrence is concerned with.

1. What does the rocking horse symbolize? Give as many details as you can to support your answer.
2. What descriptions of the rocking horse scenes help reinforce the symbolism?
3. Why do you think Lawrence chose a rocking horse as the central symbol?
4. Money is used both literally and symbolically in the text. What is its symbolic importance?

FABLE

Lawrence's story of the child who rides a rocking horse in a desperate attempt to make money for his mother is written like a **fable**, which is a short story, often with animals in it, that is told to illustrate a moral.

1. What qualities does "The Rocking-Horse Winner" share with a fable?
2. How does the opening paragraph suggest a fable?
3. What is the moral of the story? Explain it in your own words.

C   Judging for Yourself

Express yourself as personally as you like in your answers to the following questions.

1. Do you think the mother is capable of loving anybody?
2. Do you think she learns her lesson at the end of the story?
3. Would you agree with her that it is important in life to be lucky?
4. Do you think that Bassett should be punished for his role in Paul's gambling?
5. In your view, could Paul's father have helped avert the tragedy? If so, how?

D   Making Connections

1. What is the attitude toward gambling in your country?
2. Have you ever gambled? If so, in what way? Did you win or lose money?
3. Have you, or anybody you know, ever been obsessed by anything? If yes, explain the obsession.

4. Do you have superstitions in your country about what is lucky and unlucky? What are they?

5. Do you believe in the supernatural? Explain why or why not.

E Debate

Debate this proposition:

Gambling is a harmful activity that should be banned.

PART 3 Focus on Language

A Proverbs

A **proverb** is a short saying that expresses a common truth familiar to most people in a particular society. For example, in "The Rocking-Horse Winner," Uncle Oscar tells Paul, "*A bird in the hand is worth two in the bush*" (line 354). This suggests that what we already have is more valuable than what we want but have not yet acquired. English, like many languages, is rich in proverbs.

With a partner, try to work out the meaning of the following proverbs.

A fool and his money are soon parted.
A stitch in time saves nine.
A watched pot never boils.
Better late than never.
Birds of a feather flock together.
Don't count your chickens before they hatch.
His bark is worse than his bite.
Look before you leap.
Make hay while the sun shines.
Money is the root of all evil.
Money talks.
Necessity is the mother of invention.
Silence is golden.
Time is money.
Too many cooks spoil the broth.

With your partner, make up a series of dialogues in which one of you says something that makes the other one respond with an appropriate proverb. For example:

> **PARTNER A:** I've just been offered a part in a new play. However, since it's not the main role, I'm going to turn it down and wait for a better one.
>
> **PARTNER B:** I wouldn't do that. *A bird in the hand is worth two in the bush.*

Translate five proverbs from your language into English and share them with the class.

B Building Vocabulary Skills

The expressions below are all explained in the glossary accompanying the story.

> had good prospects (line 22)
>
> racked her brains (lines 26)
>
> brazen it out (line 91)
>
> in full tilt (line 127)
>
> You won't let it go any further. (lines 180–181)
>
> pursed his mouth tight (line 213)
>
> go to pieces (line 407)
>
> fought might and main (lines 438–439)
>
> eighty-odd thousand to the good (line 520)

To make sure that you understand the meaning of each expression, first give a situation in which the expression might appropriately be used. Then use it in a sentence, underlining the expression. For example:

> **SITUATION:** The future looked promising for a young graduate.
>
> **SENTENCE:** In my first job, I <u>had good prospects</u> and expected to be promoted in a few months.

PART 4 Writing Activities

1. Imagine that you have won a million dollars from gambling. In a two-page essay, first consider how you would feel acquiring such a huge sum overnight. Next explain what you think you would do with the money, and give the reasons for your decisions. In your conclusion, say whether winning so much would be morally corrupting. Try to incorporate at least one proverb concerning money into your text.

2. Would you say that your culture is particularly materialistic? After defining the term *materialistic*, examine this question in a two-page essay, giving as many reasons as possible to support your answer. In your conclusion, compare attitudes toward money in your country with attitudes in the United States.

3. Henry James wrote a famous story, "The Turn of the Screw," in which the supernatural plays an extremely important part. The story was later made into a movie and an opera. Write an essay about a story, play, movie, or opera you know in which the supernatural is a dominant element. Briefly recount the plot. Then, using lines 34–50 of "The Rocking-Horse Winner" as a model, try to recreate the atmosphere of the work and say how you were affected.

11

The Boarding House

JAMES JOYCE (1882–1941)

Born in Dublin, Ireland, James Joyce became one of the most influential writers of the twentieth century. He was a brilliant student, attending a famous Jesuit boarding school until his father's bankruptcy forced him to leave. In 1904, he left the Catholic Church and departed from Ireland for good. Joyce married and lived with his family in Trieste, Zurich, and Paris, where he taught English and wrote the works that made him famous.

In 1914, Joyce published *Dubliners,* which he described as representing "a chapter of the moral history" of Ireland. Then came *A Portrait of the Artist as a Young Man* (1916), which fictionalized Joyce's break with the Catholic Church and his assumption of the role of writer. In his great novel *Ulysses* (1922), Joyce perfected the technique of stream of consciousness, creating interior monologues in which time is disrupted to capture the inner thought processes of the characters. This novel established Joyce as a major writer who influenced the work of Virginia Woolf and William Faulkner, among others.

THE BOARDING HOUSE

*A domineering mother watches her daughter flirt with
a young man and plots their future.*

Mrs Mooney was a butcher's daughter. She was a woman who was quite able to keep things to herself:[1] a determined woman. She had married her father's foreman, and opened a butcher's shop near Spring Gardens. But as soon as his father-in-law was dead Mr Mooney began to go to the devil. He drank, plundered the till,[2] ran headlong into debt. It 5 was no use making him take the pledge:[3] he was sure to break out again a few days after. By fighting his wife in the presence of customers and by buying bad meat he ruined his business. One night he went for[4] his wife with the cleaver, and she had to sleep in a neighbour's house.

After that they lived apart. She went to the priest and got a separation 10 from him, with care of the children. She would give him neither money nor food nor house-room; and so he was obliged to enlist himself as a sheriff's man.[5] He was a shabby[6] stooped[7] little drunkard with a white face and a white moustache and white eyebrows, pencilled above his little eyes, which were pink-veined and raw; and all day long he sat in 15 the bailiff's[8] room, waiting to be put on a job. Mrs Mooney, who had taken what remained of her money out of the butcher business and set up a boarding house in Hardwicke Street, was a big imposing woman. Her house had a floating population made up of tourists from Liverpool and the Isle of Man and, occasionally, *artistes*[9] from the music halls. Its 20 resident population was made up of clerks from the city. She governed the house cunningly and firmly, knew when to give credit,[10] when to be stern and when to let things pass. All the resident young men spoke of her as *The Madam*.

Mrs Mooney's young men paid fifteen shillings a week for board and 25 lodgings (beer or stout at dinner excluded). They shared in common tastes and occupations and for this reason they were very chummy[11] with one another. They discussed with one another the chances of favourites and outsiders.[12] Jack Mooney, the Madam's son, who was clerk to a commission

---

1 **keep things to herself** keep a secret
2 **plundered the till** stole money from the cash register
3 **take the pledge** promise not to drink any alcohol
4 **went for** attacked
5 **sheriff's man** an assistant to the official responsible for the safekeeping of prisoners
6 **shabby** poorly dressed
7 **stooped** bent over
8 **bailiff** the court official who arrests people and delivers formal court documents
9 *artistes* French word for "artists"
10 **give credit** allow someone to postpone payment
11 **chummy** friendly
12 **favourites and outsiders** horse-racing terms: likely winners and unlikely winners

agent in Fleet Street, had the reputation of being a hard case. He was fond   30
of using soldiers' obscenities: usually he came home in the small hours.[13]
When he met his friends he had always a good one[14] to tell them, and
he was always sure to be on to a good thing—that is to say, a likely horse
or a likely *artiste*. He was also handy with the mits[15] and sang comic
songs. On Sunday nights there would often be a reunion in Mrs   35
Mooney's front drawing-room. The music-hall *artistes* would oblige; and
Sheridan played waltzes and polkas and vamped accompaniments. Polly
Mooney, the Madam's daughter, would also sing. She sang:

> *I'm a . . . naughty girl*
> *You needn't sham:*[16]   40
> *You know I am.*

Polly was a slim girl of nineteen; she had light soft hair and a small
full mouth. Her eyes, which were grey with a shade of green through
them, had a habit of glancing upwards when she spoke with anyone,
which made her look like a little perverse madonna.[17] Mrs Mooney had   45
first sent her daughter to be a typist in a corn-factor's[18] office, but as a
disreputable sheriff's man used to come every other day to the office,
asking to be allowed to say a word to his daughter, she had taken her
daughter home again and set her to do housework. As Polly was very
lively, the intention was to give her the run of[19] the young men. Besides,   50
young men like to feel that there is a young woman not very far away.
Polly, of course, flirted with the young men, but Mrs Mooney, who was
a shrewd judge, knew that the young men were only passing the time
away:[20] none of them meant business. Things went on so for a long time,
and Mrs Mooney began to think of sending Polly back to typewriting,   55
when she noticed that something was going on between Polly and one
of the young men. She watched the pair and kept her own counsel.[21]

Polly knew that she was being watched, but still her mother's
persistent silence could not be misunderstood. There had been no open
complicity[22] between mother and daughter, no open understanding, but   60
though people in the house began to talk of the affair, still Mrs Mooney
did not intervene.[23] Polly began to grow a little strange in her manner,
and the young man was evidently perturbed. At last, when she judged it
to be the right moment, Mrs Mooney intervened. She dealt with moral
problems as a cleaver deals with meat: and in this case she had made up   65
her mind.

---

13 **in the small hours** very late at night
14 **a good one** a good story
15 **handy with the mits** a good boxer
16 **sham** pretend
17 **perverse madonna** an improper Virgin Mary
18 **corn factor** an agent who acts as a
    middleman, buying corn from producers and
    selling it to retailers or consumers

19 **give her the run of** allow her complete
    freedom with
20 **passing the time away** flirting idly with no
    intention of getting married
21 **kept her own counsel** didn't speak to anyone
    about the matter
22 **complicity** cooperation in a wrongful act
23 **intervene** interfere

It was a bright Sunday morning of early summer, promising heat, but with a fresh breeze blowing. All the windows of the boarding house were open and the lace curtains ballooned gently towards the street beneath the raised sashes. The belfry[24] of George's Church sent out constant peals, and worshippers, singly or in groups, traversed the little circus before the church,[25] revealing their purpose by their self-contained demeanour[26] no less than by the little volumes in their gloved hands. Breakfast was over in the boarding house, and the table of the breakfast-room was covered with plates on which lay yellow streaks of eggs with morsels of bacon-fat and bacon-rind. Mrs Mooney sat in the straw arm-chair and watched the servant Mary remove the breakfast things. She made Mary collect the crusts and pieces of broken bread to help to make Tuesday's bread-pudding. When the table was cleared, the broken bread collected, the sugar and butter safe under lock and key,[27] she began to reconstruct the interview which she had had the night before with Polly. Things were as she had suspected: she had been frank[28] in her questions and Polly had been frank in her answers. Both had been somewhat awkward,[29] of course. She had been made awkward by her not wishing to receive the news in too cavalier[30] a fashion or to seem to have connived,[31] and Polly had been made awkward not merely because allusions of that kind always made her awkward, but also because she did not wish it to be thought that in her wise innocence she had divined[32] the intention behind her mother's tolerance.

Mrs Mooney glanced instinctively at the little gilt clock on the mantelpiece as soon as she had become aware through her reverie[33] that the bells of George's Church had stopped ringing. It was seventeen minutes past eleven: she would have lots of time to have the matter out[34] with Mr Doran and then catch short twelve[35] at Marlborough Street. She was sure she would win. To begin with, she had all the weight of social opinion on her side: she was an outraged mother. She had allowed him to live beneath her roof, assuming that he was a man of honour, and he had simply abused her hospitality. He was thirty-four or thirty-five years of age, so that youth could not be pleaded as his excuse; nor could ignorance be his excuse, since he was a man who had seen something of the world. He had simply taken advantage of Polly's youth and inexperience: that was evident. The question was: What reparation[36] would he make?

There must be reparation made in such a case. It is all very well for the man: he can go his ways as if nothing had happened, having had

70

75

80

85

90

95

100

105

---

24 **belfry** a bell tower
25 **traversed the little circus before the church** crossed the small circular area in front of the church
26 **self-contained demeanour** formal behavior
27 **under lock and key** locked away
28 **frank** open and honest
29 **awkward** embarrassed
30 **cavalier** casual

31 **connived** plotted
32 **divined** guessed
33 **reverie** a daydream
34 **have the matter out** discuss the problem openly
35 **catch short twelve** attend the noon service at church
36 **reparation** payment for damage done

his moment of pleasure, but the girl has to bear the brunt.[37] Some mothers would be content to patch up such an affair for a sum of money: she had known cases of it. But she would not do so. For her only one reparation could make up for the loss of her daughter's honour: marriage.

She counted all her cards[38] again before sending Mary up to Mr Doran's room to say that she wished to speak with him. She felt sure she would win. He was a serious young man, not rakish[39] or loud-voiced like the others. If it had been Mr Sheridan or Mr Meade or Bantam Lyons, her task would have been much harder. She did not think he would face publicity. All the lodgers in the house knew something of the affair; details had been invented by some. Besides, he had been employed for thirteen years in a great Catholic wine-merchant's office, and publicity would mean for him, perhaps, the loss of his job. Whereas if he agreed all might be well. She knew he had a good screw[40] for one thing, and she suspected he had a bit of stuff put by.[41]

Nearly the half-hour! She stood up and surveyed herself in the pier-glass. The decisive expression of her great florid face satisfied her, and she thought of some mothers she knew who could not get their daughters off their hands.[42]

Mr Doran was very anxious indeed this Sunday morning. He had made two attempts to shave, but his hand had been so unsteady that he had been obliged to desist. Three days' reddish beard fringed his jaws, and every two or three minutes a mist gathered on his glasses so that he had to take them off and polish them with his pocket-handkerchief. The recollection of his confession of the night before was a cause of acute pain to him; the priest had drawn out every ridiculous detail of the affair, and in the end had so magnified his sin that he was almost thankful at being afforded[43] a loophole of reparation. The harm was done. What could he do now but marry her or run away? He could not brazen it out.[44] The affair would be sure to be talked of, and his employer would be certain to hear of it. Dublin is such a small city: everyone knows everyone else's business. He felt his heart leap warmly in his throat as he heard in his excited imagination old Mr Leonard calling out in his rasping voice: "Send Mr Doran here, please."

All his long years of service gone for nothing! All his industry and diligence thrown away! As a young man he had sown his wild oats,[45] of course; he had boasted of his free-thinking and denied the existence of God to his companions in public-houses.[46] But that was all passed and done with . . . nearly. He still bought a copy of *Reynolds Newspaper* every week,

---

37 **bear the brunt** assume the major part of the responsibility
38 **counted all her cards** thought about her advantages
39 **rakish** bold and wild
40 **screw** salary
41 **he had a bit of stuff put by** he had saved some money

42 **get their daughters off their hands** get their daughters married
43 **afforded** given
44 **brazen it out** confront one's accuser confidently
45 **sown his wild oats** behaved wildly in his youth
46 **public-houses** bars (British)

but he attended to his religious duties, and for nine-tenths of the year lived [145] a regular life. He had money enough to settle down[47] on; it was not that. But the family would look down on[48] her. First of all there was her disreputable[49] father, and then her mother's boarding house was beginning to get a certain fame. He had a notion that he was being had.[50] He could imagine his friends talking of the affair and laughing. She *was* a little vulgar; [150] sometimes she said "I seen" and "If I had've known." But what would grammar matter if he really loved her? He could not make up his mind whether to like her or despise her for what she had done. Of course he had done it too. His instinct urged him to remain free, not to marry. Once you are married you are done for,[51] it said. [155]

While he was sitting helplessly on the side of the bed in shirt and trousers, she tapped lightly at his door and entered. She told him all, that she had made a clean breast of it[52] to her mother and that her mother would speak with him that morning. She cried and threw her arms around his neck, saying: [160]

"O Bob! Bob! What am I to do? What am I to do at all?"

She would put an end to herself, she said.

He comforted her feebly, telling her not to cry, that it would be all right, never fear. He felt against his shirt the agitation of her bosom.

It was not altogether his fault that it had happened. He remembered [165] well, with the curious patient memory of the celibate,[53] the first casual caresses her dress, her breath, her fingers had given him. Then late one night as he was undressing for bed she had tapped at his door, timidly. She wanted to relight her candle at his, for hers had been blown out by a gust. It was her bath night. She wore a loose open combing-jacket[54] of printed [170] flannel. Her white instep shone in the opening of her furry slippers and the blood glowed warmly behind her perfumed skin. From her hands and wrists too as she lit and steadied her candle a faint perfume arose.

On nights when he came in very late it was she who warmed up his dinner. He scarcely knew what he was eating, feeling her beside him alone, [175] at night, in the sleeping house. And her thoughtfulness! If the night was anyway cold or wet or windy there was sure to be a little tumbler of punch ready for him. Perhaps they could be happy together . . .

They used to go upstairs together on tiptoe, each with a candle, and on the third landing exchange reluctant good nights. They used to kiss. He [180] remembered well her eyes, the touch of her hand and his delirium.[55] . . .

But delirium passes. He echoed her phrase, applying it to himself: "*What am I to do?*" The instinct of the celibate warned him to hold back. But the sin was there; even his sense of honour told him that reparation must be made for such a sin. [185]

---

47 **settle down** get married
48 **look down on** feel superior to
49 **disreputable** not regarded highly
50 **he was being had** he was being tricked
51 **you are done for** you are destroyed
52 **she had made a clean breast of it** she had confessed everything

53 **the celibate** someone who does not have sex
54 **combing-jacket** a loose jacket worn in the bedroom when brushing hair
55 **delirium** feverish excitement

While he was sitting with her on the side of the bed Mary came to the door and said that the missus wanted to see him in the parlour. He stood up to put on his coat and waistcoat, more helpless than ever. When he was dressed he went over to her to comfort her. It would be all right, never fear. He left her crying on the bed and moaning softly: *"O my God!"* 190

Going down the stairs his glasses became so dimmed with moisture that he had to take them off and polish them. He longed[56] to ascend through the roof and fly away to another country where he would never hear again of his trouble, and yet a force pushed him downstairs step by step. The implacable[57] faces of his employer and of the Madam stared 195 upon his discomfiture. On the last flight of stairs he passed Jack Mooney, who was coming up from the pantry nursing[58] two bottles of *Bass*. They saluted coldly; and the lover's eyes rested for a second or two on a thick bulldog face and a pair of thick short arms. When he reached the foot of the staircase he glanced up and saw Jack regarding him from the door of 200 the return-room.

Suddenly he remembered the night when one of the music-hall *artistes,* a little blond Londoner, had made a rather free allusion to Polly. The reunion had been almost broken up on account of Jack's violence. Everyone tried to quiet him. The music-hall *artiste*, a little paler than 205 usual, kept smiling and saying that there was no harm meant; but Jack kept shouting at him that if any fellow tried that sort of game on with his sister he'd bloody well[59] put his teeth down his throat: so he would.

Polly sat for a little time on the side of the bed, crying. Then she dried her eyes and went over to the looking-glass. She dipped the end of the 210 towel in the water-jug and refreshed her eyes with cool water. She looked at herself in profile and readjusted a hairpin above her ear. Then she went back to the bed again and sat at the foot. She regarded the pillows for a long time, and the sight of them awakened in her mind secret, amiable memories. She rested the nape of her neck against the 215 cool iron bedrail and fell into a reverie. There was no longer any perturbation[60] visible on her face.

She waited on patiently, almost cheerfully, without alarm, her memories gradually giving place to hopes and visions of the future. Her hopes and visions were so intricate that she no longer saw the white pillows on 220 which her gaze was fixed, or remembered that she was waiting for anything.

At last she heard her mother calling. She started to her feet and ran to the banisters. "Polly! Polly!"

"Yes, mamma?" 225

"Come down, dear. Mr Doran wants to speak to you."

Then she remembered what she had been waiting for.

---

56 **longed** wanted badly
57 **implacable** unable or unwilling to be pacified
58 **nursing** carrying carefully

59 **bloody well** an exclamation reflecting violent anger (British slang)
60 **perturbation** anxiety

PART 1 First Reading

A Thinking About the Story

Did you object to Mrs. Mooney's attempt to influence the course of the love affair between Polly and Mr. Doran? Explain your answer.

B Understanding the Plot

1. List all the reasons why Mrs. Mooney left her husband. Did they get a divorce?

2. What do the boarding house residents mean when they refer to Mrs. Mooney as "The Madam"? (line 24) Is the title accurate? Support your answer.

3. Explain what is meant by describing Jack Mooney as having "the reputation of being a hard case." (line 30) What details are given to support that description?

4. Why did Polly have to leave her job as a typist?

5. What did Mrs. Mooney hope would happen when she brought Polly home to the boarding house?

6. Explain the sentence " . . . Mrs. Mooney . . . knew that the young men were only passing the time away: none of them meant business." (lines 52–54)

7. What is Mrs. Mooney determined to have Mr. Doran do? Is she confident of the outcome? Explain your answer.

8. Why do Polly and her mother not talk openly about what is happening in the house? When does the situation change? Does Polly understand what her mother is doing?

9. How does Mr. Doran view Polly as he sits waiting to see her mother? Draw up two columns representing her pros and cons in his eyes.

10. Who is Mr. Leonard? Why does Mr. Doran think of him that Sunday?

11. At what point does Mr. Doran finally decide what he will do? What is his decision, and why does he come to it?

PART 2 Second Reading

A   Exploring Themes

You are now ready to reread "The Boarding House." Look at how Joyce's carefully detailed descriptions of the characters and setting bring the story to life and contribute to both plot and themes.

1. What do we learn about the values of the Dublin society in which the characters live?
2. Show how the simile "she dealt with moral problems as a cleaver deals with meat" (lines 64–65) sums up Mrs. Mooney.
3. Whom do you consider to be a victim in this story? Why?
4. Show how the unspoken thoughts of the characters dominate the action and contribute to the themes. For example, Mrs. Mooney's assessment that Mr. Doran has a good salary and has saved quite a bit of money strengthens her determination to marry Polly off to him. (lines 119–121)
5. If you had to give the story a new title that sums up a dominant theme, what would you rename it?

B   Analyzing the Author's Style

For more information on the literary terms in this section, turn to the explanations of *tone* (page 309), *humor* (page 303), *irony* (page 304), and *imagery* (page 303).

TONE: Irony and Humor

"The Boarding House" has a richly **humorous** and **ironic tone**. The humor is expressed in the many descriptions Joyce builds into the story as well as in the ironic contrast between the characters' actions and their thoughts or philosophies.

An example of a humorous description is the contrast between Mr. and Mrs. Mooney's appearance. When Joyce describes Polly's father as having *a white face and a white moustache and white eyebrows, pencilled above his little eyes, which were pink-veined and raw* (lines 13–15), he makes us think of a frightened little white mouse with pink eyes. He later contrasts Mr. Mooney's small, pale, nervous appearance with that of Mrs. Mooney, whose *decisive expression of her great florid face satisfied her.* (line 123)

An example of irony is contained in the scene that Sunday morning when Mrs. Mooney sits scheming in her breakfast room, determined to ensure the ultimate success of her plan regardless of the moral cost to Polly and Mr. Doran. It is clear that she is determined to end her meeting with Mr. Doran quickly so that she can go to the noon church service. The irony lies in her inability to see that her behavior has in fact violated the teachings of her church. (lines 67–103)

1. Why is it ironic that Mrs. Mooney should worry about Polly being in communication with her disreputable father?
2. Explain the irony in the sentence, "She [Mrs. Mooney] dealt with moral problems as a cleaver deals with meat." (lines 64–65)
3. Why is it ironic for Mrs. Mooney to describe herself as "an outraged mother"? (line 96)
4. Why is Jack Mooney's outrage toward Mr. Doran ironic?
5. How does Joyce bring out the humor in the dilemma in which Mr. Doran finds himself? (lines 126–164)
6. What is comic about the scene in which Mr. Doran recalls how his affair with Polly developed? (lines 165–181)
7. Find one more example of both humor and irony in the story.

IMAGERY: Adjectives

Colorful **imagery** can be found throughout "The Boarding House." In particular, the evocative **adjectives** Joyce uses both help us see the surface pictures more clearly and enable us to grasp the depth of the passions rocking the characters. Following are three examples of the way the adjectives work in the story.

> Polly was a **slim** girl of nineteen; she had **light soft** hair and a **small full** mouth. Her eyes, which were **grey** with a shade of **green** through them, had a habit of glancing upwards when she spoke with anyone, which made her look like a **little perverse** madonna. (lines 42–45)

What information can we deduce from this description regarding the effect of Polly's appearance, her personality, and her behavior?

> He was a **serious** young man, not **rakish** or **loud-voiced** like the others. (lines 113–114)

How does this description of Mr. Doran help reinforce Mrs. Mooney's belief that she has the upper hand over him?

*He remembered well ... the first **casual** caresses her dress, her breath, her fingers had given him. ... She wore a **loose open combing**-jacket of **printed** flannel. Her **white** instep shone in the opening of her **furry** slippers and the blood glowed warmly behind her **perfumed** skin.* (lines 165–172)

1. What atmosphere do the adjectives create?
2. What senses do the adjectives appeal to?
3. What does Mr. Doran feel as he watches Polly?

OXYMORONS

An **oxymoron** is a figure of speech in which contradictory words are combined. Writers use it to heighten the effect of their texts. Following is a well-known oxymoron:

*She felt like a **living death** at the height of her illness.*

Joyce writes of Polly:

*Her eyes ... had a habit of glancing upwards ..., which made her look like a little **perverse madonna**.* (lines 43–45)

1. What contradictory facts do we learn about Polly from the description "perverse madonna"?
2. There is another example of an oxymoron in connection with Polly in lines 82–89. Say what it is and explain its meaning.

C   Judging for Yourself

Express yourself as personally as you like in your answers to the following questions.

1. What did you think Mr. Doran would do at the end? Do you agree with his decision?
2. In your view, does the couple have a future together?
3. Do you think Mrs. Mooney is a good mother?
4. What kind of a mother-in-law do you think Mrs. Mooney will be?
5. Do you approve of Mrs. Mooney's actions?
6. Would you like to have Mrs. Mooney as your landlady? Give reasons for your answer.
7. Do you feel sorry for any of the characters? Explain your answer.

D   Making Connections

1. What is the attitude toward sex before marriage in your culture?
2. How do young people meet each other in your country? What do you think of arranged marriages, Internet dating, blind dates, or advertising as methods of meeting people for dating purposes?
3. Compare dating practices in your country with those in another culture. Which do you prefer and why?
4. Have you ever been forced into taking a major step you were uncertain about? Describe the incident and the outcome.
5. Who is the dominant parent in your family? In what ways does that parent dominate? Do you relate better to one parent than the other?

E   Debate

Debate this proposition:

Parents should have influence over whom their children marry.

PART 3   Focus on Language

A   Practice with Oxymorons

Use the following oxymorons in sentences to illustrate their meaning.

a cruel kindness   a sad celebration   fiercely peaceful
an honest thief   a loud hush   a human robot

Make up five oxymorons of your own and share them with the class.

B   Adjectives

The following sentences come from the story. Circle the adjective that is closest in meaning to the boldface adjective in the sentence.

1. *He was a **shabby** stooped little drunkard . . .* (line 13)
   dishonest / ragged / unhappy
2. *. . . Mrs. Mooney, who was a **shrewd** judge, knew that the young men were only passing the time away . . .* (lines 52–54)
   clever / experienced / mean

3. *Polly knew that she was being watched, but still her mother's* **persistent** *silence could not be misunderstood.* (lines 58–59)

   continued / irritating / nagging

4. *. . . she had been* **frank** *in her questions and Polly had been frank in her answers.* (lines 82–83)

   calm / direct / tactful

5. *She had been made awkward by her not wishing to receive the news in too* **cavalier** *a fashion . . .* (lines 84–85)

   angry / lively / uncaring

6. *The decisive expression of her great* **florid** *face satisfied her . . .* (line 123)

   fat / flowery / red

7. *The recollection of his confession of the night before was a cause of* **acute** *pain to him . . .* (lines 130–131)

   embarrassing / sharp / unpleasant

8. *From her hands and wrists . . . a* **faint** *perfume arose.* (lines 172–173)

   cheap / sickly / slight

9. *They used to go upstairs together on tiptoe . . . and on the third landing exchange* **reluctant** *good nights.* (lines 179–180)

   long / passionate / unwilling

10. *Her hopes and visions were so* **intricate** *that she no longer saw the white pillows on which her gaze was fixed . . .* (lines 219–221)

    complex / confused / unrealistic

Make a list of the ten highlighted adjectives from the sentences above, and write an *antonym* (word of opposite meaning) next to each one.

C Building Vocabulary Skills

Find the following ten idioms in the story. Then complete the sentences below with the correct idiom. Use each idiom only once.

keep things to oneself (line 2)	make up for (line 109)
go for (line 8)	settle down (line 146)
have the run of (line 50)	look down on (line 147)
pass the time away (lines 53–54)	be had (line 149)
bear the brunt of (line 106)	be done for (line 155)

1. Commuters often _____ by doing crossword puzzles while riding the subway.

2. During one's teenage years, it is common to _____ rather than confide in one's parents.

3. In many societies, men are expected to
   _____ later than women.
4. It is a fact that women frequently have to
   _____ an unwanted pregnancy alone.
5. It is very arrogant to _____ other
   people.
6. Vicious dogs are known to _____ their
   victims' throats.
7. Nobody likes to _____, although it
   often occurs when one buys a secondhand car.
8. We assured our house guests that we wanted them to
   _____ our house while they were
   with us.
9. Nothing can _____ the death of my
   mother when I was seven.
10. When the stock market crashed, he felt he would soon
    _____.

PART 4 Writing Activities

1. Using lines 67–103 of "The Boarding House" as a model, create
   a scene of two to three paragraphs in which a character
   contemplates a course of action that may have far-reaching
   consequences. Concentrate on using adjectives to bring the
   surrounding environment to life as Joyce does in his extended
   description of the scene inside and outside the house. Situations
   your character might be thinking about could include whether
   to commit a crime, run away from home, or take revenge on
   someone.
2. Write an imaginary letter from Mr. Doran to a personal advice
   columnist (for example, "Dear Abby"), asking for help in his
   predicament. Include the columnist's reply to him.
3. "The Boarding House" comes from a collection of short stories
   called *Dubliners* in which James Joyce uses Dublin as a physical
   and symbolic setting for the lives of people from many different
   walks of life. Write an essay of two pages about a book you
   have read or a movie you have seen in which a city plays a major
   role in the work. In your essay describe the aspects of the city
   that stand out and explain how the setting serves to influence
   the actions and lives of the characters.

12

My Oedipus Complex

FRANK O'CONNOR (1903–1966)

Born in Cork, Ireland, Frank O'Connor, whose real name was Michael O'Donovan, was the only child of very poor, working-class parents. An Irish nationalist, he joined the Irish Republican Army (IRA), fought actively for an Ireland independent of Britain, and was imprisoned for two years. Later he spent many years in the United States, teaching at a number of prestigious universities including Harvard and Stanford. A prolific writer, O'Connor achieved the most recognition for his short-story collections, such as *Guests of the Nation* (1931), *My Oedipus Complex and Other Stories* (1963), and *A Life of Your Own and Other Stories* (1969). He also published two novels, *The Saint and Mary Kate* (1932) and *Dutch Interior* (1940); two autobiographies; poetry anthologies; plays; and books of literary criticism.

O'Connor's short stories reflect the realities of Irish life as he knew it. The naturalistic language of his writing seeks to capture the flavor of the Irish tongue, and many of his stories are infused with humor. "My Oedipus Complex" is a semiautobiographical story in which O'Connor depicts his childhood relationship with his parents.

MY OEDIPUS COMPLEX

A small boy's world is turned upside down when his father returns home from the war.

Father was in the army all through the war—the first war, I mean—so, up to the age of five, I never saw much of him, and what I saw did not worry me. Sometimes I woke and there was a big figure in khaki[1] peering down at me in the candlelight. Sometimes in the early morning I heard the slamming of the front door and the clatter of nailed boots down **5** the cobbles[2] of the lane. These were Father's entrances and exits. Like Santa Claus he came and went mysteriously.

In fact, I rather liked his visits, though it was an uncomfortable squeeze between Mother and him when I got into the big bed in the early morning. He smoked, which gave him a pleasant musty smell,[3] and **10** shaved, an operation of astounding interest. Each time he left a trail of souvenirs—model tanks and Gurkha[4] knives with handles made of bullet cases, and German helmets and cap badges and button sticks, and all sorts of military equipment—carefully stowed away in a long box on top of the wardrobe, in case they ever came in handy.[5] There was a bit of the **15** magpie[6] about Father; he expected everything to come in handy. When his back was turned, Mother let me get a chair and rummage through his treasures. She didn't seem to think so highly of them as he did.

The war was the most peaceful period of my life. The window of my attic faced southeast. My mother had curtained it, but that had small **20** effect. I always woke with the first light and, with all the responsibilities of the previous day melted, feeling myself rather like the sun, ready to illumine and rejoice. Life never seemed so simple and clear and full of possibilities as then. I put my feet out from under the clothes—I called them Mrs. Left and Mrs. Right—and invented dramatic situations for them **25** in which they discussed the problems of the day. At least Mrs. Right did; she was very demonstrative, but I hadn't the same control of Mrs. Left, so she mostly contented herself with nodding agreement.

They discussed what Mother and I should do during the day, what Santa Claus should give a fellow for Christmas, and what steps should **30** be taken to brighten the home. There was that little matter of the baby, for instance. Mother and I could never agree about that. Ours was the only house in the terrace without a new baby, and Mother said we

---

1 **khaki** material used for military uniforms
2 **cobbles** cobblestones, round stones for paving streets
3 **musty smell** a damp, stale odor
4 **Gurkha** Nepalese who served in the British army
5 **came in handy** were useful
6 **magpie** a bird that collects small articles for its nest

couldn't afford one till Father came back from the war because they cost seventeen and six.[7]

That showed how simple she was. The Geneys up the road had a baby, and everyone knew they couldn't afford seventeen and six. It was probably a cheap baby, and Mother wanted something really good, but I felt she was too exclusive.[8] The Geneys' baby would have done us fine.

Having settled my plans for the day, I got up, put a chair under the attic window, and lifted the frame high enough to stick out my head. The window overlooked the front gardens of the terrace behind ours, and beyond these it looked over a deep valley to the tall, red brick houses terraced up the opposite hillside, which were all still in shadow, while those at our side of the valley were all lit up, though with long strange shadows that made them seem unfamiliar; rigid[9] and painted.

After that I went into Mother's room and climbed into the big bed. She woke and I began to tell her of my schemes. By this time, though I never seemed to have noticed it, I was petrified[10] in my nightshirt, and I thawed as I talked until, the last frost melted, I fell asleep beside her and woke again only when I heard her below in the kitchen, making the breakfast.

After breakfast we went into town; heard Mass at St. Augustine's[11] and said a prayer for Father, and did the shopping. If the afternoon was fine we either went for a walk in the country or a visit to Mother's great friend in the convent, Mother Saint Dominic. Mother had them all praying for Father, and every night, going to bed, I asked God to send him back safe from the war to us. Little, indeed, did I know what I was praying for!

One morning, I got into the big bed, and there, sure enough, was Father in his usual Santa Claus manner, but later, instead of uniform, he put on his best blue suit, and Mother was as pleased as anything. I saw nothing to be pleased about, because, out of uniform, Father was altogether less interesting, but she only beamed, and explained that our prayers had been answered, and off we went to Mass to thank God for having brought Father safely home.

The irony of it! That very day when he came in to dinner he took off his boots and put on his slippers, donned the dirty old cap he wore about the house to save him from colds, crossed his legs, and began to talk gravely to Mother, who looked anxious. Naturally, I disliked her looking anxious, because it destroyed her good looks, so I interrupted him.

"Just a moment, Larry!" she said gently.

This was only what she said when we had boring visitors, so I attached no importance to it and went on talking.

"Do be quiet, Larry!" she said impatiently. "Don't you hear me talking to Daddy?"

---

7 **seventeen and six** seventeen shillings and six pence (British currency)
8 **exclusive** demanding
9 **rigid** stiff

10 **petrified** frozen (unusual use)
11 **heard Mass at St. Augustine's** attended a church service at St. Augustine's

This was the first time I heard those ominous[12] words, "talking to Daddy," and I couldn't help feeling that if this was how God answered prayers, he couldn't listen to them very attentively.

"Why are you talking to Daddy?" I asked with as great a show of indifference[13] as I could muster.[14]   80

"Because Daddy and I have business to discuss. Now, don't interrupt again!"

In the afternoon, at Mother's request, Father took me for a walk. This time we went into town instead of out in the country, and I thought at first, in my usual optimistic way, that it might be an improvement. It was   85
nothing of the sort. Father and I had quite different notions of a walk in town. He had no proper interest in trams, ships, and horses, and the only thing that seemed to divert him was talking to fellows as old as himself. When I wanted to stop he simply went on, dragging me behind him by the hand; when he wanted to stop I had no alternative but to do the same.   90
I noticed that it seemed to be a sign that he wanted to stop for a long time whenever he leaned against a wall. The second time I saw him do it I got wild. He seemed to be settling himself forever. I pulled him by the coat and trousers, but, unlike Mother who, if you were too persistent, got into a wax[15] and said: "Larry, if you don't behave yourself, I'll give you a good   95
slap," Father had an extraordinary capacity for amiable inattention. I sized him up[16] and wondered would I cry, but he seemed to be too remote to be annoyed even by that. Really, it was like going for a walk with a mountain! He either ignored the wrenching[17] and pummeling[18] entirely, or else glanced down with a grin of amusement from his peak. I had   100
never met anyone so absorbed in himself as he seemed.

At teatime, "talking to Daddy" began again, complicated this time by the fact that he had an evening paper, and every few minutes he put it down and told Mother something new out of it. I felt this was foul play.[19] Man for man, I was prepared to compete with him any time for Mother's   105
attention, but when he had it all made up for him by other people it left me no chance. Several times I tried to change the subject without success.

"You must be quiet while Daddy is reading, Larry," Mother said impatiently.

It was clear that she either genuinely liked talking to Father better   110
than talking to me, or else that he had some terrible hold on her[20] which made her afraid to admit the truth.

"Mummy," I said that night when she was tucking me up,[21] "do you think if I prayed hard God would send Daddy back to the war?"

She seemed to think about that for a moment.   115

---

12 **ominous** threatening
13 **show of indifference** an appearance of not
   caring
14 **muster** gather
15 **got into a wax** got angry (British slang)
16 **sized him up** judged him
17 **wrenching** fierce pulling

18 **pummeling** beating with fists
19 **foul play** not fair
20 **he had some terrible hold on her** he had
   a frightening control over her
21 **tucking me up** covering me tightly with the
   bed linen (British)

"No, dear," she said with a smile. "I don't think He would."

"Why wouldn't He, Mummy?"

"Because there isn't a war any longer, dear."

"But, Mummy, couldn't God make another war, if He liked?"

"He wouldn't like to, dear. It's not God who makes wars, but bad people." 120

"Oh!" I said.

I was disappointed about that. I began to think that God wasn't quite what He was cracked up to be.[22]

Next morning I woke at my usual hour, feeling like a bottle of 125 champagne. I put out my feet and invented a long conversation in which Mrs. Right talked of the trouble she had with her own father till she put him in the Home.[23] I didn't quite know what the Home was but it sounded the right place for Father. Then I got my chair and stuck my head out of the attic window. Dawn was just breaking, with a guilty air 130 that made me feel I had caught it in the act.[24] My head bursting with stories and schemes, I stumbled in next door, and in the half-darkness scrambled into the big bed. There was no room at Mother's side so I had to get between her and Father. For the time being I had forgotten about him, and for several minutes I sat bolt upright,[25] racking my brains[26] to 135 know what I could do with him. He was taking up more than his fair share of the bed, and I couldn't get comfortable, so I gave him several kicks that made him grunt and stretch. He made room all right, though. Mother waked and felt for me. I settled back comfortably in the warmth of the bed with my thumb in my mouth. 140

"Mummy!" I hummed, loudly and contentedly.

"Sssh! dear," she whispered. "Don't wake Daddy!"

This was a new development, which threatened to be even more serious than "talking to Daddy." Life without my early-morning conferences was unthinkable. 145

"Why?" I asked severely.

"Because poor Daddy is tired."

This seemed to me a quite inadequate reason, and I was sickened by the sentimentality of her "poor Daddy." I never liked that sort of gush,[27] it always struck me as insincere. 150

"Oh!" I said lightly. Then in my most winning tone:[28] "Do you know where I want to go with you today, Mummy?"

"No, dear," she sighed.

"I want to go down the Glen and fish for thornybacks with my new net, and then I want to go out to the Fox and Hounds, and—" 155

---

22 **God wasn't quite what He was cracked up to be** God didn't live up to His reputation
23 **the Home** an institution for old people
24 **caught it in the act** caught it doing something bad
25 **sat bolt upright** sat very straight
26 **racking my brains** thinking as hard as I could
27 **gush** sentimentality
28 **winning tone** charming voice

"Don't-wake-Daddy!" she hissed angrily, clapping her hand across my mouth.

But it was too late. He was awake, or nearly so. He grunted and reached for the matches. Then he stared incredulously at his watch.

"Like a cup of tea, dear?" asked Mother in a meek, hushed voice I had never heard her use before. It sounded almost as though she were afraid. 160

"Tea?" he exclaimed indignantly. "Do you know what the time is?"

"And after that I want to go up the Rathcooney Road," I said loudly, afraid I'd forget something in all those interruptions.

"Go to sleep at once, Larry!" she said sharply. 165

I began to snivel. [29] I couldn't concentrate, the way that pair went on, and smothering my early-morning schemes was like burying a family from the cradle. [30]

Father said nothing, but lit his pipe and sucked it, looking out into the shadows without minding [31] Mother or me. I knew he was mad. Every time 170 I made a remark Mother hushed me irritably. I was mortified. [32] I felt it wasn't fair, there was even something sinister in it. Every time I had pointed out to her the waste of making two beds when we could both sleep in one, she had told me it was healthier like that, and now here was this man, this stranger, sleeping with her without the least regard for her health! 175

He got up early and made tea, but though he brought Mother a cup he brought none for me.

"Mummy," I shouted, "I want a cup of tea, too."

"Yes, dear," she said patiently. "You can drink from Mummy's saucer."

That settled it. Either Father or I would have to leave the house. I 180 didn't want to drink from Mother's saucer; I wanted to be treated as an equal in my own home, so, just to spite her, I drank it all and left none for her. She took that quietly, too.

But that night when she was putting me to bed she said gently: "Larry, I want you to promise me something." 185

"What is it?" I asked.

"Not to come in and disturb poor Daddy in the morning. Promise?"

"Poor Daddy" again! I was becoming suspicious of everything involving that quite impossible man.

"Why?" I asked. 190

"Because poor Daddy is worried and tired and he doesn't sleep well."

"Why doesn't he, Mummy?"

"Well, you know, don't you, that while he was at the war Mummy got the pennies from the post office?"

"From Miss MacCarthy?" 195

---

29 **snivel** whine, complain weakly
30 **smothering my early-morning schemes was like burying a family from the cradle** destroying or suffocating my early-morning

plans was like burying babies before they had a chance to grow up
31 **minding** paying attention to
32 **mortified** very embarrassed

"That's right. But now, you see, Miss MacCarthy hasn't any more pennies, so Daddy must go out and find us some. You know what would happen if he couldn't?"

"No," I said, "tell us."

"Well, I think we might have to go out and beg for them like the poor old woman on Fridays. We wouldn't like that, would we?"

"No," I agreed. "We wouldn't."

"So you'll promise not to come in and wake him?"

"Promise."

Mind you,[33] I meant that. I knew pennies were a serious matter, and I was all against having to go out and beg like the old woman on Fridays. Mother laid out all my toys in a complete ring round the bed so that, whatever way I got out, I was bound to fall over one of them.

When I woke I remembered my promise all right. I got up and sat on the floor and played—for hours, it seemed to me. Then I got my chair and looked out the attic window for more hours. I wished it was time for Father to wake; I wished someone would make me a cup of tea. I didn't feel in the least like the sun; instead, I was bored and so very, very cold! I simply longed for the warmth and depth of the big feather bed.

At last I could stand it no longer. I went into the next room. As there was still no room at Mother's side I climbed over her and she woke with a start.

"Larry," she whispered, gripping my arm very tightly, "what did you promise?"

"But I did, Mummy," I wailed, caught in the very act. "I was quiet for ever so long."

"Oh, dear, and you're perished!"[34] she said sadly, feeling me all over. "Now, if I let you stay will you promise not to talk?"

"But I want to talk, Mummy," I wailed.

"That has nothing to do with it," she said with a firmness that was new to me. "Daddy wants to sleep. Now, do you understand that?"

I understood it only too well. I wanted to talk, he wanted to sleep, whose house was it, anyway?

"Mummy," I said with equal firmness, "I think it would be healthier for Daddy to sleep in his own bed."

That seemed to stagger[35] her, because she said nothing for a while.

"Now, once for all," she went on, "you're to be perfectly quiet or go back to your own bed. Which is it to be?"

The injustice of it got me down.[36] I had convicted her out of her own mouth of inconsistency and unreasonableness, and she hadn't even attempted to reply. Full of spite, I gave Father a kick, which she didn't notice but which made him grunt and open his eyes in alarm.

---

33 **Mind you** an expression used for emphasis
34 **perished** frozen (unusual use)
35 **stagger** amaze
36 **got me down** depressed me

"What time is it?" he asked in a panic-stricken voice, not looking at mother but at the door, as if he saw someone there.

"It's early yet," she replied soothingly. "It's only the child. Go to sleep again. . . . Now, Larry," she added, getting out of bed, "you've wakened Daddy and you must go back."   240

This time, for all her quiet air, I knew she meant it, and knew that my principal rights and privileges were as good as lost[37] unless I asserted them at once. As she lifted me, I gave a screech, enough to wake the   245 dead, not to mind Father.[38] He groaned.

"That damn child! Doesn't he ever sleep?"

"It's only a habit, dear," she said quietly, though I could see she was vexed.[39]

"Well, it's time he got out of it," shouted Father, beginning to heave in   250 the bed. He suddenly gathered all the bedclothes about him, turned to the wall, and then looked back over his shoulder with nothing showing only two small, spiteful, dark eyes. The man looked very wicked.

To open the bedroom door, Mother had to let me down, and I broke free and dashed for the farthest corner, screeching. Father sat bolt upright   255 in bed.

"Shut up, you little puppy!" he said in a choking voice.

I was so astonished that I stopped screeching. Never, never had anyone spoken to me in that tone before. I looked at him incredulously and saw his face convulsed with rage. It was only then that I fully   260 realized how God had codded[40] me, listening to my prayers for the safe return of this monster.

"Shut up, you!" I bawled, beside myself.

"What's that you said?" shouted Father, making a wild leap out of the bed.   265

"Mick, Mick!" cried Mother. "Don't you see the child isn't used to you?"

"I see he's better fed than taught," snarled Father, waving his arms wildly. "He wants his bottom smacked."[41]

All his previous shouting was as nothing to these obscene words referring to my person. They really made my blood boil.   270

"Smack your own!" I screamed hysterically. "Smack your own! Shut up! Shut up!"

At this he lost his patience and let fly[42] at me. He did it with the lack of conviction you'd expect of a man under Mother's horrified eyes, and it ended up as a mere tap, but the sheer indignity of being struck at all   275 by a stranger, a total stranger who had cajoled[43] his way back from the

---

37 **were as good as lost** were just about lost
38 **not to mind Father** more than loudly enough to wake Father
39 **vexed** annoyed, irritated
40 **codded** played a joke on, tricked (unconventional use)

41 **He wants his bottom smacked.** He deserves to be punished with a spanking.
42 **let fly** attacked suddenly
43 **cajoled** persuaded unfairly, coaxed

war into our big bed as a result of my innocent intercession,[44] made me completely dotty.[45] I shrieked and shrieked, and danced in my bare feet, and Father, looking awkward and hairy in nothing but a short gray army shirt, glared down at me like a mountain out for murder. I think it must have been then that I realized he was jealous too. And there stood Mother in her nightdress, looking as if her heart was broken between us. I hoped she felt as she looked. It seemed to me that she deserved it all.

From that morning out my life was a hell. Father and I were enemies, open and avowed. We conducted a series of skirmishes[46] against one another, he trying to steal my time with Mother and I his. When she was sitting on my bed, telling me a story, he took to looking for some pair of old boots which he alleged he had left behind him at the beginning of the war. While he talked to Mother I played loudly with my toys to show my total lack of concern. He created a terrible scene one evening when he came in from work and found me at his box, playing with his regimental badges, Gurkha knives and button sticks. Mother got up and took the box from me.

"You mustn't play with Daddy's toys unless he lets you, Larry," she said severely. "Daddy doesn't play with yours."

For some reason Father looked at her as if she had struck him and then turned away with a scowl.

"Those are not toys," he growled, taking down the box again to see had I lifted[47] anything. "Some of those curios are very rare and valuable."

But as time went on I saw more and more how he managed to alienate[48] Mother and me. What made it worse was that I couldn't grasp his method or see what attraction he had for Mother. In every possible way he was less winning than I. He had a common accent and made noises at his tea. I thought for a while that it might be the newspapers she was interested in, so I made up bits of news of my own to read to her. Then I thought it might be the smoking, which I personally thought attractive, and took his pipes and went round the house dribbling[49] into them till he caught me. I even made noises at my tea, but Mother only told me I was disgusting. It all seemed to hinge round[50] that unhealthy habit of sleeping together, so I made a point of dropping into their bedroom and nosing round, talking to myself, so that they wouldn't know I was watching them, but they were never up to anything[51] that I could see. In the end it beat me. It seemed to depend on being grown-up and giving people rings, and I realized I'd have to wait.

But at the same time I wanted him to see that I was only waiting, not giving up the fight. One evening when he was being particularly

---

44 **intercession** prayer
45 **dotty** crazy
46 **skirmishes** small battles
47 **lifted** taken, stolen
48 **alienate** put a distance between
49 **dribbling** dropping saliva
50 **hinge round** depend on
51 **were never up to anything** were never misbehaving

obnoxious,[52] chattering away well above my head, I let him have it.[53] "Mummy," I said, "do you know what I'm going to do when I grow up?"

"No, dear," she replied. "What?"

"I'm going to marry you," I said quietly.   320

Father gave a great guffaw[54] out of him, but he didn't take me in.[55] I knew it must only be pretense. And Mother, in spite of everything, was pleased. I felt she was probably relieved to know that one day Father's hold on her would be broken. "Won't that be nice?" she said with a smile.

"It'll be very nice," I said confidently. "Because we're going to have   325
lots and lots of babies."

"That's right, dear," she said placidly. "I think we'll have one soon, and then you'll have plenty of company."

I was no end pleased about that because it showed that in spite of the way she gave in to Father she still considered my wishes. Besides, it   330
would put the Geneys in their place.[56]

It didn't turn out like that, though. To begin with, she was very preoccupied[57]—I supposed about where she would get the seventeen and six—and though Father took to[58] staying out late in the evenings it did me no particular good. She stopped taking me for walks, became as   335
touchy as blazes,[59] and smacked me for nothing at all. Sometimes I wished I'd never mentioned the confounded baby—I seemed to have a genius for bringing calamity on myself.

And calamity it was! Sonny arrived in the most appalling hullabaloo[60]— even that much he couldn't do without a fuss—and from the first moment   340
I disliked him. He was a difficult child—so far as I was concerned he was always difficult—and demanded far too much attention.

Mother was simply silly about him, and couldn't see when he was only showing off. As company he was worse than useless. He slept all day, and I had to go round the house on tiptoe to avoid waking him. It   345
wasn't any longer a question of not waking Father. The slogan now was "Don't-wake-Sonny!" I couldn't understand why the child wouldn't sleep at the proper time, so whenever Mother's back was turned I woke him. Sometimes to keep him awake I pinched him as well. Mother caught me at it one day and gave me a most unmerciful flaking.[61]   350

One evening, when Father was coming in from work, I was playing trains in the front garden.

I let on[62] not to notice him; instead, I pretended to be talking to myself, and said in a loud voice: "If another bloody[63] baby comes into this house, I'm going out."   355

---

52 **obnoxious** very unpleasant, offensive
53 **let him have it** attacked him (slang)
54 **guffaw** a loud laugh
55 **take me in** deceive me
56 **put the Geneys in their place** humble the
   Geneys
57 **preoccupied** absorbed, deep in thought

58 **took to** began to
59 **as touchy as blazes** quick to lose
   one's temper
60 **hullabaloo** confused noise
61 **flaking** beating (British slang)
62 **let on** pretended
63 **bloody** (negative expression—British)

Father stopped dead and looked at me over his shoulder.

"What's that you said?" he asked sternly.

"I was only talking to myself," I replied, trying to conceal my panic. "It's private."

He turned and went in without a word. Mind you, I intended it as a solemn warning, but its effect was quite different. Father started being quite nice to me. I could understand that, of course. Mother was quite sickening about Sonny. Even at mealtimes she'd get up and gawk at [64] him in the cradle with an idiotic smile, and tell Father to do the same. He was always polite about it, but he looked so puzzled you could see he didn't know what she was talking about. He complained of the way Sonny cried at night, but she only got cross and said that Sonny never cried except when there was something up with him [65]—which was a flaming [66] lie, because Sonny never had anything up with him, and only cried for attention. It was really painful to see how simpleminded she was. Father wasn't attractive, but he had a fine intelligence. He saw through Sonny, and now he knew that I saw through him as well.

One night I woke with a start. There was someone beside me in the bed. For one wild moment I felt sure it must be Mother, having come to her senses and left Father for good, but then I heard Sonny in convulsions in the next room, and Mother saying: "There! There! There!" and I knew it wasn't she. It was Father. He was lying beside me, wide-awake, breathing hard and apparently as mad as hell.

After a while it came to me what he was mad about. It was his turn now. After turning me out of the big bed, he had been turned out himself. Mother had no consideration now for anyone but that poisonous pup, Sonny. I couldn't help feeling sorry for Father. I had been through it all myself, and even at that age I was magnanimous. [67] I began to stroke him down and say: "There! There!" He wasn't exactly responsive.

"Aren't you asleep either?" he snarled.

"Ah, come on and put your arm around us, can't you?" I said, and he did, in a sort of way. Gingerly, [68] I suppose, is how you'd describe it. He was very bony but better than nothing.

At Christmas he went out of his way [69] to buy me a really nice model railway.

---

64 **gawk at** stare stupidly at
65 **there was something up with him** there was something wrong with him
66 **flaming** glaring, obvious
67 **magnanimous** generous
68 **Gingerly** Carefully
69 **went out of his way** went to a lot of trouble

PART 1 First Reading

A Thinking About the Story

Were you able to identify with the boy's feelings of displacement? Did you enjoy the warm humor of the piece? Say why.

B Understanding the Plot

1. How does Larry view his father's brief visits home during the war?
2. What is Larry's attitude toward the war?
3. Why does Larry play the imaginary game with his feet?
4. About what time does Larry usually wake up? How do his parents respond to this?
5. What religion does the family practice? How do we know?
6. What prayers are referred to in line 78? Why is Larry disappointed in God's powers? (lines 123–124)
7. Why do Larry's two feet "talk" about putting a parent in a Home?
8. Whom does Larry accuse of destroying his early-morning schemes? (lines 167–168) With what does he compare the destruction of his plans?
9. Why isn't Larry's father sleeping well, according to his mother?
10. For how long do you think Larry played alone when he says it seemed "for hours"? (line 210)
11. Why does Larry's father sound panic-stricken about the time? (line 238)
12. How hard does Larry's father hit him? Explain your answer.
13. Why does Larry's father begin to stay out late in the evenings when his wife is pregnant? Where do you think he goes?
14. How does Larry feel about his long-awaited baby brother?
15. What causes Larry's father to become more sympathetic toward him?

PART 2 Second Reading

A   Exploring Themes

You are now ready to reread "My Oedipus Complex." Look carefully at how Frank O'Connor uses humor to lessen the impact of Larry's painful feelings of jealousy and alienation.

1. How are the first and last paragraphs of the story related?
2. In what way does Larry mature and change in the story?
3. How does the jealousy that Larry and his father feel for each other express itself?
4. How does being an only child affect Larry's behavior?
5. How does Larry's mother deal with the conflicting pull on her loyalties?
6. What is the turning point in the relationship between Larry and his father? What brings about the change?

B   Analyzing the Author's Style

For more information on the literary term in this section, turn to the explanation of *humor* (page 303).

HUMOROUS EFFECTS

The **humor** in "My Oedipus Complex" arises from several sources. The first one revolves around the oedipal behavior that five-year-old Larry innocently exhibits. The Austrian psychoanalyst Sigmund Freud developed his theory of the Oedipus complex to explain the jealous sexual attachment of a young child for a parent of the opposite sex. For example, when Larry declares to his mother his intention to marry her, he is expressing his desire to take his father's place in her affections and causes the reader to smile at his innocent ignorance.

1. What other examples of oedipal behavior can you find in the text? How do they help create the humor?

The second source of humor arises from the gap between the child's point of view or perception and the adult language he uses to express himself. For example, Larry exhibits his naivete about sex when he accepts his mother's statement that babies can be bought for *seventeen and six*, yet at the same time comments that his mother was perhaps too *exclusive* (lines 36–39).

2. What other examples can you find of sophisticated language that conflicts with the child's-eye view of the world that is being expressed?

A third area of humor lies in Larry's desperate attempts to be the man of the house, while, not surprisingly, he is incapable of filling that role. So, when he thinks, *I wanted to be treated as an equal in my own home* (lines 181–182), he follows this up by drinking all the tea his father had made for his mother.

3. Pick out other instances where Larry jealously tries to act, speak, or think like a man but humorously undercuts his own attempts by his childish behavior.

Finally, there is warm humor in the two scenes where father and son are alone with each other and start the process of adapting to each other's existence and slowly identifying with each other.

4. In the first of these scenes (lines 83–101), how are the contrasts between father and son comically magnified in the child's eyes?
5. In the second scene (lines 373–388), what makes the reconciliation between Larry and his father touchingly funny?

C Judging for Yourself

Express yourself as personally as you like in your answers to the following questions.

1. Do you think Larry's mother handled her son's oedipal behavior wisely?
2. In your view, is Larry's mother a good wife? Justify your answer.
3. Do you anticipate that Larry and his father will strengthen their newfound bond in the future?
4. Would you call Larry's strong attachment to his mother unhealthy? Give reasons for your answer.

D Making Connections

1. Is the Oedipus complex recognized in your culture? Do you feel that it is a valid description and explanation of a young child's relationship with a parent of the opposite sex? Are there other periods in life when children feel closer to one parent than the other?

2. What is the ideal number of children per family in your country? Does religion, economics, or population control play a role in deciding the number?

3. Has your country experienced wars in which men have spent long periods of time away from home? How has this affected their relationship with their families?

4. Is there a particular *hierarchy* (order of importance) in the family in your country? Who is traditionally the most important or influential member of the family? Who is the least important?

E   Debate

Debate this proposition:

The saying "Children should be seen but not heard" is a sensible child-rearing philosophy.

PART 3   Focus on Language

A   Denotation and Connotation

All words have a **denotation,** or specific meaning, which is the dictionary definition of the word. For example, the denotation of *mother* is a female parent. In addition to their denotation, many words have a **connotation,** which is an association suggested by the word and is usually separate from its meaning. Words can have positive and/or negative associations. For example, some positive connotations of *mother* might be love, security, kisses, food, warmth, comforter, bedtime stories, and being spoiled when sick. Some negative connotations of *mother* might include nagging, overanxiousness, overprotectiveness, guilt, restrictiveness, and hysteria.

Look at the following list of words from the story.

father (line 1)	mountain (lines 99, 280)
candlelight (line 4)	a bottle of champagne (lines 125–126)
slamming (line 5)	dawn (line 130)
Santa Claus (line 7)	hissed (line 156)
shadow (line 44)	feather bed (line 214)

With the aid of a dictionary, write the denotation of each word. Then look at the words again. Write the connotation(s) that come to mind. Your connotations may be positive or negative or both.

B Building Vocabulary Skills

Following is a list of idioms from the text. Review the context in which each idiom is used in the story. (Some of the verb tenses have been changed.)

come in handy (line 16)	take to (line 287)
size someone up (lines 96–97)	be up to (line 312)
foul play (line 104)	let someone have it (line 317)
cracked up to be (line 124)	take someone in (line 321)
sit bolt upright (line 135)	give in to (line 330)
rack one's brains (line 135)	turn out (lines 332 and
as good as lost (line 244)	380)—two different
let fly (line 273)	meanings
	show off (line 344)

With a partner, create a minidialogue relating to each idiom to demonstrate that you understand the meaning of the idiom and a correct situation in which it is used. For example:

A: That chocolate bar you gave me sure *came in handy* today.

B: Really? In what way?

A: I didn't have time for lunch, so I was happy to find it in my pocket.

PART 4 Writing Activities

1. Compose a short story of three to four pages centering on a conflict between a young child and his or her parents. Tell the story through the child's eyes. Base your story on a real-life conflict you recall. Using Frank O'Connor's narrative technique as a model, try to capture the child's voice in your story without necessarily using childish language.

2. Write two descriptive paragraphs, the first concentrating on words with a positive connotation and the second centering on words with a negative connotation. Begin your first paragraph with *I woke up with the scent of honey in the air.* Begin your second paragraph with *The earth began to heave ominously.*

3. Write an essay of two to three pages in which you take a position both for and against the statement that children in single-child families are ultimately disadvantaged. For instance, some people say that such children benefit from the exclusive attention they receive, while other people think that such attention spoils a child. When you have stated the case for both sides as well as you can, reread your essay. Then in a concluding paragraph, state which side of your argument you were more convinced by.

4. The oedipal theme runs through many novels, plays, and movies. The ancient Greek playwright Sophocles dramatized the Oedipus legend in his famous tragedy *Oedipus Rex*. In modern times D. H. Lawrence's novel *Sons and Lovers* centers on this theme. Similarly, Woody Allen takes up the subject in a humorous vein in his segment of the movie *New York Stories* entitled "Oedipus Wrecks." Write an essay of two pages in which you briefly describe a work you have read or seen that is dominated by the oedipal theme. Say whether the subject is treated seriously or humorously.

LONELINESS
AND ALIENATION

Edward Hopper, *Sunlight in a Cafeteria*, 1958

13

The Model

BERNARD MALAMUD (1914–1986)

Born in Brooklyn, New York, Bernard Malamud grew up in the Depression years. His parents were Russian-Jewish immigrants who worked long hours in their grocery store to make ends meet. Young Bernard began writing in a room at the back of the store when he was in high school.

Malamud published numerous novels and short stories and received many literary honors. In 1967, he was awarded the Pulitzer Prize for his novel *The Fixer*, and in 1981, the gold medal for fiction from the American Academy and Institute for Arts and Letters. His collection of short stories *The Magic Barrel* was given the National Book Award for fiction in 1959. Two novels—*The Fixer* and *The Natural*—were made into movies, the latter starring Robert Redford.

Most of Malamud's writing draws on his and his family's experiences on the Lower East Side of Manhattan. His work reflects his Jewish consciousness and deals with the struggle of ordinary people to survive in a harsh world.

THE MODEL

An old man asks an agency to send him a model so that he can revive his painting skills, but the sitting does not go as planned.

Early one morning, Ephraim Elihu rang up the Art Students League and asked the woman who answered the phone how he could locate an experienced female model he could paint nude. He told the woman that he wanted someone of about thirty. "Could you possibly help me?"

"I don't recognize your name," said the woman on the telephone. 5 "Have you ever dealt with us before? Some of our students will work as models, but usually only for painters we know." Mr. Elihu said he hadn't. He wanted it understood he was an amateur painter who had once studied at the League.

"Do you have a studio?" 10

"It's a large living room with lots of light. I'm no youngster," he said, "but after many years I've begun painting again and I'd like to do some nude studies to get back my feeling for form.[1] I'm not a professional painter, but I'm serious about painting. If you want any references as to[2] my character, I can supply them." 15

He asked her what the going rate[3] for models was, and the woman, after a pause, said, "Six dollars the hour."

Mr. Elihu said that was satisfactory to him. He wanted to talk longer, but she did not encourage him to. She wrote down his name and address and said she thought she could have someone for him the day after 20 tomorrow. He thanked her for her consideration.[4]

That was on Wednesday. The model appeared on Friday morning. She had telephoned the night before, and they had settled on[5] a time for her to come. She rang his bell shortly after nine, and Mr. Elihu went at once to the door. He was a gray-haired man of seventy who lived in a 25 brownstone house near Ninth Avenue, and he was excited by the prospect of painting this young woman.

The model was a plain-looking woman of twenty-seven or so, and the painter decided her best features were her eyes. She was wearing a blue raincoat, though it was a clear spring day. The old painter liked her but 30 kept that to himself. She barely glanced at him as she walked firmly into the room.

"Good day," he said, and she answered, "Good day."

"It's like spring," said the old man. "The foliage[6] is starting up again."

---

1 **form** shape and structure
2 **as to** regarding
3 **going rate** the usual fee
4 **consideration** thoughtfulness
5 **settled on** agreed to
6 **foliage** the growth of leaves

"Where do you want me to change?" asked the model. 35

Mr. Elihu asked her name, and she responded, "Ms. Perry."

"You can change in the bathroom, I would say, Miss Perry, or if you like, my own room—down the hall—is empty, and you can change there also. It's warmer than the bathroom."

The model said it made no difference to her but she thought she 40
would rather change in the bathroom.

"That is as you wish," said the elderly man.

"Is your wife around?" she then asked, glancing into the room.

"No, I happen to be a widower."

He said he had had a daughter once, but she had died in an accident. 45

The model said she was sorry. "I'll change and be out in a few fast minutes."

"No hurry at all," said Mr. Elihu, glad he was about to[7] paint her.

Ms. Perry entered the bathroom, undressed there, and returned quickly. She slipped off her terry-cloth[8] robe. Her head and shoulders were 50
slender and well formed. She asked the old man how he would like her to pose. He was standing by an enamel-top kitchen table near a large window. On the tabletop he had squeezed out, and was mixing together, the contents of two small tubes of paint. There were three other tubes, which he did not touch. The model, taking a last drag[9] of a cigarette, 55
pressed it out against a coffee-can lid on the kitchen table.

"I hope you don't mind if I take a puff once in a while?"

"I don't mind, if you do it when we take a break."

"That's all I meant."

She was watching him as he slowly mixed his colors. 60

Mr. Elihu did not immediately look at her nude body but said he would like her to sit in the chair by the window. They were facing a back yard with an ailanthus[10] tree whose leaves had just come out.

"How would you like me to sit, legs crossed or not crossed?"

"However you prefer that. Crossed or uncrossed doesn't make much 65
of a difference to me. Whatever makes you feel comfortable."

The model seemed surprised at that, but she sat down in the yellow chair by the window and crossed one leg over the other. Her figure was good.

"Is this okay for you?" 70

Mr. Elihu nodded. "Fine," he said. "Very fine."

He dipped his brush into the paint he had mixed on the table-top, and after glancing[11] at the model's nude body, began to paint. He would look at her, then look quickly away, as if he were afraid of affronting[12] her. But his expression was objective. He painted apparently casually, 75
from time to time gazing up at the model. He did not often look at her.

---

7 **about to** ready to do something
8 **terry cloth** a cotton material that absorbs water
9 **drag** a puff on a cigarette

10 **ailanthus** a tropical tree commonly grown in New York City
11 **glancing** looking quickly
12 **affronting** insulting

She seemed not to be aware of him. Once she turned to observe the ailanthus tree, and he studied her momentarily [13] to see what she might have seen in it.

Then she began to watch the painter with interest. She watched his eyes and she watched his hands. He wondered if he was doing something wrong. At the end of about an hour she rose impatiently from the yellow chair.

"Tired?" he asked.

"It isn't that," she said, "but I would like to know what in the name of Christ you think you are doing? I frankly don't think you know the first thing about painting."

She had astonished him. He quickly covered the canvas with a towel.

After a long moment, Mr. Elihu, breathing shallowly, [14] wet his dry lips and said he was making no claims for himself as a painter. [15] He said he had tried to make that absolutely clear to the woman he talked to at the art school when he called.

Then he said, "I might have made a mistake in asking you to come to this house today. I think I should have tested myself a while longer, just so I wouldn't be wasting anybody's time. I guess I am not ready to do what I would like to do."

"I don't care how long you have tested yourself," said Ms. Perry. "I honestly don't think you have painted me at all. In fact, I felt you weren't interested in painting me. I think you're interested in letting your eyes go over my naked body for certain reasons of your own. I don't know what your personal needs are, but I'm damn well sure that most of them have nothing to do with painting."

"I guess I have made a mistake."

"I guess you have," said the model. She had her robe on now, the belt pulled tight.

"I'm a painter," she said, "and I model because I am broke, [16] but I know a fake [17] when I see one."

"I wouldn't feel so bad," said Mr. Elihu, "if I hadn't gone out of my way [18] to explain the situation to that lady at the Art Students League.

"I'm sorry this happened," Mr. Elihu said hoarsely. "I should have thought it through [19] more than I did. I'm seventy years of age. I have always loved women and felt a sad loss that I have no particular women friends at this time of my life. That's one of the reasons I wanted to paint again, though I make no claims that I was ever greatly talented. Also, I guess I didn't realize how much about painting I have forgotten. Not only about that, but also about the female body. I didn't realize I would be so moved by yours, and, on reflection, about the way my life has gone. I

---

13 **momentarily** quickly and briefly
14 **shallowly** superficially, not deeply
15 **making no claims for himself as a painter** not maintaining that he could paint well
16 **am broke** have no money

17 **a fake** someone who is not genuine
18 **gone out of my way** taken extra care
19 **thought it through** considered it carefully

hoped painting again would refresh my feeling for life. I regret that I have inconvenienced and disturbed you."

"I'll be paid for my inconvenience," Ms. Perry said, "but what you can't pay me for is the insult of coming here and submitting myself to your eyes crawling on my body." 120

"I didn't mean it as an insult."

"That's what it feels like to me."

She then asked Mr. Elihu to disrobe. 125

"I?" he said, surprised. "What for?"

"I want to sketch you. Take your pants and shirt off."

He said he had barely got rid of his winter underwear, but she did not smile.

Mr. Elihu disrobed, ashamed of how he must look to her. 130

With quick strokes she sketched his form. He was not a bad-looking man, but felt bad. When she had the sketch, she dipped his brush into a blob[20] of black pigment she had squeezed out of a tube and smeared his features,[21] leaving a black mess.

He watched her hating him, but said nothing. 135

Ms. Perry tossed the brush into a wastebasket and returned to the bathroom for her clothing.

The old man wrote out a check for her for the sum they had agreed on. He was ashamed to sign his name, but he signed it and handed it to her. Ms. Perry slipped the check into her large purse and left. 140

He thought that in her way she was not a bad-looking woman, though she lacked grace.[22] The old man then asked himself, "Is there nothing more to my life than it is now? Is this all that is left to me?"

The answer seemed to be yes, and he wept at how old he had so quickly become. 145

Afterward he removed the towel over his canvas and tried to fill in her face, but he had already forgotten it.

---

20 **blob** a lump
21 **smeared his features** spread paint across his face

22 **grace** charm

PART 1 First Reading

A Thinking About the Story

How did you feel when you finished reading the story? Would you have reacted as strongly as the model? Give reasons for your answer.

B Understanding the Plot

1. What information does the woman at the Art Students League request from Mr. Elihu?
2. Why does she question him so closely?
3. Why do you think Mr. Elihu asks for a model around thirty years old?
4. What do we learn about his family situation?
5. What kind of painter is he?
6. List all the things Mr. Elihu does and says that make the model uneasy about him.
7. Why does Ms. Perry choose to undress in the bathroom?
8. What does she accuse Mr. Elihu of?
9. What does she do to take revenge on Mr. Elihu?

PART 2 Second Reading

A Exploring Themes

You are now ready to reread "The Model." Look carefully at how the writer sets the scene for the sad misunderstanding that arises between Mr. Elihu and the model.

1. In what season does the story take place? List all the details that support your answer. How does the season relate to a central theme in the story?
2. What are the different expectations of the two characters regarding the modeling session? How do these expectations influence their behavior?
3. How does the tone of Mr. Elihu's greeting differ from the tone of the model's response in lines 33–35?

4. Does Mr. Elihu have another reason for requesting a model than the one he gave the woman at the League?

5. What do you think Mr. Elihu means when he says, "I think I should have tested myself a while longer . . ."? (line 94)

6. What expression does the model use that describes most vividly her feelings of disgust at Mr. Elihu? Explain the expression fully.

7. What was the model trying to achieve by her act of revenge? Did she succeed?

8. What do you think the ending means?

B   Analyzing the Author's Style

For more information on the literary term in this section, turn to the explanation of *inference* (page 304).

INFERENCE

On several occasions in "The Model," instead of spelling out the details, Bernard Malamud prefers to use **inference**, requiring the reader to discover the inner meaning of a character's thoughts or actions. For example, when the model chooses to change in the bathroom rather than the bedroom, we can infer that she is uncomfortable with the notion of undressing in a strange man's bedroom.

1. What is suggested by the pause the woman from the Art Students League makes before answering Mr. Elihu? (lines 16–17)

2. What can be inferred about the state of mind of Mr. Elihu and the woman from the Art Students League from the sentence, "He wanted to talk longer, but she did not encourage him to"? (lines 18–19)

3. What is implied by the description of the model as "wearing a blue raincoat, though it was a clear spring day"? (lines 29–30)

4. What inference is contained in the reference to the model's robe and belt in lines 104–105? Which word reinforces the inference?

C   Judging for Yourself

Express yourself as personally as you like in your answers to the following questions.

1. Would you agree with the model's view of Mr. Elihu as a "dirty old man"?

2. What do you think of the model's act of revenge?

3. Do you think Mr. Elihu will ever paint again? Give reasons for your answer.

4. What do you imagine a typical day in Mr. Elihu's life is like?

5. Do you prefer one character over another in this story? Why?

D   Making Connections

1. Are the elderly treated with respect in your country? What have you read and/or observed about the situation of old people in the United States or another foreign country?

2. Are you afraid of growing old?

3. What do you think you could learn from an old person?

4. How is nudity regarded in your culture? Would you agree to model in the nude?

E   Debate

Debate this proposition:

Old age is a curse.

PART 3   Focus on Language

A   Euphemism

Euphemism is a device by which a writer or speaker softens a word or expression by substituting something pleasant-sounding for something more uncomfortable. For example, in the story when Mr. Elihu says, *"I'm no youngster"* (line 11), he is really saying, "I'm old." Two other common euphemisms are:

She passed away. (She died.)

He was economical with the truth. (He lied.)

With a partner, match the euphemisms in the right column with the words in the left column.

_h_ 1. ill   a. grease someone's palm

_____ 2. die   b. homely

_____ 3. beggar   c. liquidity crisis

_____ 4. bankruptcy d. let go

——— 5. deaf   e. meet one's maker

——— 6. pregnant   f. hearing impaired

——— 7. fire   g. well-padded

——— 8. bribe   h. under the weather

——— 9. ugly   i. panhandler

——— 10. fat   j. expecting

The following sentences contain italicized euphemisms. First guess what the euphemisms mean in context. Then check your answers with your teacher. Share other euphemisms you know with the class.

1. Now that I am *getting on*, I regret to say that my memory is failing.
2. *The happy event* is only six weeks away.
3. Movies in which people *sleep together* often draw large audiences.
4. "Unless you do what I say, you'll *go home in a box*!" he threatened.
5. Would you excuse me while I *powder my nose*?
6. He's had *a glass too many* again.
7. You'd better get some qualifications since you won't be able to rely on *a sugar daddy* all your life.
8. I wasn't at all surprised to hear about their *shotgun marriage*.
9. There's a special class for *late developers* at my son's school.
10. We *put* our old dog *to sleep* yesterday.

B Building Vocabulary Skills

1. The word *about* is used in three different ways in the story. Explain each meaning. Then make up sentences of your own, using *about* in these three ways.

   a. *He told the woman that he wanted someone of **about** thirty.* (line 4)

   b. *"No hurry at all," said Mr. Elihu, glad he was **about** to paint her.* (line 48)

   c. *"Also, I guess I didn't realize how much **about** painting I have forgotten."* (lines 114–115)

2. There are many other ways of using *about*. Use your dictionary to help you find out what the following expressions mean.

   a. out and about _____

   b. look about _____

   c. about-face _____

   d. bring about _____

   e. beat about the bush _____

   f. about time _____

3. Complete each of the sentences that follow with the correct expression from the preceding list.

   a. In an unexpected _____, the model began to sketch Mr. Elihu.

   b. The model didn't _____ when she accused Mr. Elihu of insulting her.

   c. Mr. Elihu felt that it was _____ he took steps to try to live again.

   d. The model immediately began to _____ the room for signs of the old man's family.

   e. The old man failed to _____ the changes in his life that he'd hoped for.

   f. He'd been at home for so long, he desperately wanted to go _____ .

4. "The Model" has many examples of words and expressions that can be used in more than one way. With the help of your dictionary, explain the difference between the italicized words in the following pairs of sentences. The first sentence of the pair is taken directly from the story, while the second uses the italicized word in an entirely different manner.

   a. He thanked her for her *consideration*. (line 21)
      For a small *consideration*, I will paint your child's room.

      _____

   b. . . . they had *settled on* a time for her to come. (line 23)
      The early pioneers faced many dangers when they *settled on* the land.

      _____

   c. The model, taking a last *drag* of a cigarette, pressed it out against a coffee-can lid on the kitchen table. (lines 55–56)
      Most children consider it a *drag* to do household chores.

      _____

d. "I don't mind, if you do it when we take a *break*." (line 58)

If there's a *break* in relations between the two countries, there's sure to be a war.

_____

e. They were facing a backyard with an ailanthus tree whose leaves had just *come out*. (lines 62–63)

It was difficult for my gay nephew to *come out* and speak to his parents about his lifestyle.

_____

f. But his expression was *objective*. (line 75)

I have been trying hard to discover what your *objective* in life is.

_____

g. Then she began to watch the painter with *interest*. (line 80)

Including the *interest*, your loan comes to $10,000.

_____

h. Afterward he removed the towel over his canvas and tried to *fill in* her face . . . (lines 146–147)

The student teacher was very nervous when he heard that there was an emergency and he had to *fill in* for the regular teacher.

_____

PART Writing Activities

1. Write an essay of about two pages on what could be done to improve the condition of old people in your country. First, describe their condition. Then suggest a number of specific ways to improve it. In your conclusion, say whether you think the authorities would be willing to adopt your proposals.

2. Describe a situation in which you have actually taken revenge on someone or fantasized about doing it. Explain clearly the nature of the situation and the steps you took (or imagined taking) to remedy it.

3. *Driving Miss Daisy* (American) and *Ikiru* (Japanese) are two famous movies in which the main characters are old. Write an essay of one to two pages on any movie you have seen that stars old people. How are they presented in the movie? What does the movie convey about old age?

4. Write three extended paragraphs showing how the time of year in which the story takes place is central to the themes of "The Model," "Miss Brill" (page 199), and "The Story of an Hour" (page 13). Devote one paragraph to each story.

14

Disappearing

MONICA WOOD (b. 1953)

Born in Maine, the American writer Monica Wood grew up listening to her mother and father tell wonderful stories in the tradition of their homeland, Prince Edward Island, Canada. Wood lives in Portland, Maine, and writes almost daily in a special cabin adjoining her house. Her short stories, which have appeared in numerous publications, have been nominated for the National Magazine Awards, and in 1991 she received a special mention from the Pushcart Prize. *Ernie's Ark,* her collection of linked short stories set in a fictional paper-mill town in Maine, was published in 2002 to critical acclaim.

Wood is the author of *Secret Language* (1993), *My Only Story* (2000), and *Any Bitter Thing* (2005). She has edited *Short Takes: 15 Contemporary Stories,* and has written a fiction-writing handbook, *The Pocket Muse: Ideas and Inspirations for Writing* (2002). A recurring theme in her work is the sense of loss and retrieval felt by her characters.

DISAPPEARING

Her obsession with swimming radically changes the life of a severely overweight woman.

When he starts in, I don't look anymore, I know what it looks like, what he looks like, tobacco on his teeth. I just lie in the deep sheets and shut my eyes. I make noises that make it go faster and when he's done he's as far from me as he gets. He could be dead he's so far away.

Lettie says leave then stupid but who would want me. Three hundred 5 pounds anyway but I never check. Skin like tapioca pudding,[1] I wouldn't show anyone. A man.

So we go to the pool at the junior high, swimming lessons. First it's blow bubbles and breathe, blow and breathe. Awful, hot nosefuls of chlorine.[2] My eyes stinging red and patches on my skin. I look worse. We'll 10 get caps and goggles[3] and earplugs and body cream Lettie says. It's better.

There are girls there, what bodies. Looking at me and Lettie out the side of their eyes. Gold hair, skin like milk, chlorine or no.

They thought when I first lowered into the pool, that fat one parting the Red Sea.[4] I didn't care. Something happened when I floated. Good 15 said the little instructor. A little redhead in an emerald suit, no stomach, a depression almost, and white wet skin. Good she said you float just great. Now we're getting somewhere. The whistle around her neck blinded my eyes. And the water under the fluorescent lights. I got scared and couldn't float again. The bottom of the pool was scarred, drops of 20 gray shadow rippling.[5] Without the water I would crack open my head, my dry flesh would sound like a splash on the tiles.

At home I ate a cake and a bottle of milk. No wonder you look like that he said. How can you stand yourself. You're no Cary Grant[6] I told him and he laughed and laughed until I threw up. 25

When this happens I want to throw up again and again until my heart flops[7] out wet and writhing[8] on the kitchen floor. Then he would know I have one and it moves.

So I went back. And floated again. My arms came around and the groan of the water made the tight blondes smirk[9] but I heard Good that's 30

---

1 **tapioca pudding** a dessert made from a grainy starch (has a lumpy look)
2 **chlorine** a chemical used to purify swimming pool water
3 **goggles** protective glasses for underwater swimming
4 **parting the Red Sea** a Biblical reference to the parting of the Red Sea by God to enable the Israelites to flee from Egypt

5 **rippling** flowing in small waves
6 **Cary Grant** a movie star famous for his good looks and charm
7 **flops** drops down in a heavy or clumsy way
8 **writhing** twisting in pain
9 **smirk** smile in an unpleasant way

the crawl that's it in fragments[10] from the redhead when I lifted my face. Through the earplugs I heard her skinny[11] voice. She was happy that I was floating and moving too.

Lettie stopped the lessons and read to me things out of magazines. You have to swim a lot to lose weight. You have to stop eating too. [35] Forget cake and ice cream. Doritos[12] are out.[13] I'm not doing it for that I told her but she wouldn't believe me. She couldn't imagine.

Looking down that shaft[14] of water I know I won't fall. The water shimmers and eases up and down, the heft[15] of me doesn't matter I float anyway. [40]

He says it makes no difference I look the same. But I'm not the same. I can hold myself up in deep water. I can move my arms and feet and the water goes behind me, the wall comes closer. I can look down twelve feet to a cold slab of tile and not be afraid. It makes a difference I tell him. Better believe it mister. [45]

Then this other part happens. Other men interest me. I look at them, real ones, not the ones on TV that's something else entirely. These are real. The one with the white milkweed[16] hair who delivers the mail. The meter man from the light company, heavy thick feet in boots. A smile. Teeth. I drop something out of the cart in the supermarket to see who [50] will pick it up. Sometimes a man. One had yellow short hair and called me ma'am. Young. Thin legs and an accent. One was older. Looked me in the eyes. Heavy, but not like me. My eyes are nice. I color the lids. In the pool it runs off in blue tears. When I come out my face is naked.

The lessons are over, I'm certified. A little certificate signed by the [55] redhead. She says I can swim and I can. I'd do better with her body, thin calves hard as granite.[17]

I get a lane to myself, no one shares. The blondes ignore me now that I don't splash the water, know how to lower myself silently. And when I swim I cut the water cleanly. [60]

For one hour every day I am thin, thin as water, transparent, invisible, steam or smoke.

The redhead is gone, they put her at a different pool and I miss the glare of the whistle dangling[18] between her emerald breasts. Lettie won't come over at all now that she is fatter than me. You're so uppity[19] she [65] says. All this talk about water and who do you think you are.

He says I'm looking all right, so at night it is worse but sometimes now when he starts in I say no. On Sundays the pool is closed I can't say no. I haven't been invisible. Even on days when I don't say no it's all right, he's better. [70]

---

10 **fragments** little pieces
11 **skinny** very thin
12 **Doritos** a brand of spicy corn chips
13 **are out** are not allowed
14 **shaft** a column
15 **heft** weight

16 **milkweed** a plant with milky sap and seeds with fine white hairs
17 **granite** hard rock
18 **dangling** hanging loosely
19 **uppity** snobbish

One night he says it won't last, what about the freezer full of low-cal dinners[20] and that machine in the basement. I'm not doing it for that and he doesn't believe me either. But this time there is another part. There are other men in the water I tell him. Fish he says. Fish in the sea. Good luck.

Ma you've lost says my daughter-in-law, the one who didn't want me in the wedding pictures. One with the whole family, she couldn't help that. I learned how to swim I tell her. You should try it, it might help your ugly disposition.[21]

They closed the pool for two weeks and I went crazy. Repairing the tiles. I went there anyway, drove by in the car. I drank water all day.

Then they opened again and I went every day, sometimes four times until the green paint and new stripes looked familiar as a face. At first the water was heavy as blood but I kept on until it was thinner and thinner, just enough to hold me up. That was when I stopped with the goggles and cap and plugs, things that kept the water out of me.

There was a time I went the day before a holiday and no one was there. It was echoey silence just me and the soundless empty pool and a lifeguard behind the glass. I lowered myself so slow it hurt every muscle but not a blip[22] of water not a ripple not one sound and I was under in that other quiet, so quiet some tears got out, I saw their blue trail swirling.

The redhead is back and nods, she has seen me somewhere. I tell her I took lessons and she still doesn't remember.

This has gone too far he says I'm putting you in the hospital. He calls them at the pool and they pay no attention. He doesn't touch me and I smile into my pillow, a secret smile in my own square of the dark.

Oh my God Lettie says what the hell are you doing what the hell do you think you're doing. I'm disappearing I tell her and what can you do about it not a blessed thing.

For a long time in the middle of it people looked at me. Men. And I thought about it. Believe it, I thought. And now they don't look at me again. And it's better.

I'm almost there. Almost water.

The redhead taught me how to dive, how to tuck my head[23] and vanish like a needle into skin, and every time it happens, my feet leaving the board, I think, this will be the time.

---

20 **low-cal dinners** low-calorie dinners
21 **disposition** temper, personality
22 **blip** an interruption

23 **tuck my head** bend my neck, drawing my head to my chest

PART 1 First Reading

A Thinking About the Story

Did your attitude toward the narrator change as the story progressed? Did you feel optimistic or pessimistic at the end of the story? Explain your answer.

B Understanding the Plot

1. Who is the man referred to in the first paragraph?
2. What activity is being described in the opening paragraph? How do the participants feel about it?
3. Who is Lettie? What advice does she give the narrator regarding her marriage?
4. Why is the narrator's entry into the pool compared with the parting of the Red Sea? (lines 14–15) Is this description still accurate at the end of the story? Explain your answer.
5. What details give you an idea about the quantity of food the narrator consumes?
6. Why did Lettie stop swimming?
7. What does "that" in line 36 refer to?
8. What do the men in lines 46–53 have in common?
9. What day of the week is the most difficult for the narrator? Explain why.
10. What does the narrator's husband predict about her weight loss? What is the basis for his prediction?
11. What is the relationship between the narrator and her daughter-in-law? Why is it like this?
12. How does the narrator react when the pool is closed?
13. Why does the narrator's husband threaten to put her in the hospital? (line 93)
14. What does "in the middle of it" (line 99) refer to? What did the narrator consider doing then?
15. What word in the conclusion is a synonym for *disappear*?

PART 2 Second Reading

Before starting the second reading, do the first exercise on ellipsis in Analyzing the Author's Style (pages 194–195).

A Exploring Themes

You are now ready to reread "Disappearing." Try to decide what the connection is between the nature of the narrator's personal relationships and her obsession with swimming.

1. How does swimming change the narrator's relationship with her husband? Give examples from the story.
2. Why is the narrator unable to follow through on the new interest in her shown by other men? Give some psychological reasons that you can infer from the story.
3. What do you think the ending means? What imagery in the story reinforces your answer?
4. What are the probable roots of the narrator's obsession with disappearing?
5. Discuss the symbolic nature of water in the story.
   Note: For information on symbolism, see page 308.

B Analyzing the Author's Style

For more information on the literary terms in this section, turn to the explanations of *ellipsis* (page 301) and *imagery* (page 303).

ELLIPSIS

In "Disappearing," Monica Wood uses a narrative style in which the language is for the most part informal and crisp. She relies on **ellipsis,** in which parts of sentences—in particular, verbs—are left out but are nevertheless easily understood or inferred. For example, when the narrator compares herself unfavorably with the thin swimmers around her, she describes them as *Gold hair, skin like milk, chlorine or no.* (line 13) Here the absence of verbs makes the visual impact stronger and reminds us of her less flattering description of herself as *skin like tapioca pudding.* (line 6)

1. Supply what has been left out but implied in these sentences and phrases from the story. Refer to the text before answering.
   a. When he starts in (line 1)
   b. Three hundred pounds anyway (lines 5–6)

    c. A man. (line 7)

    d. Awful, hot nosefuls of chlorine. (lines 9–10)

    e. And the water under the fluorescent lights. (line 19)

    f. You're no Cary Grant (line 24)

    g. She couldn't imagine. (line 37)

    h. A smile. Teeth. (lines 49–50)

    i. Fish in the sea. (line 74)

    j. Ma you've lost (line 75)

    k. Believe it, I thought. (line 100)

2. Explain how the elliptical style of writing helps convey the narrator's thoughts and feelings.

IMAGERY

There are moments when the narrator's voice in "Disappearing" becomes less colloquial and more poetic, and we feel keenly the pathos underlying her situation. This change is accomplished through the employment of powerful **imagery,** or pictures that appeal to our visual (sight), auditory (hearing), and tactile (touch) senses. For example, *the groan of the water* (lines 29–30) encourages one to hear the water's strained sounds as the very fat woman labors through it.

Look at the following images from the story. Say whether they are visual, auditory, or tactile. Explain the effect of each image as fully as possible.

1. my dry flesh would sound like a splash on the tiles (line 22)
2. my heart flops out wet and writhing on the kitchen floor (lines 26–27)
3. tight blondes (line 30)
4. skinny voice (line 32)
5. a cold slab of tile (line 44)
6. it runs off in blue tears (line 54)
7. thin calves hard as granite (lines 56–57)
8. thin as water (line 61)
9. emerald breasts (line 64)
10. the water was heavy as blood (line 83)
11. my own square of the dark (line 95)
12. vanish like a needle into skin (line 104)

C Judging for Yourself

Express yourself as personally as you like in your answers to the following questions.

1. In your view, was Lettie a good friend?
2. Is it fair to blame the husband for his wife's problems?
3. Should the wife have followed Lettie's advice and left her husband?
4. Would it have made a great difference to the narrator's life if she had encouraged one of the men who began to look at her as her figure and her morale improved?
5. Do you think the narrator is being courageous or cowardly in her quest to disappear? Support your answer.

D Making Connections

1. What is your society's attitude toward fat people?
2. Would you say that fat people are discriminated against in your culture? Give examples to substantiate your answer.
3. Are eating disorders common in your society? What do you think causes people deliberately to overeat or to starve themselves?
4. Does the concept of marital rape exist in your country? Do you think a man is raping his wife if he insists on having sex with her against her wishes? Should he be punished?

E Debate

Debate this proposition:

A person's weight is a reflection of his or her willpower.

PART 3 Focus on Language

A Building Vocabulary Skills

Complete the following sentences with appropriate glossed words from the text. You may need to change the form or tense of some verbs. First try to do the exercise by referring to the story without looking at the definitions of the words.

1. Monuments are frequently made of _____ because it is a material that lasts.

2. I have never met anyone as popular as my sister. Everybody is attracted to her because of her sunny _____.

3. They did not feel comfortable with the new people in the neighborhood, who were very _____ and didn't want to mix with the other residents.

4. Because of his illness, he _____ into bed straight after dinner every evening.

5. When you stir your tea, you will see the liquid _____.

6. If you want to avoid burning your eyes under water, always wear _____.

7. The athlete _____ in agony from a broken ankle when I rushed up to help her.

8. My cousin always looked uncomfortable in his school photos as he gazed out _____ at the unseen face of the photographer.

9. It was a terrifying sight to see a leg _____ out of the car after the accident.

10. As a result of the concussion she suffered, only _____ of her memory returned.

The following words appear in the story but are not glossed. First define each word, using its context in the story as a guide. Then fill in each blank in the paragraph below with the correct word from the list. You may have to change the tense or form of the word.

lowered (line 14) _____

floated (line 15) _____

scarred (line 20) _____

transparent (line 61) _____

vanish (line 104) _____

Since she was feeling nervous, she tried to _____ herself into the _____ water, looking anxiously at the chipped, _____ tiles. But after a while her fears _____, and she felt as if she were _____ on air as she swam successfully from one end of the pool to the other.

PART 4 Writing Activities

1. Imagine that you have woken up one morning one hundred pounds (forty-five kilos) heavier or lighter than your usual weight. Using the informal narrative voice in "Disappearing" as a guideline, write a monologue in which you express your immediate thoughts and feelings about this extraordinary event.

2. Have you or has anybody you know been obsessed with something? Write an essay of two to three pages in which you first outline the nature and source of the obsession. Next consider its effect on the obsessed person as well as on the people around this individual. In your conclusion, say whether you think the person can be "cured" of this obsession and if so, how.

3. In *Hedda Gabler,* a play by the Norwegian playwright Henrik Ibsen, the heroine shoots herself at the end as a way out of an unhappy marriage that she feels is killing her. Outline the plot of a book or movie you know in which a character feels forced to take drastic action to escape from an unloved spouse. In your discussion of the plot, try to convey the desperation of the character. Then give your opinion of the action the character took.

4. Both "The Rocking-Horse Winner" (page 123) and "Disappearing" are centered on an obsession and its drastic repercussions for the characters concerned. In a two-page essay, briefly describe the main characters of both stories and their obsessions. Consider which story was more disturbing to you, and analyze the reasons for your response. Say whether you empathized more with one character than the other.

15

Miss Brill

KATHERINE MANSFIELD (1888–1923)

Born in Wellington, New Zealand, Katherine Mansfield was the daughter of a wealthy businessman and a cold, sickly mother. In 1908, determined to become a writer, she left for London, where she adopted a highly unconventional lifestyle while relishing the city's intellectual stimulation. She married twice, bore a child out of wedlock, and became a close friend of D. H. Lawrence. She was at the height of her literary powers when she was diagnosed with tuberculosis in 1918.

During her life, Mansfield worked tirelessly to refine the technique of impressionist writing. Ironically, she was to find almost all the material she needed for her stories in her early life with her family in New Zealand. She drew on her past for many of her themes, especially those that highlighted the price paid by a woman in marriage and the plight of a woman on her own in an unfriendly world.

Mansfield's volumes of short stories include *In a German Pension* (1911), *Prelude* (1918), *Bliss and Other Stories* (1923), and *Stories by Katherine Mansfield* (1930).

MISS BRILL

A lonely woman enjoys her Sunday afternoon outings to the park until her encounter with a thoughtless young couple.

Although it was so brilliantly fine—the blue sky powdered with gold and great spots of light like white wine splashed over the Jardins Publiques¹—Miss Brill was glad that she had decided on her fur. The air was motionless, but when you opened your mouth there was just a faint chill, like a chill from a glass of iced water before you sip, and now and again a leaf came drifting²—from nowhere, from the sky. Miss Brill put up her hand and touched her fur. Dear little thing! It was nice to feel it again. She had taken it out of its box that afternoon, shaken out the moth-powder, given it a good brush, and rubbed the life back into the dim little eyes. "What has been happening to me?" said the sad little eyes. Oh, how sweet it was to see them snap at her again from the red eiderdown!³ . . . But the nose, which was of some black composition, wasn't at all firm. It must have had a knock, somehow. Never mind—a little dab of black sealing-wax⁴ when the time came—when it was absolutely necessary. . . . Little rogue!⁵ Yes, she really felt like that about it. Little rogue biting its tail just by her left ear. She could have taken it off and laid it on her lap and stroked it. She felt a tingling⁶ in her hands and arms, but that came from walking, she supposed. And when she breathed, something light and sad—no, not sad, exactly—something gentle seemed to move in her bosom.

There were a number of people out this afternoon, far more than last Sunday. And the band sounded louder and gayer.⁷ That was because the Season had begun. For although the band played all the year round on Sundays, out of season⁸ it was never the same. It was like some one playing with only the family to listen; it didn't care how it played if there weren't any strangers present. Wasn't the conductor wearing a new coat, too? She was sure it was new. He scraped with his foot and flapped his arms like a rooster about to crow,⁹ and the bandsmen sitting in the green rotunda¹⁰ blew out their cheeks and glared at the music. Now there came a little "flutey"¹¹ bit—very pretty!— a little chain of bright drops. She was sure it would be repeated. It was; she lifted her head and smiled.

Only two people shared her "special" seat: a fine old man in a velvet coat, his hands clasped over a huge carved walking-stick, and a big old

---

1 **Jardins Publiques** Public Gardens (French)
2 **drifting** floating down
3 **eiderdown** a warm bed cover
4 **dab of black sealing-wax** a tiny amount of black patching material
5 **rogue** a mischievous person
6 **tingling** a prickly sensation
7 **gayer** happier

8 **out of season** socially, during the less important months
9 **about to crow** getting ready to make a rooster's cry
10 **rotunda** a round building covered by a dome
11 **"flutey"** like a flute (usually spelled *fluty*)

woman, sitting upright, with a roll of knitting on her embroidered apron. They did not speak. This was disappointing, for Miss Brill always looked forward to the conversation. She had become really quite expert, she thought, at listening as though she didn't listen, at sitting in other people's lives just for a minute while they talked round her.

She glanced, sideways, at the old couple. Perhaps they would go soon. Last Sunday, too, hadn't been as interesting as usual. An Englishman and his wife, he wearing a dreadful Panama hat[12] and she button boots. And she'd gone on[13] the whole time about how she ought to wear spectacles; she knew she needed them; but that it was no good getting any; they'd be sure to break and they'd never keep on. And he'd been so patient. He'd suggested everything—gold rims, the kind that curved round your ears, little pads inside the bridge. No, nothing would please her. "They'll always be sliding down my nose!" Miss Brill had wanted to shake her.

The old people sat on the bench, still as statues. Never mind, there was always the crowd to watch. To and fro,[14] in front of the flower-beds and the band rotunda, the couples and groups paraded, stopped to talk, to greet, to buy a handful of flowers from the old beggar who had his tray fixed to the railings. Little children ran among them, swooping[15] and laughing; little boys with big white silk bows under their chins, little girls, little French dolls, dressed up in velvet and lace. And sometimes a tiny staggerer[16] came suddenly rocking into the open from under the trees, stopped, stared, as suddenly sat down "flop," until its small high-stepping mother, like a young hen, rushed scolding[17] to its rescue. Other people sat on the benches and green chairs, but they were nearly always the same, Sunday after Sunday, and—Miss Brill had often noticed—there was something funny about nearly all of them. They were odd, silent, nearly all old, and from the way they stared they looked as though they'd just come from dark little rooms or even—even cupboards![18]

Behind the rotunda the slender trees with yellow leaves down drooping, and through them just a line of sea, and beyond the blue sky with gold-veined clouds.

Tum-tum-tum tiddle-um! tiddle-um! tum tiddley-um tum ta! blew the band.

Two young girls in red came by and two young soldiers in blue met them, and they laughed and paired and went off arm-in-arm. Two peasant women with funny straw hats passed, gravely, leading beautiful smoke-coloured donkeys. A cold, pale nun hurried by. A beautiful woman came along and dropped her bunch of violets, and a little boy ran after to hand them to her, and she took them and threw them away as if they'd been poisoned. Dear me! Miss Brill didn't know whether to admire that or not! And now an ermine toque[19] and a gentleman in grey

---

12 **Panama hat** a lightweight straw hat
13 **gone on** talked endlessly
14 **To and fro** Forward and backward
15 **swooping** moving downward quickly
16 **staggerer** someone who moves very unsteadily

17 **scolding** expressing disapproval
18 **cupboards** closets
19 **ermine toque** a small, close-fitting woman's hat made of the fur of an ermine, a small white animal

met just in front of her. He was tall, stiff, dignified, and she was wearing 75
the ermine toque she'd bought when her hair was yellow. Now everything,
her hair, her face, even her eyes, was the same colour as the shabby[20]
ermine, and her hand, in its cleaned glove, lifted to dab her lips, was a
tiny yellowish paw. Oh, she was so pleased to see him—delighted! She
rather thought they were going to meet that afternoon. She described 80
where she'd been—everywhere, here, there, along by the sea. The day
was so charming—didn't he agree? And wouldn't he, perhaps? . . . But
he shook his head, lighted a cigarette, slowly breathed a great deep puff
into her face, and, even while she was still talking and laughing, flicked
the match away and walked on. The ermine toque was alone; she smiled 85
more brightly than ever. But even the band seemed to know what she
was feeling and played more softly, played tenderly, and the drum beat,
"The Brute! The Brute!" over and over. What would she do? What was
going to happen now? But as Miss Brill wondered, the ermine toque
turned, raised her hand as though she'd seen some one else, much nicer, 90
just over there, and pattered[21] away. And the band changed again and
played more quickly, more gaily than ever, and the old couple on Miss
Brill's seat got up and marched away, and such a funny old man with
long whiskers[22] hobbled[23] along in time to the music and was nearly
knocked over by four girls walking abreast.[24] 95

Oh, how fascinating it was! How she enjoyed it! How she loved sitting
here, watching it all! It was like a play. It was exactly like a play. Who could
believe the sky at the back wasn't painted? But it wasn't till a little brown
dog trotted on solemn and then slowly trotted off, like a little "theatre" dog,
a little dog that had been drugged, that Miss Brill discovered what it was that 100
made it so exciting. They were all on the stage. They weren't only the
audience, not only looking on; they were acting. Even she had a part and
came every Sunday. No doubt somebody would have noticed if she hadn't
been there; she was part of the performance after all. How strange she'd
never thought of it like that before! And yet it explained why she made such 105
a point of[25] starting from home at just the same time each week—so as not
to be late for the performance—and it also explained why she had quite a
queer, shy feeling at telling her English pupils how she spent her Sunday
afternoons. No wonder! Miss Brill nearly laughed out loud. She was on the
stage. She thought of the old invalid[26] gentleman to whom she read the 110
newspaper four afternoons a week while he slept in the garden. She had got
quite used to the frail head on the cotton pillow, the hollowed eyes, the
open mouth and the high pinched[27] nose. If he'd been dead she mightn't
have noticed for weeks; she wouldn't have minded. But suddenly he knew
he was having the paper read to him by an actress! "An actress!" The old 115
head lifted; two points of light quivered in the old eyes. "An actress—are ye?"

---

20 **shabby** worn and old-looking
21 **pattered** ran with light, quick steps
22 **whiskers** a beard or sometimes a mustache
23 **hobbled** walked with great difficulty

24 **walking abreast** walking side by side
25 **made such a point of** insisted on
26 **invalid** a sickly person
27 **pinched** narrow

And Miss Brill smoothed the newspaper as though it were the manuscript of her part and said gently: "Yes, I have been an actress for a long time."

The band had been having a rest. Now they started again. And what they played was warm, sunny, yet there was just a faint chill—a something, what was it?— not sadness—no, not sadness—a something that made you want to sing. The tune lifted, lifted, the light shone; and it seemed to Miss Brill that in another moment all of them, all the whole company, would begin singing. The young ones, the laughing ones who were moving together, they would begin, and the men's voices, very resolute and brave, would join them. And then she too, she too, and the others on the benches—they would come in with a kind of accompaniment—something low, that scarcely rose or fell, something so beautiful—moving. . . . And Miss Brill's eyes filled with tears and she looked smiling at all the other members of the company. Yes, we understand, we understand, she thought—though what they understood she didn't know.

Just at that moment a boy and girl came and sat down where the old couple had been. They were beautifully dressed; they were in love. The hero and heroine, of course, just arrived from his father's yacht.[28] And still soundlessly singing, still with that trembling smile, Miss Brill prepared to listen.

"No, not now," said the girl. "Not here, I can't."

"But why? Because of that stupid old thing at the end there?" asked the boy. "Why does she come here at all—who wants her? Why doesn't she keep her silly old mug[29] at home?"

"It's her fu-fur which is so funny," giggled the girl. "It's exactly like a fried whiting."[30]

"Ah, be off with you!" said the boy in an angry whisper. Then: "Tell me, ma petite chérie—"[31]

"No, not here," said the girl. "Not *yet*."

On her way home she usually bought a slice of honey-cake at the baker's. It was her Sunday treat. Sometimes there was an almond[32] in her slice, sometimes not. It made a great difference. If there was an almond it was like carrying home a tiny present—a surprise—something that might very well not have been there. She hurried on the almond Sundays and struck the match for the kettle[33] in quite a dashing way.

But to-day she passed the baker's by, climbed the stairs, went into the little dark room—her room like a cupboard—and sat down on the red eiderdown. She sat there for a long time. The box that the fur came out of was on the bed. She unclasped the necklet quickly; quickly, without looking, laid it inside. But when she put the lid on she thought she heard something crying.

---

28 **yacht** a small sailing ship, a cruise boat
29 **mug** an ugly face (slang)
30 **whiting** a kind of fish
31 **ma petite chérie** my little darling (French)

32 **almond** a type of small nut
33 **struck the match for the kettle** lit her stove to boil water for tea

PART 1 First Reading

A Thinking About the Story

Did you feel the sadness that lay beneath the story, even when Miss Brill seemed at her happiest? Were you moved by the ending? Why?

B Understanding the Plot

1. In what season does the story take place? How do you know?
2. What is unusual about the way Miss Brill regards her fur?
3. How long has it been since Miss Brill last wore her fur?
4. What is special about the band that Sunday afternoon?
5. Why is Miss Brill disappointed in the old man and woman who are sharing the bench? With whom does she compare them?
6. What word would you use to describe what the gentleman in gray does to the woman in the ermine toque?
7. With what does Miss Brill compare the Sunday afternoon scenes she witnesses? How does she see herself? How does she initially see the young couple?
8. How often does Miss Brill go to the park?
9. How does she earn her living?
10. What is different for Miss Brill about this Sunday afternoon's return from the park?
11. What is Miss Brill's financial situation? Give details to support your answer.

PART 2 Second Reading

A Exploring Themes

You are now ready to reread "Miss Brill." Note how Katherine Mansfield unfolds in painstaking detail the scenes that Miss Brill witnesses until everything is as vivid as it would be in a movie, a play, or a complex painting. Be sensitive to the gently sad atmosphere that pervades the story.

1. What role does the season play in the story?
2. What does the fur symbolize in the story? Be as detailed as possible in your answer.
   Note: For information on symbol, see page 308.
3. What does the thrill Miss Brill gets from eavesdropping (listening in on other people's conversations) tell us about the kind of life she leads?
4. What is ironic about the way Miss Brill sees the silent old people who frequent the park? (lines 56–61)
   Note: For information on irony, see page 304.
5. What later scene does the incident with the "ermine toque" foreshadow? (lines 74–91) Explain the parallels.
6. Discuss the implications of the ending.

B   Analyzing the Author's Style

For more information on the literary terms in this section, turn to the explanations of *synecdoche* (page 308) and *simile* (page 307).

SYNECDOCHE

Katherine Mansfield makes interesting use of **synecdoche,** a figure of speech in which a part is used to describe a whole. For example, Miss Brill refers to the woman she sees and pities as *an ermine toque.* (line 74) In this example, the woman's fur hat both represents her person and also draws attention to the symbolic parallels between her fur hat and Miss Brill's fur wrap.

With a partner, decide what the following sentences mean. Point out the synecdoche in each sentence, and explain the whole that the part stands for. Then see what other examples of synecdoche you can think of.

1. The rancher who owns 50,000 head of cattle was arrested last week.
2. Their brother had the reputation of being the heart and soul of any party he attended.
3. Since I have to earn my bread, I cannot afford to take a long vacation.
4. The orchestra's strong point is its strings.
5. Our neighbor recently won an important award for his rhyme.
6. Let me introduce you to the brains behind this project.
7. The captain yelled for all hands on deck during the storm.
8. In spite of all our misfortunes, we still have a roof over our head.

SIMILE

"Miss Brill" resonates with **similes** (explicit comparisons that use *like* or *as* to unite the two elements). For example, the story opens with a description of a blue sky with *great spots of light like white wine*. (line 2) Here, the two elements compared are light and wine, and the effect is an image of crisp, sparkling afternoon light.

1. What other simile can be found in the first paragraph? What two elements are being compared?
2. As Miss Brill observes the passing parade, she often registers what the people are doing in terms of similes. How many such similes can you find? Name them. How do these similes add color to the descriptions?
3. What does the young girl compare Miss Brill's fur to? What does this simile suggest about the appearance of the fur? How does it contradict Miss Brill's own image of her fur?
4. What simile is used to describe Miss Brill's room? What is the full effect of using this simile?

C   Judging for Yourself

Express yourself as personally as you like in your answers to the following questions.

1. Do you think Miss Brill will return to the park on the following Sunday? Justify your answer.
2. In your view, was Miss Brill wrong to eavesdrop? Should eavesdroppers always be prepared to hear something hurtful about themselves?
3. Do you feel that Miss Brill will ever take her fur out of the box again? Explain your answer.
4. What do you imagine a regular weekday to be like for Miss Brill?
5. Did you sympathize with Miss Brill's need for fantasy?

D   Making Connections

1. Who are the loneliest segments of the population in your country? Explain why they are so lonely.
2. What facilities are there in your hometown for people to get together and socialize? Have you made use of any of these facilities?

3. Is there a correlation between age, gender, and poverty in your country?

4. Have you ever witnessed anybody being humiliated or been in that situation yourself? Describe what happened.

E   Debate

Debate this proposition:

Lonely people have only themselves to blame.

PART 3   Focus on Language

A   Verbs of Movement

Katherine Mansfield employs a variety of verbs to describe the leg, arm, and hand movements of her characters.

Look at the following list of verbs taken from the text, although not necessarily in the same form or tense.

stroke (line 16)	dab (line 78)
flap (line 26)	flick (line 84)
clasp (line 32)	patter (line 91)
parade (line 49)	hobble (line 94)
stagger (line 54)	trot (line 99)

Make two columns—one for leg movements and one for hand/arm movements—and list each word in the appropriate column. Then complete the paragraph that follows with the appropriate verbs. Make sure you use the correct form and tense of each verb.

Miss Brill _____ her forehead with her handkerchief as she sat watching the scene unfold in front of her. As the people _____ before her in twos and threes, she _____ her fur absentmindedly. She felt sorry for the old man who came _____ forward, _____ his cane tightly. She watched as a puppy _____ up to the playing children and wagged its tail. An anxious mother rushed up, _____ her arms wildly to shoo it away, but the puppy, unafraid, went on lightly _____ after them. Miss Brill smiled when a toddler began _____ uncertainly toward her, then gasped as she witnessed the man in gray ———————— the cigarette ash off his jacket while he brutally turned his back on the woman in the ermine toque.

B Building Vocabulary Skills

Look at the following adjectives from the story.

embroidered (line 33)

slender (line 62)

drooping (line 63)

dignified (line 75)

queer (line 108)

frail (line 112)

resolute (line 125)

trembling (line 135)

dashing (line 151)

With the help of your dictionary, find a synonym for each adjective. Then write sentences using each adjective in a context that illustrates its meaning.

PART 4 Writing Activities

1. Write an essay of two to three pages examining the situation of older single women in your culture. Begin your essay with this statement: *In general, my culture extends/does not extend the same respect to an older single woman as it gives to an older married woman.* Go on to explain the reasons and show the economic and social consequences. Conclude your essay with a comment on whether the present situation is likely to change and why.

2. Select a place where you can watch a parade of people. Note carefully what they are doing, saying, and wearing. Then, using the lively pictorial writing in lines 31–95 of "Miss Brill" as a model, write three paragraphs on what you have observed. Try to include original similes in your piece.

3. The aging single woman is frequently treated as a lonely, tragic figure in literature, epitomized by the fading beauty Blanche DuBois in Tennessee Williams's play *A Streetcar Named Desire*. Write an essay of one to two pages about a play, book, or movie you are familiar with in which an older unmarried woman plays a central role. Briefly describe her role and say whether the woman is presented in a positive or negative light.

16

Teenage Wasteland

ANNE TYLER (b. 1941)

Born in Minneapolis, Minnesota, Anne Tyler has spent most of her life in Baltimore, Maryland, which is a recurring location in her novels. She studied at Duke University, from which she graduated with the highest academic honors. At the age of twenty-two, she published her first novel, *If Morning Ever Comes*, which attracted critical notice. The *New York Times Book Review* called it "a subtle and mature story."

A prolific writer, Tyler regularly brings out a new novel every few years. In 1988, she won the Pulitzer Prize for *Breathing Lessons*, and she is also well known for *Dinner at the Homesick Restaurant* (1983) and *The Accidental Tourist* (1985), which won the National Book Critics Circle Award and was made into a movie. More recent novels include *Ladder of Years* (1995), *A Patchwork Planet* (1998), and *The Amateur Marriage* (2004). Her books and short stories examine minutely the complexities of family life as her characters struggle to make sense of their relationships and choices in a bewildering world.

TEENAGE WASTELAND

A teenage boy withdraws from his family and comes under the influence of an unconventional tutor whose methods have questionable results.

He used to have very blond hair—almost white—cut shorter than other children's so that on his crown a little cowlick[1] always stood up to catch the light. But this was when he was small. As he grew older, his hair grew darker, and he wore it longer—past his collar even. It hung in lank,[2] taffy-colored ropes around his face, which was still an endearing   5
face, fine-featured, the eyes an unusual aqua blue. But his cheeks, of course, were no longer round, and a sharp new Adam's apple jogged in his throat when he talked.

In October, they called from the private school he attended to request a conference with his parents. Daisy went alone; her husband was at   10
work. Clutching her purse, she sat on the principal's couch and learned that Donny was noisy, lazy, and disruptive;[3] always fooling around with his friends, and he wouldn't respond in class.

In the past, before her children were born, Daisy had been a fourth-grade teacher. It shamed her now to sit before this principal as a parent, a   15
delinquent[4] parent, a parent who struck[5] Mr. Lanham, no doubt, as unseeing or uncaring. "It isn't that we're not concerned," she said. "Both of us are. And we've done what we could, whatever we could think of. We don't let him watch TV on school nights. We don't let him talk on the phone till he's finished his homework. But he tells us he doesn't *have* any homework or he   20
did it all in study hall. How are we to know what to believe?"

From early October through November, at Mr. Lanham's suggestion, Daisy checked Donny's assignments every day. She sat next to him as he worked, trying to be encouraging, sagging[6] inwardly as she saw the poor quality of everything he did—the sloppy[7] mistakes in math, the illogical   25
leaps in his English themes, the history questions left blank if they required any research.

Daisy was often late starting supper, and she couldn't give as much attention to Donny's younger sister. "You'll never guess what happened at . . ." Amanda would begin, and Daisy would have to tell her, "Not now,   30
honey."

By the time her husband, Matt, came home, she'd be snappish.[8] She would recite the day's hardships—the fuzzy instructions in English, the

---

1 **cowlick** a curl of hair growing in the wrong direction	5 **struck** affected, impressed
2 **lank** hanging straight and thin	6 **sagging** drooping as if under a heavy weight
3 **disruptive** disturbing the order	7 **sloppy** careless
4 **delinquent** not carrying out one's duties	8 **snappish** irritable

botched history map, the morass of unsolvable algebra equations. Matt would look surprised and confused, and Daisy would gradually wind down.[9] There was no way, really, to convey how exhausting all this was.

In December, the school called again. This time, they wanted Matt to come as well. She and Matt had to sit on Mr. Lanham's couch like two bad children and listen to the news: Donny had improved only slightly, raising a D in history to a C, and a C in algebra to a B-minus. What was worse, he had developed new problems. He had cut classes[10] on at least three occasions. Smoked in the furnace room. Helped Sonny Barnett break into a freshman's locker. And last week, during athletics, he and three friends had been seen off the school grounds; when they returned, the coach had smelled beer on their breath.

Daisy and Matt sat silent, shocked. Matt rubbed his forehead with his fingertips. Imagine, Daisy thought, how they must look to Mr. Lanham: an overweight housewife in a cotton dress and a too-tall, too-thin insurance agent in a baggy, frayed suit.[11] Failures, both of them—the kind of people who are always hurrying to catch up, missing the point of things that everyone else grasps at once. She wished she'd worn nylons instead of knee socks.

It was arranged that Donny would visit a psychologist for testing. Mr. Lanham knew just the person. He would set this boy straight,[12] he said.

When they stood to leave, Daisy held her stomach in and gave Mr. Lanham a firm, responsible handshake.

Donny said the psychologist was a jackass and the tests were really dumb; but he kept all three of his appointments, and when it was time for the follow-up conference with the psychologist and both parents, Donny combed his hair and seemed unusually sober and subdued. The psychologist said Donny had no serious emotional problems. He was merely going through a difficult period in his life. He required some academic help and a better sense of self-worth. For this reason, he was suggesting a man named Calvin Beadle, a tutor[13] with considerable psychological training.

In the car going home, Donny said he'd be damned if he'd let them drag him to some stupid fairy[14] tutor. His father told him to watch his language in front of his mother.

That night, Daisy lay awake pondering[15] the term "self-worth." She had always been free with her praise. She had always told Donny he had talent, was smart, was good with his hands. She had made a big to-do[16] over every little gift he gave her. In fact, maybe she had gone too far, although, Lord knows, she had meant every word. Was that his trouble?

9 **wind down** relax
10 **cut classes** deliberately missed classes
11 **a baggy, frayed suit** a suit that is too large and is old and worn-out
12 **set this boy straight** help this boy to reform himself
13 **tutor** a private teacher
14 **fairy** an insulting reference to a male homosexual
15 **pondering** thinking deeply
16 **to-do** fuss

She remembered when Amanda was born. Donny had acted lost and 75
bewildered. Daisy had been alert to that, of course, but still, a new baby
keeps you so busy. Had she really done all she could have? She longed—
she ached—for a time machine. Given one more chance, she'd do it
perfectly—hug him more, praise him more, or perhaps praise him less.
Oh, who can say . . . 80

The tutor told Donny to call him Cal. All his kids did, he said. Daisy
thought for a second that he meant his own children, then realized her
mistake. He seemed too young, anyhow, to be a family man. He wore a
heavy brown handlebar mustache. His hair was as long and stringy as
Donny's, and his jeans as faded. Wire-rimmed spectacles slid down his 85
nose. He lounged[17] in a canvas director's chair with his fingers laced
across his chest, and he casually, amiably questioned Donny, who sat
upright and glaring in an armchair.

"So they're getting on your back[18] at school," said Cal. "Making a big
deal about anything you do wrong." 90

"Right," said Donny.

"Any idea why that would be?"

"Oh, well, you know, stuff like homework and all," Donny said.

"You don't do your homework?"

"Oh, well, I might do it sometimes but not just exactly like they want 95
it." Donny sat forward and said, "It's like a prison there, you know? You've
got to go to every class, you can never step off the school grounds."

"You cut classes sometimes?"

"Sometimes," Donny said, with a glance at his parents.

Cal didn't seem perturbed.[19] "Well," he said, "I'll tell you what. Let's 100
you and me try working together three nights a week. Think you could
handle that? We'll see if we can show that school of yours a thing or two.
Give it a month; then if you don't like it, we'll stop. If *I* don't like it, we'll
stop. I mean, sometimes people just don't get along,[20] right? What do you
say to that?" 105

"Okay," Donny said. He seemed pleased.

"Make it seven o'clock till eight, Monday, Wednesday, and Friday,"
Cal told Matt and Daisy. They nodded. Cal shambled to his feet, gave
them a little salute, and showed them to the door.

This was where he lived as well as worked, evidently. The interview 110
had taken place in the dining room, which had been transformed into a
kind of office. Passing the living room, Daisy winced[21] at the rock music
she had been hearing, without registering it, ever since she had entered
the house. She looked in and saw a boy about Donny's age lying on a

---

17 **lounged** sat in a relaxed fashion	19 **perturbed** disturbed
18 **getting on your back** being a persistent nuisance (slang)	20 **get along** like one another, feel good together
	21 **winced** moved one's body in response to pain

sofa with a book. Another boy and a girl were playing Ping-Pong in front   115
of the fireplace. "You have several here together?" Daisy asked Cal.

"Oh, sometimes they stay on after their sessions, just to rap.[22] They're
a pretty sociable group, all in all. Plenty of goof-offs[23] like young Donny
here."

He cuffed Donny's shoulder playfully. Donny flushed and grinned.   120
Climbing into the car, Daisy asked Donny, "Well? What did you think?"

But Donny had returned to his old evasive[24] self. He jerked his chin
toward the garage. "Look," he said. "He's got a basketball net."

Now on Mondays, Wednesdays, and Fridays, they had supper early—
the instant Matt came home. Sometimes, they had to leave before they   125
were really finished. Amanda would still be eating her dessert. "Bye,
honey. Sorry," Daisy would tell her.

Cal's first bill sent a flutter of panic through Daisy's chest, but it was
worth it, of course. Just look at Donny's face when they picked him up:
alight and full of interest. The principal telephoned Daisy to tell her how   130
Donny had improved. "Of course, it hasn't shown up in his grades yet,
but several of the teachers have noticed how his attitude's changed. Yes,
sir, I think we're onto something[25] here."

At home, Donny didn't act much different. He still seemed to have a
low opinion of his parents. But Daisy supposed that was unavoidable—   135
part of being fifteen. He said his parents were too "controlling"— a word
that made Daisy give him a sudden look. He said they acted like wardens.
On weekends, they enforced a curfew.[26] And any time he went to a party,
they always telephoned first to see if adults would be supervising. "For
God's sake!" he said. "Don't you trust me?"   140

"It isn't a matter of trust, honey . . ." But there was no explaining to him.

His tutor called one afternoon. "I get the sense," he said, "that this
kid's feeling . . . underestimated, you know? Like you folks expect the
worst of him. I'm thinking we ought to give him more rope."[27]

"But see, he's still so suggestible,"[28] Daisy said. "When his friends   145
suggest some mischief—smoking or drinking or such—why, he just finds
it hard not to go along with[29] them."

"Mrs. Coble," the tutor said, "I think this kid is hurting. You know?
Here's a serious, sensitive kid, telling you he'd like to take on[30] some
grown-up challenges, and you're giving him the message that he can't be   150
trusted. Don't you understand how that hurts?"

"Oh," said Daisy.

"It undermines his self-esteem—don't you realize that?"

---

22 **rap** talk informally
23 **goof-offs** people who regularly avoid work
    (slang)
24 **evasive** secretive
25 **we're onto something** we're in the
    process of discovering something

26 **curfew** a strict time by which one
    has to be home or else be punished
27 **give him more rope** give him more freedom
28 **suggestible** easily influenced
29 **go along with** agree with, support
30 **take on** assume

"Well, I guess you're right," said Daisy. She saw Donny suddenly from a whole new angle: his pathetically poor posture, that slouch so forlorn that his shoulders seemed about to meet his chin . . . oh, wasn't it awful being young? She'd had a miserable adolescence herself and had always sworn no child of hers would ever be that unhappy.

They let Donny stay out later, they didn't call ahead to see if the parties were supervised, and they were careful not to grill[31] him about his evening. The tutor had set down so many rules! They were not allowed any questions at all about any aspect of school, nor were they to speak with his teachers. If a teacher had some complaint, she should phone Cal. Only one teacher disobeyed—the history teacher, Miss Evans. She called one morning in February. "I'm a little concerned about Donny, Mrs. Coble."

"Oh, I'm sorry, Miss Evans, but Donny's tutor handles these things now . . ."

"I always deal directly with the parents. You are the parent," Miss Evans said, speaking very slowly and distinctly. "Now, here is the problem. Back when you were helping Donny with his homework, his grades rose from a D to a C, but now they've slipped back, and they're closer to an F."

"They are?"

"I think you should start overseeing his homework again."

"But Donny's tutor says . . ."

"It's nice that Donny has a tutor, but you should still be in charge of his homework. With you, he learned it. Then he passed his tests. With the tutor, well, it seems the tutor is more of a crutch.[32] 'Donny,' I say, 'a quiz is coming up on Friday. Hadn't you better be listening instead of talking?' 'That's okay, Miss Evans,' he says. 'I have a tutor now.' Like a talisman![33] I really think you ought to take over,[34] Mrs. Coble."

"I see," said Daisy. "Well, I'll think about that. Thank you for calling."

Hanging up, she felt a rush of anger at Donny. A talisman! For a talisman, she'd given up all luxuries, all that time with her daughter, her evenings at home!

She dialed Cal's number. He sounded muzzy. "I'm sorry if I woke you," she told him, "but Donny's history teacher just called. She says he isn't doing well."

"She should have dealt with me."

"She wants me to start supervising his homework again. His grades are slipping."

"Yes," said the tutor, "but you and I both know there's more to it than mere grades, don't we? I care about the *whole* child—his happiness, his self-esteem. The grades will come. Just give them time."

When she hung up, it was Miss Evans she was angry at. What a narrow woman!

---

31 **grill** question intensely
32 **crutch** support

33 **talisman** a magic charm
34 **take over** take control

It was Cal this, Cal that, Cal says this, Cal and I did that. Cal lent Donny an album by the Who. He took Donny and two other pupils to a rock concert. In March, when Donny began to talk endlessly on the phone with a girl named Miriam, Cal even let Miriam come to one of the tutoring sessions. Daisy was touched that Cal would grow so involved in Donny's life, but she was also a little hurt, because she had offered to have Miriam to dinner and Donny had refused. Now he asked them to drive her to Cal's house without a qualm. [35]

This Miriam was an unappealing girl with blurry lipstick and masses of rough red hair. She wore a short, bulky jacket that would not have been out of place on a motorcycle. During the trip to Cal's she was silent, but coming back, she was more talkative. "What a neat guy, [36] and what a house! All those kids hanging out, [37] like a club. And the stereo playing rock . . . gosh, he's not like a grown-up at all! Married and divorced and everything, but you'd think he was our own age."

"Mr. Beadle was married?" Daisy asked.

"Yeah, to this really controlling lady. She didn't understand him a bit."

"No, I guess not," Daisy said.

Spring came, and the students who hung around at Cal's drifted out to the basketball net above the garage. Sometimes, when Daisy and Matt arrived to pick up Donny, they'd find him there with the others—spiky [38] and excited, jittering on his toes beneath the backboard. It was staying light much longer now, and the neighboring fence cast narrow bars across the bright grass. Loud music would be spilling from Cal's windows. Once it was the Who, which Daisy recognized from the time that Donny had borrowed the album. "*Teenage Wasteland,*" she said aloud, identifying the song, and Matt gave a short, dry laugh. "It certainly is," he said. He'd misunderstood; he thought she was commenting on the scene spread before them. In fact, she might have been. The players looked like hoodlums, [39] even her son. Why, one of Cal's students had recently been knifed in a tavern. One had been shipped off to boarding school in midterm; two had been withdrawn by their parents. On the other hand, Donny had mentioned someone who'd been studying with Cal for five years. "Five years!" said Daisy. "Doesn't anyone ever stop needing him?"

Donny looked at her. Lately, whatever she said about Cal was read as criticism. "You're just feeling competitive," he said. "And controlling."

She bit her lip and said no more.

In April, the principal called to tell her that Donny had been expelled. There had been a locker check, and in Donny's locker they found five cans of beer and half a pack of cigarettes. With Donny's previous record, this offense meant expulsion.

---

35 **without a qualm** confidently
36 **a neat guy** a wonderful man (slang)
37 **hanging out** not doing anything in particular (slang)
38 **spiky** sharp and pointy
39 **hoodlums** young people who do bad, often illegal things

Daisy gripped the receiver tightly and said, "Well, where is he now?"

"We've sent him home," said Mr. Lanham. "He's packed up all his belongings, and he's coming home on foot." 240

Daisy wondered what she would say to him. She felt him looming[40] closer and closer, bringing this brand-new situation that no one had prepared her to handle. What other place would take him? Could they enter him in public school? What were the rules? She stood at the living 245 room window, waiting for him to show up. Gradually, she realized that he was taking too long. She checked the clock. She stared up the street again.

When an hour had passed, she phoned the school. Mr. Lanham's secretary answered and told her in a grave, sympathetic voice that yes, Donny Coble had most definitely gone home. Daisy called her husband. 250 He was out of the office. She went back to the window and thought awhile, and then she called Donny's tutor.

"Donny's been expelled from school," she said, "and now I don't know where he's gone. I wonder if you've heard from him?"

There was a long silence. "Donny's with me, Mrs. Coble," he finally said. 255

"With you? How'd he get there?"

"He hailed a cab, and I paid the driver."

"Could I speak to him, please?"

There was another silence. "Maybe it'd be better if we had a conference," Cal said. 260

"I don't *want* a conference. I've been standing at the window picturing him dead or kidnapped or something, and now you tell me you want a—"

"Donny is very, very upset. Understandably so," said Cal. "Believe me, Mrs. Coble, this is not what it seems. Have you asked Donny's side 265 of the story?"

"Well, of course not, how could I? He went running off to you instead."

"Because he didn't feel he'd be listened to."

"But I haven't even—"

"Why don't you come out and talk? The three of us," said Cal, "will 270 try to get this thing in perspective."

"Well, all right," Daisy said. But she wasn't as reluctant as she sounded. Already, she felt soothed by the calm way Cal was taking this.

Cal answered the doorbell at once. He said, "Hi, there," and led her into the dining room. Donny sat slumped in a chair, chewing the knuckle of one 275 thumb. "Hello, Donny," Daisy said. He flicked his eyes in her direction.

"Sit here, Mrs. Coble," said Cal, placing her opposite Donny. He himself remained standing, restlessly pacing. "So," he said.

Daisy stole a look at Donny. His lips were swollen, as if he'd been crying. 280

"You know," Cal told Daisy, "I kind of expected something like this. That's a very punitive[41] school you've got him in—you realize that. And

---

40 **looming** appearing large and threatening   41 **punitive** punishing

any half-decent lawyer will tell you they've violated his civil rights. Locker checks! Where's their search warrant?"[42]

"But if the rule is—" Daisy said.

"Well, anyhow, let him tell you his side."

She looked at Donny. He said, "It wasn't my fault. I promise."

"They said your locker was full of beer."

"It was a put-up job![43] See, there's this guy that doesn't like me. He put all these beers in my locker and started a rumor going, so Mr. Lanham ordered a locker check."

"What was the boy's name?" Daisy asked.

"Huh?"

"Mrs. Coble, take my word, the situation is not so unusual," Cal said. "You can't imagine how vindictive kids can be sometimes."

"What was the boy's *name,*" said Daisy, "so that I can ask Mr. Lanham if that's who suggested he run a locker check."

"You don't believe me," Donny said.

"And how'd this boy get your combination in the first place?"

"Frankly," said Cal, "I wouldn't be surprised to learn the school was in on[44] it. Any kid that marches to a different drummer, why, they'd just love an excuse to get rid of[45] him. The school is where I lay the blame."

"Doesn't *Donny* ever get blamed?"

"Now, Mrs. Coble, you heard what he—"

"Forget it," Donny told Cal. "You can see she doesn't trust me."

Daisy drew in a breath to say that of course she trusted him—a reflex. But she knew that bold-faced, wide-eyed look of Donny's. He had worn that look when he was small, denying some petty misdeed with the evidence plain as day all around him. Still, it was hard for her to accuse him outright. She temporized[46] and said, "The only thing I'm sure of is that they've kicked you out[47] of school, and now I don't know what we're going to do."

"We'll fight it," said Cal.

"We can't. Even you must see we can't."

"I could apply to Brantly," Donny said.

Cal stopped his pacing to beam down at him. "Brantly! Yes. They're really onto where a kid is coming from, at Brantly. Why, *I* could get you into Brantly. I work with a lot of their students."

Daisy had never heard of Brantly, but already she didn't like it. And she didn't like Cal's smile, which struck her now as feverish and avid— a smile of hunger.

On the fifteenth of April, they entered Donny in a public school, and they stopped his tutoring sessions. Donny fought both decisions bitterly. Cal, surprisingly enough, did not object. He admitted he'd made no

---

42 **search warrant** official written documents
   permitting a search (legal term)
43 **a put-up job** an attempt to trap
   someone secretly (slang)

44 **was in on** was involved in
45 **get rid of** be free of
46 **temporized** compromised
47 **kicked out** expelled (slang)

headway[48] with Donny and said it was because Donny was emotionally   325
disturbed.

Donny went to his new school every morning, plodding[49] off alone
with his head down. He did his assignments, and he earned average
grades, but he gathered no friends, joined no clubs. There was something
exhausted and defeated about him.   330

The first week in June, during final exams, Donny vanished. He simply
didn't come home one afternoon, and no one at school remembered
seeing him. The police were reassuring, and for the first few days, they
worked hard. They combed[50] Donny's sad, messy room for clues; they
visited Miriam and Cal. But then they started talking about the number   335
of kids who ran away every year. Hundreds, just in this city. "He'll show
up, if he wants to," they said. "If he doesn't, he won't."

Evidently, Donny didn't want to.

It's been three months now and still no word. Matt and Daisy still
look for him in every crowd of awkward, heartbreaking teenage boys.   340
Every time the phone rings, they imagine it might be Donny. Both
parents have aged. Donny's sister seems to be staying away from home
as much as possible.

At night, Daisy lies awake and goes over Donny's life. She is trying
to figure out what went wrong, where they made their first mistake. Often,   345
she finds herself blaming Cal, although she knows he didn't begin it. Then
at other times she excuses him, for without him, Donny might have left
earlier. Who really knows? In the end, she can only sigh and search for a
cooler spot on the pillow. As she falls asleep, she occasionally glimpses
something in the corner of her vision. It's something fleet and round, a   350
ball—a basketball. It flies up, it sinks through the hoop, descends, lands
in a yard littered with last year's leaves and striped with bars of sunlight
as white as bones, bleached and parched and cleanly picked.[51]

---

48 **headway** progress
49 **plodding** walking slowly and heavily
50 **combed** searched thoroughly

51 **bleached and parched and cleanly picked**
lightened and dried out, with all the flesh
removed

PART 1 First Reading

A Thinking About the Story

Did you feel that the story would end well or badly? What gave you that feeling?

B Understanding the Plot

1. Why does the school principal initially request to see Donny's parents?
2. What new information does Daisy receive about Donny in her second interview with Mr. Lanham?
3. What is the psychologist's diagnosis of Donny's problems?
4. What is Daisy's state of mind after they return from the psychologist's office?
5. What are Daisy's first impressions of Cal?
6. What does Donny compare his school to?
7. Why is Miss Evans determined to speak to Daisy? Does she succeed in her mission?
8. What information about Cal does Daisy learn from Miriam?
9. Why was Donny expelled from school?
10. How do Cal's and Daisy's reactions to the expulsion differ? What does Donny claim happened?
11. Over what period of time does the story take place?

PART 2 Second Reading

A Exploring Themes

You are now ready to reread "Teenage Wasteland." Try to understand how the weaknesses of the main characters affect their actions, and pay particular attention to the connection between the title and a major theme of the story.

1. How does the description of Donny's changing appearance in paragraph 1 relate to the story?
2. How do Donny's problems affect his sister, Amanda?

3. Is Cal generally successful in helping his students? Explain your answer by giving examples from the story.
4. Does Daisy's personality contribute to Donny's problems? If so, how?
5. What is the role of Donny's father in the story?
6. How does the ending relate to the title of the story?

B Analyzing the Author's Style

For more information on the literary terms in this section, turn to the explanations of *point of view* (page 306) and *inference* (page 304).

POINT OF VIEW: Third-Person Narration

One of the decisions Anne Tyler had to make in writing "Teenage Wasteland" was whether her **third-person narrator** would have *total omniscience* (the narrator is not a participant in the story and has a complete picture of the characters and events) or *limited omniscience* (the narrator can penetrate the thoughts of only one or two characters and provides a subjective view of characters and events).

1. Does the narrator display total or limited omniscience? Explain your answer.
2. Which character's point of view dominates the story?
3. How does this character's point of view affect the way we see Donny?
4. Choose another character and say how the story might be different if it were told from his or her perspective.

INFERENCE

In "Teenage Wasteland," not everything is immediately accessible to the reader. Anne Tyler requires you to **infer,** or deduce, hidden meanings throughout the story.

For example, Tyler writes *Daisy was often late starting supper . . .* (line 28), leaving us to infer that because she was spending so much time with Donny, the other family members suffered.

And when Tyler describes Cal with hair *as long and stringy as Donny's, and his jeans as faded* (lines 84–85), she is implying that Daisy sees him more as a teenager than an adult.

1. What can you infer about the teenage years from the title of the story?

2. What is implied by Donny's keeping "all three of his appointments" even though he criticized the psychologist and his tests? (lines 57–58)

3. What can you infer about the Cobels' financial situation in lines 47–52?

4. What does Daisy's wince imply when she hears the rock music? (line 112)

5. The history teacher refers to Cal as "a crutch" (line 179) and "like a talisman" (lines 181–182). What is she implying about Cal's effectiveness as a tutor?

C Judging for Yourself

Express yourself as personally as you like in your answers to the following questions.

1. Do you agree with the opinion of Donny's psychologist—and later of Cal—that his problem is mainly one of self-esteem?

2. Do you feel that Donny's parents are "too controlling"? If you were Donny's parent, would you give him more freedom? Give reasons for your answer.

3. In your view, does Daisy relate to how a teenager feels?

4. Do you agree with the principal's reasons for expelling Donny?

5. In your view, is Cal good or bad for Donny?

6. Who do you think is to blame for Donny's problems? Why?

7. Do you think Donny will come home? Explain your answer.

D Making Connections

1. Are the teenage years particularly difficult in your culture?

2. Does your country have a problem with runaway teenagers? If so, what happens to most of them? If not, what do you think the reasons are?

3. If you and your friends faced problems as teenagers, what were they?

4. How do you think parents should deal with their teenage children? Would you handle your teenage child in the same way your parents handled you? Why or why not?

E Debate

Debate this proposition:

Children should have a lot of discipline when growing up.

PART 3 Focus on Language

A   Conditionals

Conditionals, or *if-clauses*, can be divided into two categories: the *real* or *true* conditional and the *unreal* or *untrue* conditional.

A **real conditional** contains a situation that is likely to happen. When the verb in the conditional clause (cc) is in the present tense, the verb in the main clause (mc) can also be in the present, or can consist of a present modal (such as *may*) plus the base form of the verb. For example:

            cc   mc

*If Donny **feels** talkative, he **speaks** only to Miriam.*

            cc   mc

*If Amanda **continues** to stay out late, she **may turn out** like Donny.*

            cc   mc

*If the school rules **are** repeatedly **broken**, the offending student **will be expelled**.*

An **unreal conditional** contains a situation that is impossible or unlikely to happen. To express an unreal situation in the present or future, the verb in the conditional clause (cc) is in the past tense, while the verb in the main clause (mc) is a past modal (*would/could/might*) plus the base form of the verb. This suggests that if something were true (but it isn't at the time or can never be), something else would happen (but it won't). For example:

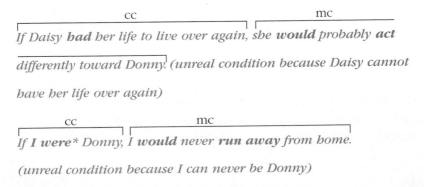

            cc   mc

*If Daisy **had** her life to live over again, she **would** probably **act** differently toward Donny.* (unreal condition because Daisy cannot have her life over again)

            cc   mc

*If **I were*** Donny, I **would** never **run away** from home.*

(unreal condition because I can never be Donny)

*Note: If you use the verb *to be* in a present unreal condition, use *were* for all persons in the conditional clause.

To express an unreal situation in the past, the verb in the conditional clause (cc) is in the past perfect tense, while the verb in the main clause (mc) is composed of *would have/could have/might have* plus the past participle. This suggests that if something had been true (but it wasn't at the time), something else would have happened (but it didn't). For example:

```
         cc                    mc
 ┌───────────────┐  ┌──────────────────────┐
If Donny had studied, he would have passed his exams.
```

(unreal condition because Donny did not study)

Complete the following dialogue with the correct form of the verb in parentheses. If the condition used is real, write *R* above your answer. If the condition is unreal, write *U*.

PARENT: If you _____ home by twelve tonight, you _____. (not be, punish)

TEENAGER: Why are you always so mean to me? Everybody else is allowed to stay out much later. And I know that even if I _____ home early, you _____ on my back. (get, be)

PARENT: No, we won't. And remember, if you _____ home on time last Saturday, we _____ now. (come, not argue)

TEENAGER: You're always looking for an excuse to punish me. If you _____ so unreasonable, I _____ to you more. (not be, listen)

PARENT: Perhaps if you _____ with us more, you _____ we aren't so difficult to get along with after all. (cooperate, see)

TEENAGER: This is getting us nowhere. If I _____ you, I _____ my child. (be, trust) You're both jerks!

PARENT: If this conversation _____, we _____ even more hurtful things to each other. (continue, say) So let's stop now.

With a partner, write a few more sentences to resolve the conflict, also using the conditional. Act out the dialogue for the class.

B   Building Vocabulary Skills

The following idioms appear in the story, and most are explained in the accompanying glosses. Complete the sentences with the correct idioms from the list. Be sure to put the verb in the correct person and tense.

get along (line 104)	hang out (line 210)
goof off (line 118)	show up (line 246)
go along with (line 147)	be in on (lines 300–301)
take on (line 149)	get rid of (line 302)
take over (line 182)	kick out (line 311)

1. He always _____ when he needs money.

2. When we were in the army, we relied on our captain to _____ in a difficult situation.

3. As people mature, they tend to _____ more responsibility.

4. If you had _____ our plan to demonstrate, you too might have been arrested.

5. We like to _____ at our neighborhood club on Saturdays.

6. Will she be _____ of the class because of her disruptive behavior?

7. Please reveal to us how you _____ for so many years without having a single serious quarrel.

8. My husband has great difficulty in _____ his old possessions.

9. Since I was elected to office, I've _____ all the latest political gossip.

10. How can you expect to pass your exams if you're always _____?

PART 4 Writing Activities

1. Choose one of the characters in "Teenage Wasteland." Compose diary entries for your character, covering an imaginary week in that troubled year. Try to imagine how your character would think, feel, and act during that week, based on what you have learned about him or her from the story. Try to incorporate examples of real and unreal conditional clauses in some of your entries.

2. In an essay of two to three pages, compare and contrast teenagers of your generation with those of your parents' time. You might begin your essay with the sentence *In general, teenagers today have a more difficult/an easier time than their parents did.* In your supporting paragraphs, consider aspects like economic conditions, personal freedom, exposure to harmful substances, peer pressure, and the structure of the family.

3. *The Catcher in the Rye* by J. D. Salinger is a famous American novel about the teenage years. In an essay of one to two pages, describe a book you've read or movie you've seen that deals with the problems of adolescence. Could you identify with the teens as they were portrayed?

Social Change
and Injustice

Douglass Crockwell, *Paper Workers*, 1934

17

Like a Winding Sheet

ANN PETRY (1908–1997)

Born into an African-American family, Ann Petry grew up in the mainly white community of Old Saybrook, Connecticut. Although the family was middle class and reasonably well off, Petry was exposed to racism from an early age and has recalled many of the incidents in her writing. After earning a Ph.D. in pharmacy, she worked in the profession for seven years. In 1938, Petry married and went to live in Harlem, a large African-American neighborhood in New York City, where she began her writing career. As a journalist there, she learned at close hand about the struggle for survival of urban blacks.

Petry's best-selling first novel, *The Street* (1946), catapulted her to fame. It was followed by *Country Place* (1947) and *The Narrows* (1953); a collection of short stories, *Miss Muriel and Other Stories* (1971); as well as children's books and historical biographies. Her writing focuses on the troubled relationships between blacks and whites. Her story "Like a Winding Sheet" received critical acclaim and was included in Martha Foley's *Best American Short Stories of 1946*.

LIKE A WINDING SHEET

*The accumulated stress of living in a racist society takes
a terrible toll on a factory worker.*

He had planned to get up before Mae did and surprise her by fixing breakfast.[1] Instead he went back to sleep and she got out of bed so quietly he didn't know she wasn't there beside him until he woke up and heard the queer soft gurgle[2] of water running out of the sink in the bathroom. 5

He knew he ought to get up but instead he put his arms across his forehead to shut the afternoon sunlight out of his eyes, pulled his legs up close to his body, testing them to see if the ache was still in them.

Mae had finished in the bathroom. He could tell because she never closed the door when she was in there and now the sweet smell of 10 talcum powder was drifting down the hall and into the bedroom. Then he heard her coming down the hall.

"Hi, babe," she said affectionately.

"Hum," he grunted, and moved his arms away from his head, opened one eye. 15

"It's a nice morning."

"Yeah." He rolled over and the sheet twisted around him, outlining his thighs, his chest. "You mean afternoon, don't ya?"

Mae looked at the twisted sheet and giggled. "Looks like a winding sheet,"[3] she said. "A shroud—" Laughter tangled with her words and she 20 had to pause for a moment before she could continue. "You look like a huckleberry[4]—in a winding sheet—"

"That's no way to talk. Early in the day like this," he protested.

He looked at his arms silhouetted against the white of the sheets. They were inky black by contrast and he had to smile in spite of himself 25 and he lay there smiling and savoring[5] the sweet sound of Mae's giggling.

"Early?" She pointed a finger at the alarm clock on the table near the bed and giggled again. "It's almost four o'clock. And if you don't spring up out of there, you're going to be late again."

"What do you mean 'again'?" 30

"Twice last week. Three times the week before. And once the week before and—"

"I can't get used to sleeping in the daytime," he said fretfully. He pushed his legs out from under the covers experimentally. Some of the

---

1 **fixing breakfast** making breakfast
2 **gurgle** the bubbling sound of running water
3 **winding sheet** the sheet in which a dead body is wrapped

4 **huckleberry** a dark blue-black berry
5 **savoring** enjoying

ache had gone out of them but they weren't really rested yet. "It's too light 35
for good sleeping. And all that standing beats the hell out of my legs."⁶

"After two years you oughta be used to it," Mae said.

He watched her as she fixed her hair, powdered her face, slipped
into a pair of blue denim overalls. She moved quickly and yet she didn't
seem to hurry. 40

"You look like you'd had plenty of sleep," he said lazily. He had to
get up but he kept putting the moment off, not wanting to move, yet he
didn't dare let his legs go completely limp⁷ because if he did he'd go
back to sleep. It was getting later and later but the thought of putting his
weight on his legs kept him lying there. 45

When he finally got up he had to hurry, and he gulped his breakfast
so fast that he wondered if his stomach could possibly use food thrown
at it at such a rate of speed. He was still wondering about it as he and
Mae were putting their coats on in the hall.

Mae paused to look at the calendar. "It's the thirteenth," she said. Then 50
a faint excitement in her voice, "Why, it's Friday the thirteenth." She had
one arm in her coat sleeve and she held it there while she stared at the
calendar. "I oughta stay home," she said. "I shouldn't go outa the house."

"Aw, don't be a fool," he said. "Today's payday. And payday is a good
luck day everywhere, any way you look at it." And as she stood hesitating 55
he said, "Aw, come on."

And he was late for work again because they spent fifteen minutes
arguing before he could convince her she ought to go to work just the
same. He had to talk persuasively, urging her gently, and it took time.
But he couldn't bring himself to talk to her roughly or threaten to strike 60
her like a lot of men might have done. He wasn't made that way.

So when he reached the plant he was late and he had to wait to
punch the time clock⁸ because the day-shift workers were streaming out
in long lines, in groups and bunches that impeded⁹ his progress.

Even now just starting his workday his legs ached. He had to force 65
himself to struggle past the outgoing workers, punch the time clock, and
get the little cart he pushed around all night, because he kept toying
with¹⁰ the idea of going home and getting back in bed.

He pushed the cart out on the concrete floor, thinking that if this was
his plant he'd make a lot of changes in it. There were too many standing- 70
up jobs for one thing. He'd figure out some way most of 'em could be
done sitting down and he'd put a lot more benches around. And this job
he had—this job that forced him to walk ten hours a night, pushing this
little cart, well, he'd turn it into a sitting-down job. One of those little
trucks they used around railroad stations would be good for a job like 75

---

6 **beats the hell out of my legs** makes my legs
  hurt badly
7 **go limp** become weak
8 **punch the time clock** register on a special
  clock one's time of arrival and departure

9 **impeded** blocked
10 **toying with** considering (but not seriously)

this. Guys sat on a seat and the thing moved easily, taking up little room and turning in hardly any space at all, like on a dime.[11]

He pushed the cart near the foreman. He never could remember to refer to her as the forelady even in his mind. It was funny to have a white woman for a boss in a plant like this one.   80

She was sore[12] about something. He could tell by the way her face was red and her eyes were half-shut until they were slits.[13] Probably been out late and didn't get enough sleep. He avoided looking at her and hurried a little, head down, as he passed her though he couldn't resist stealing a glance at her out of the corner of his eye. He saw the edge of   85
the light-colored slacks she wore and the tip end of a big tan shoe.

"Hey, Johnson!" the woman said.

The machines had started full blast.[14] The whirr and the grinding[15] made the building shake, made it impossible to hear conversations. The men and women at the machines talked to each other but looking at   90
them from just a little distance away, they appeared to be simply moving their lips because you couldn't hear what they were saying. Yet the woman's voice cut across the machine sounds—harsh, angry.

He turned his head slowly. "Good evenin', Mrs. Scott," he said, and waited.   95

"You're late again."

"That's right. My legs were bothering me."

The woman's face grew redder, angrier looking. "Half this shift comes in late," she said. "And you're the worst one of all. You're always late. Whatsa matter with ya?"   100

"It's my legs," he said. "Somehow they don't ever get rested. I don't seem to get used to sleeping days. And I just can't get started."

"Excuses. You guys always got excuses," her anger grew and spread. "Every guy comes in here late always has an excuse. His wife's sick or his grandmother died or somebody in the family had to go to the hospital,"   105
she paused, drew a deep breath. "And the niggers[16] is the worse. I don't care what's wrong with your legs. You get in here on time. I'm sick of you niggers—"

"You got the right to get mad," he interrupted softly. "You got the right to cuss me four ways to Sunday[17] but I ain't letting nobody call me   110
a nigger."

He stepped closer to her. His fists were doubled. His lips were drawn back in a thin narrow line. A vein in his forehead stood out swollen, thick.

And the woman backed away from him, not hurriedly but slowly— two, three steps back.   115

"Aw, forget it," she said. "I didn't mean nothing by it. It slipped out.[18] It was an accident." The red of her face deepened until the small blood

---

11 **turning . . . on a dime** turning accurately in a
   very small space
12 **sore** angry (colloquialism)
13 **slits** narrow openings
14 **full blast** at full speed

15 **whirr and grinding** noises made by a machine
16 **niggers** an insulting reference to black people
17 **cuss me four ways to Sunday** curse me every
   possible way (slang)
18 **slipped out** came out suddenly

vessels in her cheeks were purple. "Go on and get to work," she urged. And she took three more slow backward steps.

He stood motionless for a moment and then turned away from the sight of the red lipstick on her mouth that made him remember that the foreman was a woman. And he couldn't bring himself[19] to hit a woman. He felt a curious tingling[20] in his fingers and he looked down at his hands. They were clenched[21] tight, hard, ready to smash some of those small purple veins in her face. 120 125

He pushed the cart ahead of him, walking slowly. When he turned his head, she was staring in his direction, mopping[22] her forehead with a dark blue handkerchief. Their eyes met and then they both looked away.

He didn't glance in her direction again but moved past the long work benches, carefully collecting the finished parts, going slowly and steadily up and down, and back and forth the length of the building, and as he walked he forced himself to swallow his anger, get rid of it. 130

And he succeeded so that he was able to think about what had happened without getting upset about it. An hour went by but the tension stayed in his hands. They were clenched and knotted on the handles of the cart as though ready to aim a blow. 135

And he thought he should have hit her anyway, smacked her hard in the face, felt the soft flesh of her face give under the hardness of his hands. He tried to make his hands relax by offering them a description of what it would have been like to strike her because he had the queer feeling that his hands were not exactly a part of him anymore—they had developed a separate life of their own over which he had no control. So he dwelt on[23] the pleasure his hands would have felt—both of them cracking at her, first one and then the other. If he had done that his hands would have felt good now—relaxed, rested. 140 145

And he decided that even if he'd lost his job for it, he should have let her have it[24] and it would have been a long time, maybe the rest of her life, before she called anybody else a nigger.

The only trouble was he couldn't hit a woman. A woman couldn't hit back the same way a man did. But it would have been a deeply satisfying thing to have cracked her narrow lips wide open with just one blow, beautifully timed and with all his weight in back of it. That way he would have gotten rid of all the energy and tension his anger had created in him. He kept remembering how his heart had started pumping blood so fast he had felt it tingle even in the tips of his fingers. 150 155

With the approach of night, fatigue[25] nibbled[26] at him. The corners of his mouth drooped,[27] the frown between his eyes deepened, his shoulders sagged; but his hands stayed tight and tense. As the hours dragged by[28]

---

19 **he couldn't bring himself** he was unable to persuade himself
20 **tingling** a prickly sensation
21 **clenched** tightly closed
22 **mopping** wiping
23 **dwelt on** concentrated on

24 **he should have let her have it** he should have hit her (slang)
25 **fatigue** tiredness
26 **nibbled** took little bites
27 **drooped** turned down
28 **dragged by** passed very slowly

he noticed that the women workers had started to snap and snarl[29] at each other. He couldn't hear what they said because of the sound of machines but he could see the quick lip movements that sent words tumbling from the sides of their mouths. They gestured irritably with their hands and scowled[30] as their mouths moved. 160

Their violent jerky motions told him that it was getting close on to quitting time but somehow he felt that the night still stretched ahead of him, composed of endless hours of steady walking on his aching legs. When the whistle finally blew he went on pushing the cart, unable to believe that it had sounded. The whirring of the machines died away to a murmur and he knew then that he'd really heard the whistle. He stood still for a moment, filled with a relief that made him sigh. 165

170

Then he moved briskly, putting the cart in the storeroom, hurrying to take his place in the line forming before the paymaster. That was another thing he'd change, he thought. He'd have the pay envelopes handed to the people right at their benches so there wouldn't be ten or fifteen minutes lost waiting for the pay. He always got home about fifteen minutes late on payday. They did it better in the plant where Mae worked, brought the money right to them at their benches. 175

He stuck his pay envelope in his pants' pocket and followed the line of workers heading for the subway in a slow-moving stream. He glanced up at the sky. It was a nice night, the sky looked packed full to running over with stars. And he thought if he and Mae would go right to bed when they got home from work they'd catch a few hours of darkness for sleeping. But they never did. They fooled around[31]—cooking and eating and listening to the radio and he always stayed in a big chair in the living room and went almost but not quite to sleep and when they finally got to bed it was five or six in the morning and daylight was already seeping around the edges of the sky. 180

185

He walked slowly, putting off the moment when he would have to plunge into the crowd hurrying toward the subway. It was a long ride to Harlem and tonight the thought of it appalled[32] him. He paused outside an all-night restaurant to kill time,[33] so that some of the first rush of workers would be gone when he reached the subway. 190

The lights in the restaurant were brilliant, enticing.[34] There was life and motion inside. And as he looked through the window he thought that everything within range of his eyes gleamed—the long imitation marble counter, the tall stools, the white porcelain-topped tables and especially the big metal coffee urn right near the window. Steam issued from its top and a gas flame flickered under it—a lively, dancing, blue flame. 195

A lot of the workers from his shift—men and women—were lining up near the coffee urn. He watched them walk to the porcelain-topped 200

---

29 **snap and snarl** speak angrily
30 **scowled** made an angry facial expression
31 **fooled around** wasted time
32 **appalled** shocked
33 **kill time** spend time doing nothing in particular
34 **enticing** inviting

tables carrying steaming cups of coffee and he saw that just the smell of the coffee lessened the fatigue lines in their faces. After the first sip their faces softened, they smiled, they began to talk and laugh.

On a sudden impulse he shoved the door open and joined the line in front of the coffee urn. The line moved slowly. And as he stood there 205 the smell of the coffee, the sound of the laughter and of the voices, helped dull the sharp ache in his legs.

He didn't pay any attention to the white girl who was serving the coffee at the urn. He kept looking at the cups in the hands of the men who had been ahead of him. Each time a man stepped out of the line with one of 210 the thick white cups, the fragrant steam got in his nostrils. He saw that they walked carefully so as not to spill a single drop. There was a froth[35] of bubbles at the top of each cup and he thought about how he would let the bubbles break against his lips before he actually took a big deep swallow.

Then it was his turn. "A cup of coffee," he said, just as he had heard 215 the others say.

The white girl looked past him, put her hands up to her head and gently lifted her hair away from the back of her neck, tossing her head back a little.

"No more coffee for a while," she said. 220

He wasn't certain he'd heard her correctly and he said "What?" blankly.

"No more coffee for a while," she repeated.

There was silence behind him and then uneasy movement. He thought someone would say something, ask why or protest, but there was only silence and then a faint shuffling sound as though the men 225 standing behind him had simultaneously shifted their weight from one foot to the other.

He looked at the girl without saying anything. He felt his hands begin to tingle and the tingling went all the way down to his finger tips so that he glanced down at them. They were clenched tight, hard, into fists. Then 230 he looked at the girl again. What he wanted to do was to hit her so hard that the scarlet lipstick on her mouth would smear and spread over her nose, her chin, out toward her cheeks, so hard that she would never toss her head again and refuse a man a cup of coffee because he was black.

He estimated the distance across the counter and reached forward, 235 balancing his weight on the balls of his feet, ready to let the blow go. And then his hands fell back down to his sides because he forced himself to lower them, to unclench them and make them dangle[36] loose. The effort took his breath away because his hands fought against him. But he couldn't hit her. He couldn't even now bring himself to hit a woman, not even this 240 one, who had refused him a cup of coffee with a toss of her head. He kept seeing the gesture with which she had lifted the length of her blond hair from the back of her neck as expressive of her contempt for him.

When he went out the door he didn't look back. If he had he would have seen the flickering blue flame under the shiny coffee urn being 245

---

35 **froth** bubbles on a liquid   36 **dangle** hang loosely

extinguished.[37] The line of men who had stood behind him lingered[38] a moment to watch the people drinking coffee at the tables and then they left just as he had without having had the coffee they wanted so badly. The girl behind the counter poured water in the urn and swabbed it out[39] and as she waited for the water to run out, she lifted her hair gently from the back of her neck and tossed her head before she began making a fresh lot of coffee. 250

But he had walked away without a backward look, his head down, his hands in his pockets, raging at himself and whatever it was inside of him that had forced him to stand quiet and still when he wanted to strike out. 255

The subway was crowded and he had to stand. He tried grasping an overhead strap and his hands were too tense to grip it. So he moved near the train door and stood there swaying[40] back and forth with the rocking of the train. The roar of the train beat inside his head, making it ache and throb, and the pain in his legs clawed up into his groin so that he seemed 260 to be bursting with pain and he told himself that it was due to all that anger-born energy that had piled up in him and not been used and so it had spread through him like a poison—from his feet and legs all the way up to his head.

Mae was in the house before he was. He knew she was home before 265 he put the key in the door of the apartment. The radio was going. She had it turned up loud and she was singing along with it.

"Hello, babe," she called out, as soon as he opened the door.

He tried to say "hello" and it came out half grunt and half sigh.

"You sure sound cheerful," she said. 270

She was in the bedroom and he went and leaned against the doorjamb. The denim overalls she wore to work were carefully draped over the back of a chair by the bed. She was standing in front of the dresser, tying the sash of a yellow housecoat around her waist and chewing gum vigorously as she admired her reflection in the mirror over the dresser. 275

"Whatsa matter?" she said. "You get bawled out[41] by the boss or somep'n?"

"Just tired," he said slowly. "For God's sake, do you have to crack that gum like that?"

"You don't have to lissen to me," she said complacently.[42] She patted 280 a curl in place near the side of her head and then lifted her hair away from the back of her neck, ducking her head forward and then back.

He winced[43] away from the gesture. "What you got to be always fooling with your hair for?" he protested.

"Say, what's the matter with you anyway?" She turned away from the 285 mirror to face him, put her hands on her hips. "You ain't been in the house two minutes and you're picking on me."[44]

---

37 **extinguished** put out
38 **lingered** stayed behind
39 **swabbed it out** cleaned it out
40 **swaying** moving unsteadily

41 **get bawled out** be severely criticized (informal)
42 **complacently** with self-satisfaction
43 **winced** made a quick facial movement of pain
44 **picking on me** criticizing me

He didn't answer her because her eyes were angry and he didn't want to quarrel with her. They'd been married too long and got along too well and so he walked all the way into the room and sat down in the chair by the bed and stretched his legs out in front of him, putting his weight on the heels of his shoes, leaning way back in the chair, not saying anything. **290**

"Lissen," she said sharply. "I've got to wear those overalls again tomorrow. You're going to get them all wrinkled up[45] leaning against them like that." **295**

He didn't move. He was too tired and his legs were throbbing[46] now that he had sat down. Besides the overalls were already wrinkled and dirty, he thought. They couldn't help but be[47] for she'd worn them all week. He leaned farther back in the chair.

"Come on, get up," she ordered. **300**

"Oh, what the hell,"[48] he said wearily, and got up from the chair. "I'd just as soon live in a subway.[49] There'd be just as much place to sit down."

He saw that her sense of humor was struggling with her anger. But her sense of humor won because she giggled.

"Aw, come on and eat," she said. There was a coaxing[50] note in her **305** voice. "You're nothing but an old hungry nigger trying to act tough and—" she paused to giggle and then continued, "You—"

He had always found her giggling pleasant and deliberately said things that might amuse her and then waited, listening for the delicate sound to emerge from her throat. This time he didn't even hear the **310** giggle. He didn't let her finish what she was saying. She was standing close to him and that funny tingling started in his finger tips, went fast up his arms and sent his fist shooting straight for her face.

There was the smacking sound of soft flesh being struck by a hard object and it wasn't until she screamed that he realized he had hit her in **315** the mouth—so hard that the dark red lipstick had blurred and spread over her full lips, reaching up toward the tip of her nose, down toward her chin, out toward her cheeks.

The knowledge that he had struck her seeped through him slowly and he was appalled but he couldn't drag his hands away from her face. **320** He kept striking her and he thought with horror that something inside him was holding him, binding him to this act, wrapping and twisting about him so that he had to continue it. He had lost all control over his hands. And he groped for[51] a phrase, a word, something to describe what this thing was like that was happening to him and he thought it was like **325** being enmeshed[52] in a winding sheet—that was it—like a winding sheet. And even as the thought formed in his mind, his hands reached for her face again and yet again.

---

45 **wrinkled up** creased, looking unironed
46 **throbbing** beating with pain
47 **They couldn't help but be** They would have to be
48 **what the hell** what difference does it make? (slang exclamation)

49 **I'd just as soon live in a subway** I'd prefer to live in a subway
50 **coaxing** pleading
51 **groped for** searched for
52 **enmeshed** trapped

PART 1 First Reading

A Thinking About the Story

Could you feel the rage that was building up in Mr. Johnson, and were you able to sympathize with him at the end? Did you predict that the story would end so badly? What made you think that?

B Understanding the Plot

1. What kind of relationship do Mae and her husband have at the start of the story? Illustrate your answer with concrete examples.
2. What does Mr. Johnson look like when he is lying in bed? Explain the comparison.
3. How does Mr. Johnson feel about working the night shift?
4. Is Mae superstitious?
5. What was offensive about the forewoman's behavior to Mr. Johnson? Give examples.
6. Why didn't Mr. Johnson hit the forewoman as he desperately wanted to do?
7. What aspects of Mr. Johnson's job increase his stress? List as many as possible.
8. What part of Mr. Johnson's body continually suggests the suppressed rage he feels?
9. Why does Mr. Johnson delay going home?
10. Where do he and Mae live?
11. Why doesn't the girl serve coffee to Mr. Johnson? What does he think the reason is?
12. What is the final act of the day that causes Mr. Johnson to snap and beat up Mae?

PART 2 | Second Reading

A   Exploring Themes

You are now ready to reread "Like a Winding Sheet." Look at Mr. Johnson's swelling rage and frustration, and consider how the day's events are connected.

1. What is the significance of the title to the central theme of the story?

2. How does the story serve as a critique of factory working conditions?

3. Examine closely what links the three women in the story. What is the importance of these connections?

4. Is Mr. Johnson naturally violent? Explain your answer.

5. Whose point of view dominates the story? How is this character's point of view crucial to an understanding of what happened in the restaurant?

   Note: For information on point of view, see page 306.

6. Explain how the reference to Mr. Johnson's anger being "like a poison" (line 263) contributes to our understanding of his actions.

B   Analyzing the Author's Style

For more information on the literary terms in this section, turn to the explanations of *colloquialism* (page 299), *dialect* (page 300), and *imagery* (page 303).

COLLOQUIALISM AND DIALECT

The dialogue in "Like a Winding Sheet" is very **colloquial,** or informal, and makes liberal use of New York working-class **dialect,** in which words are often changed, left out, or elided (joined). By using language in this way, Petry reinforces the authenticity of her characters and effectively establishes their social class, as well as their prejudices. For example, when Mr. Johnson remarks that the forewoman was *sore about something* (line 81), it could be more formally rephrased as she was *angry about something.* Later the forewoman snaps, *"Whatsa matter with ya?"* (line 100), which can be rewritten in standard English as *"What's the matter with you?"* and then she adds in a racist aside, *"I'm sick of you niggers—."* (lines 107–108)

Rewrite the following expressions from the text in more formal English, correcting the grammatical errors.

1. "After two years you oughta be used to it," Mae said. (line 37)
2. "I shouldn't go outa the house." (line 53)
3. "Every guy comes in here late always has an excuse." (line 104)
4. "And the niggers is the worse." (line 106)
5. "You got the right to cuss me four ways to Sunday but I ain't letting nobody call me a nigger." (lines 109–111)
6. "Aw, forget it," she said. "I didn't mean nothing by it." (line 116)

Can you find at least three more examples of colloquial language in the story?

IMAGERY

The restaurant scene (lines 193–214) in "Like a Winding Sheet" is packed with distinctive **images,** or verbal pictures, that engage the senses (taste, touch, sight, hearing, and smell), sometimes more than one at the same time. For example:

> *He watched them walk to the porcelain-topped tables carrying steaming cups of coffee . . .* (lines 200–201)

In this one sentence, Petry conveys the image of the man taking in the cool shining table tops while feeling the heat from the steaming cups that people were carrying, as if he were already carrying one himself, and then, in his imagination, gratefully tasting the hot liquid.

Reread lines 193–214 carefully. Then analyze how the following sentences appeal to the senses.

1. The lights in the restaurant were brilliant, enticing. (line 193)
2. Steam issued from its top and a gas flame flickered under it—a lively, dancing, blue flame. (lines 197–198)
3. And as he stood there the smell of the coffee, the sound of the laughter and of the voices, helped dull the sharp ache in his legs. (lines 205–207)
4. Each time a man stepped out of the line with one of the thick white cups, the fragrant steam got in his nostrils. (lines 210–211)
5. There was a froth of bubbles at the top of each cup and he thought about how he would let the bubbles break against his lips before he actually took a big deep swallow. (lines 212–214)

C Judging for Yourself

Express yourself as personally as you like in your answers to the following questions.

1. Why do you think Mr. Johnson hit his wife instead of one of the other two women?
2. Do you blame Mr. Johnson for finally boiling over? Should he have exercised more self-control? What other options were open to him to release his anger?
3. What kinds of racial insults do you imagine Mr. Johnson encountered daily?
4. Do you suppose that Mr. Johnson is likely to be violent again?
5. In your view, can Mae ever forgive her husband?

D Making Connections

1. Is there a tendency in your country to solve disputes by violence?
2. Are many women beaten by their husbands, fathers, or boyfriends in your country? How does the society at large view such acts? Are there shelters women can go to in order to escape such violence?
3. What are factory conditions like where you live? Is there an attempt to humanize life for the workers?
4. Which groups of people are discriminated against in your society? What is the discrimination based on—race, gender, caste, religion, other categories?
5. Is Friday the thirteenth considered an unlucky date in your culture? What other numbers have a positive or negative significance?

E Debate

Debate this proposition:

Violence is never justified.

PART 3 Focus on Language

A Adverbial Clauses

An **adverbial clause** is a subordinate, or dependent, clause introduced by a subordinating conjunction such as *when, after, because, in order that, if,* or *although.* Since it is a dependent clause, it cannot stand alone in a sentence but must be accompanied by an independent (main) clause, and like all clauses, it has its own subject and verb. Adverbial clauses may be grouped into categories of time, reason, result, condition, and concession.

1. An **adverbial clause of time** may start with words such as *before, after, when, as, until,* or *as soon as.* For example:

   *He had planned to get up **before Mae did** and surprise her by fixing breakfast.* (lines 1–2)

   __As the hours dragged by__ he noticed that the women workers had started to snap and snarl at each other. (lines 158–160)

2. An **adverbial clause of reason** may start with words such as *because, since,* or *as.* For example:

   *... they appeared to be simply moving their lips **because you couldn't hear** what they were saying.* (lines 91–92)

3. An **adverbial clause of result** starts with *so that, so . . . that,* or *such . . . that.* For example:

   *The roar of the train beat inside his head, making it ache and throb, and the pain in his legs clawed up into his groin **so that he seemed to be bursting with pain**....* (lines 259–261)

   This sentence could be rewritten as follows:

   *The pain in his legs was **so great that he seemed to be bursting with pain.***

4. An **adverbial clause of condition** starts with words such as *if, provided that, unless,* or *whether or not.* For example:

   *"And **if you don't spring up out of there,** you're going to be late again."* (lines 28–29)

If you use the verb *to be* in an unreal condition, use *were* for all persons in the conditional clause. For example:

*"**If I were you,** I'd get up quickly or you'll be late."*

5. An **adverbial clause of concession** starts with words such as *although, though,* or *whereas.* For example:

*He avoided looking at her and hurried a little, head down, as he passed her **though he couldn't resist stealing a glance at her out of the corner of his eye.*** (lines 83–85)

Note: If one adverbial clause is linked to another clause by *and, but,* or *or,* the second clause is also an adverbial clause. For example:

*He didn't answer her **because her eyes were angry and [because] he didn't want to quarrel with her.*** (lines 288–289)

PUNCTUATION OF ADVERBIAL CLAUSES

If the adverbial clause comes after the independent clause, no commas are used to set it off from the independent clause. For example:

*Mae was in the house **before he was.*** (line 265)

If the adverbial clause precedes the independent clause, a comma is used to set it off from the independent clause. For example:

***Before he reached the house,** Mae had already arrived and was preparing dinner.*

Note: These punctuation rules are frequently *not* followed in "Like a Winding Sheet." Authors often bend punctuation rules to fit their individual writing styles. However, it is good practice to follow the rules in your own writing.

In the following sentences about the story, underline the adverbial clause and write what kind of adverbial clause it is (time, reason, result, condition, or concession).

1. And he was late for work again because they spent fifteen minutes arguing . . . (lines 57–58) _____
2. If he had done that, his hands would have felt good now—relaxed, rested. (lines 144–145) _____

3. What he wanted to do was hit her so hard that the scarlet lipstick on her mouth would smear and spread over her nose . . . (lines 231–233) _____

4. "Hello, babe," she called out, as soon as he opened the door. (line 268) _____

5. Although Mae was exhausted at the end of the day, she always folded her clothes neatly over the chair. _____

The following sentences are all related to the plot of "Like a Winding Sheet." Complete them with adverbial clauses that would be appropriate to the story. Use a different kind of adverbial clause in each sentence.

1. _____, he was unable to hit the two women.

2. He managed to control his explosive anger _____.

3. _____, he would reform many of the working conditions in the factory.

4. He felt so insulted by the women _____ and _____.

5. Mae was annoyed with him _____.

Write five sentences of your own using an adverbial clause from each category. In one sentence join two adverbial clauses with *and, but,* or *or.* Relate your sentences to the story.

B   Building Vocabulary Skills

Complete each of the following sentences with a suitable synonym from the list below. Both the italicized word and its synonym appear in the story. You may need to change the tense or form of the word. Try to do this exercise first without referring to the story.

bunch	strike	sag	snarl
rock	froth	twist	knot

1. He stood *swaying* and _____ in the subway train as it rushed toward Harlem.

2. She was so tired after a hard day's work that her shoulders *drooped* and _____ as she collapsed into the chair.

3. The workers in the factory would *snap* and _____ at each other toward the end of the day.

4. He saw the people in the restaurant standing in *groups* or _____ as they waited for the coffee to be poured.

5. He could feel his poisonous anger *wrapping* and _____ around him as he struggled to control himself.

6. His hands were *clenched* and _____ after the forewoman insulted him.

7. The coffee looked so enticing with the steaming *bubbles* and _____.

8. He felt himself *smack* and _____ her over and over, but he could do nothing about it.

PART 4 Writing Activities

1. Write a two-page essay discussing domestic violence in your country. Consider what forms the violence takes; for example, violence can include verbal insults as well as physical blows. Explain who the chief victims are and who usually inflicts the violence. Analyze the reasons for this behavior. In your conclusion, say whether the victims are treated sympathetically by society.

2. Imagine that you are extremely hungry and for some reason you cannot satisfy your craving to eat. Write two to three paragraphs in which you either see or imagine the food you desperately want. Use the story's restaurant scene, with its intensely evocative imagery, as a model to convey your situation, as well as your feelings at the time. Make clear in your writing why you are unable to eat immediately.

3. Write a dialogue between Mae and her husband five hours after the beating takes place. Have them speak frankly to each other about what happened and the reasons for it. According to the way the dialogue is constructed, convey whether their relationship can be saved or not.

4. Novels such as *The Color Purple* by Alice Walker and *The Joy Luck Club* by Amy Tan deal with, among other themes, the anguish of domestic violence. Write an essay of one or two pages on a book you have read or a movie you have seen in which a woman or child is subject to violence from a husband or father. Describe the relationship and analyze the reasons for this situation. Does the victim try to do anything about this abuse? Say what happens.

18

The Lily-White Boys

WILLIAM MAXWELL (1908–2000)

Born in Lincoln, Illinois, William Maxwell had an idyllic childhood until his mother died in the 1918 worldwide influenza epidemic. He was sent to live with relatives until his father remarried and moved the family to Chicago in 1922. Maxwell often asserted that the first fourteen years of his life were the source of much of his fiction. After graduating from the University of Illinois and Harvard University, he moved to New York and joined *The New Yorker* magazine, where he remained on staff for forty years. He became a legendary editor, working with some of the most eminent authors of his time, including J. D. Salinger, John Cheever, Eudora Welty, and Frank O'Connor.

In addition to his editing, Maxwell was a prolific writer. He published six novels, including *Bright Center of Heaven* (1934) and *So Long, See You Tomorrow* (1980), which won the American Book Award. His many short stories have been collected into three anthologies, the most recent of which, *All the Days and Nights* (1995), is composed of stories written between 1939 and 1992. In addition, he wrote a memoir, *Ancestors* (1972), and a book of essays, *The Outermost Dream* (1989). In his novels, Maxwell's spare, beautifully crafted prose captures without sentimentality or falseness the childhood events of his central characters.

THE LILY-WHITE BOYS

A couple receives an unpleasant surprise when they return home after a party on Christmas Day.

The Follansbees' Christmas party was at teatime on Christmas Day, and it was for all ages. Ignoring the fire laws, the big Christmas tree standing between the two front windows in the living room of the Park Avenue apartment had candles on it. When the last one was lit, somebody flipped a light switch, and in the hush that fell over the room the soft ⁵ yellow candlelight fell on the upturned faces of the children sitting on the floor in a ring around the base of the tree, bringing tears to the eyes of the susceptible.[1] The tree was strung with loops of gold and silver tinsel[2] and popcorn and colored paper, and some of the glass ornaments—the hardy tin soldier, the drum, the nutmeg, and the Man in the Moon—went ¹⁰ all the way back to Beth Follansbee's childhood. While the presents were being distributed, Mark Follansbee stood by with a bucket of water and a broom. The room smelled of warm wax and balsam.[3]

The big red candles on the mantlepiece burned down slowly in their nest of holly. In the dining room, presiding over the cut-glass punch ¹⁵ bowl,[4] Beth Follansbee said, "You let the peaches sit all day in a quart of vodka, and then you add two bottles of white wine and a bottle of champagne. Be a little careful. It isn't as innocuous[5] as you might think," and with her eyebrows signaled to the maid that the plate of watercress sandwiches needed refilling. Those that liked to sing had gathered ²⁰ around the piano in the living room and, having done justice to[6] all the familiar carols, were singing with gusto,[7] "Seven for the seven stars in the sky and six for the six proud walkers. Five for the symbols at your door and four for the Gospel makers,[8] Three, three, the rivals, Two, two, two the lily-white boys, clothed all in green-ho. One is one and all alone and ²⁵ evermore shall *be* so." And an overexcited little boy with a plastic spaceship was running up and down the hall and shouting "Blast off!"

The farewells at the elevator door were followed by a second round down below on the sidewalk while the doorman was blowing his whistle for cabs. ³⁰

"Can we drop you?" Ellen Hunter called.

"No. You're going downtown, and it would be out of your way," Celia Coleman said.

---

1 **susceptible** especially sensitive, easily influenced
2 **tinsel** thin strips of glittering material
3 **balsam** a sweet-smelling fir tree
4 **punch bowl** a bowl that holds a spiced fruit and alcohol drink
5 **innocuous** harmless
6 **done justice to** shown full appreciation of
7 **gusto** great enthusiasm
8 **Gospel makers** the four evangelists: Matthew, Mark, Luke, and John (Biblical reference)

The Colemans walked two blocks north on Park and then east. The sidewalks of Manhattan[9] were bare, the snow the weatherman promised having failed to come. There were no stars, and the night sky had a brownish cast.[10] From a speaker placed over the doorway of a darkened storefront human voices sang "O Little Town of Bethlehem." The drugstore on the corner was brightly lighted but locked, with the iron grating pulled down and no customers inquiring about cosmetics at the cash register or standing in front of the revolving Timex display unable to make up their minds.

The Venetian red door of the Colemans' house was level with the sidewalk and had a Christmas wreath on it. In an eerie[11] fashion it swung open when Dan Coleman tried to fit his key in the lock.

"Did we forget to close it?" Celia said and he shook his head. The lock had been jimmied.[12]

"I guess it's our turn," he said grimly as they walked in. At the foot of the stairs they stood still and listened. Nothing on the first floor was disturbed. There was even a silver spoon and a small silver tray on the dining room sideboard. Looking at each other they half managed to believe that everything was all right: The burglars had been frightened by somebody coming down the street, or a squad car perhaps, and had cleared out[13] without taking anything. But the house felt queer, not right somehow, not the way it usually felt, and they saw why when they got to the top of the first flight of stairs.

"Sweet Jesus!" he exclaimed softly, and she thought of her jewelry.

The shades were drawn to the sills, so that people on the sidewalk or in the apartments across the way could not see in the windows. One small detail caught his eye in the midst of the general destruction. A Limoges jar[14] that held potpourri[15] lay in fragments on the hearth and a faint odor of rose petals hung on the air.

With her heart beating faster than usual and her mouth as dry as cotton she said, "I can understand why they might want to look behind the pictures, but why walk on them?"

"Saves time," he said.

"And why break the lamps?"

"I don't know," he said. "I have never gone in for[16] house-breaking."

A cigarette had been placed at the edge of a tabletop, right next to an ashtray, and allowed to burn all the way down. The liquor cupboard was untouched. In the study, on that same floor at the back of the house, where the hi-fi, the tape deck, and the TV should have been there was a blank space. Rather than bother to unscrew the cable, the burglars had

---

9 **Manhattan** the most well-known area of New York City
10 **cast** slight color
11 **eerie** strange and frightening
12 **jimmied** forced open with a metal bar
13 **cleared out** left quickly (informal)

14 **Limoges jar** an expensive piece of eighteenth-century pottery
15 **potpourri** a mixture of scented dried flowers and spices
16 **have never gone in for** have never had an interest in, have never taken part in

snipped it with wire cutters. All the books had been pulled from the shelves and lay in mounds on the floor. 75

"Evidently they are not readers," he said, and picked up volume seven of *Hakluyt's Voyages*[17] and stood it on an empty shelf.

She tried to think of a reason for not going up the next flight to the bedrooms, to make the uncertainty last a little longer. Rather than leave her jewelry in the bank and never have the pleasure of wearing it, she 80 had hidden it in a place that seemed to her very clever.

It was not clever enough. The star ruby ring, the cabochon emeralds, the gold bracelets, the moonstones, the garnet necklace that had been her father's wedding present to her mother, the peridot and tourmaline pin[18] that she found in an antiquity shop on a back street in Toulon, the 85 diamond earrings—gone. All gone. Except for the things Dan had given her they were all inherited and irreplaceable, and so what would be the point of insuring them.

"In a way it's a relief," she said, in what sounded to her, though not to him, like her normal voice. 90

"Meaning?"

"Meaning that you can't worry about possessions you no longer have."

She opened the top right-hand drawer of her dressing table and saw that the junk jewelry was still there. As she pushed the drawer shut he said, "The standard procedure," and took her in his arms. 95

The rest was also pretty much the standard procedure. Mattresses were pulled half off the beds and ripped open with a razor blade, drawers turned upside down, and his clothes closet completely empty, which meant that his wardrobe now consisted of the dark blue suit he had put on earlier this evening to go to the Follansbees' Christmas party. 100 Her dresses lay in a colored confusion that spilled out into the room from the floor of her walk-in closet. Boxes from the upper shelves had been pulled down and ransacked[19]—boxes containing hats, evening purses, evening dresses she no longer had occasion to wear, since they seldom went out at night except to go to the theater or dine with friends. 105

When the police came she let him do the talking. Christmas Eve, Christmas Day, were the prime moments for break-ins, they said. The house had probably been watched. They made a list of the more important things and suggested that Dan send them an inventory.[20] They were pleasant and held out no hope. There were places they could 110 watch, they said, to see if anything belonging to the Colemans turned up, but chances were that. . . . When they left he put the back of a chair against the doorknob of the street door and started up the stairs.

---

17 *Hakluyt's Voyages* a series of books by the sixteenth-century British explorer Richard Hakluyt

18 **peridot and tourmaline pin** a brooch composed of two semiprecious gemstones

19 **ransacked** searched violently for valuables

20 **inventory** a record of (stolen) items

From the stairs he could see into their bedroom. To his astonishment Celia had on an evening dress he hadn't seen for twenty years. Turning this way and that, she studied her reflection in the full-length mirror on the back of a closet door. Off the dress came, over her head, and she worked her way into a scarlet chiffon sheath[21] that had a sooty footprint on it. Her hair had turned from dark brown to grey and when she woke up in the morning her back was as stiff as a board, but the dress fit her perfectly. While he stood there, watching, and unseen, she tried them on, one after another—the black taffeta with the bouffant skirt,[22] the pale sea-green silk with bands of matching silk fringe, all her favorite dresses that she had been too fond of to take to a thrift shop,[23] and that had been languishing[24] on the top shelf of her closet. As she stepped back to consider critically the effect of a white silk evening suit, her high heels ground splinters of glass into the bedroom rug.

Its load lightened by a brief stop in the Bronx at a two-story warehouse that was filled from floor to ceiling with hi-fi sets and color TVs, the Chrysler sedan proceeded along the Bruckner Elevated Expressway to Route 95. When the car slowed down for the tollgate at the Connecticut state line, the sandy-haired[25] recidivist,[26] slouched down[27] in the right-hand front seat, opened his eyes. The false license plates aroused no interest whatever as the car came to a stop and then drove on.

In the middle of the night, the material witnesses[28] to the breaking and entering communicated with one another, a remark at a time. A small spotlight up near the ceiling that was trained on an area over the living room sofa said, *When I saw the pictures being ripped from the walls I was afraid. I thought I was going to go the same way.*

So fortunate, they were, the red stair-carpet said, and the stair-rail said, *Fortunate? How?*

The intruders[29] were gone when they came home.

I had a good look at them, said the mirror over the lowboy[30] in the downstairs hall. *They were not at all like the Colemans' friends or the delivery boys from Gristede's[31] and the fish market.*

The Colemans' friends don't break in the front door, the Sheraton sideboard said. *They ring and then wait for somebody to come and open it.*

She will have my top refinished, said the table with the cigarette scar. *The number is in the telephone turnaround. She knows about that sort of thing and he doesn't. But it will take a while. And the room will look odd without me.*

---

21 **chiffon sheath** a tight-fitting dress made of light material
22 **the black taffeta with the bouffant skirt** full-skirted, shiny black dress
23 **thrift shop** a shop that sells used articles, especially clothing, to benefit a charity
24 **had been languishing** had been lying neglected
25 **sandy-haired** with light yellowish-brown hair
26 **recidivist** a repeat criminal
27 **slouched down** sitting low in the seat
28 **material witnesses** important, relevant witnesses
29 **intruders** uninvited people
30 **lowboy** a low, tablelike chest of drawers
31 **Gristede's** a supermarket chain

It took a long time to make that star ruby, said a small seashell on the mantelpiece.

Precious stones you can buy, said the classified directory. *Van Cleef and Arpels. Harry Winston.*[32] *And auctions at Christie's and Sotheby Parke-Bernet. It is the Victorian and Edwardian settings that were unusual. I don't suppose the thieves will know enough to value them.* 155

They will be melted down, said the brass fire irons, *into unidentifiability. It happens every day.*

Antique jewelry too can be picked up[33] *at auction places. Still, it is disagreeable to lose things that have come down in the family. It isn't something one would choose to have happen.* 160

There are lots of things one would not choose to have happen that do happen, said the fire irons.

With any unpleasantness, said the orange plastic Design Research kitchen wall clock, *it is better to take the long view.* 165

Very sensible of them to fall asleep the minute their heads hit the pillow, said the full-length mirror in the master bedroom. *Instead of turning and tossing and going over in their minds the things they have lost, that are gone forever.* 170

They have each other, a small bottle of Elizabeth Arden perfume spray said. *They will forget about what happened this evening. Or, if they remember, it will be something they have ceased to have much feeling about, a story they tell sometimes at dinner parties, when the subject of robberies comes up. He will tell how they walked home from the Follansbees'* 175 *on Christmas night and found the front door ajar, and she will tell about the spoon and the silver tray the thieves didn't take, and he will tell how he stood on the stairs watching while she tried on all her favorite evening dresses.*

---

32 **Van Cleef and Arpels, Harry Winston.** two well-known New York jewelers

33 **picked up** easily acquired

PART **1** First Reading

A   Thinking About the Story

Were you surprised by the couple's reaction to the burglary? What was your response to the talking objects? Explain your answer.

B   Understanding the Plot

1. In what city and in what neighborhood does the story take place?
2. What details illustrate that the Follansbees and the Colemans are wealthy people? List as many as possible.
3. What is Dan Coleman referring to when he says, "I guess it's our turn"? (line 48)
4. In what ways were the burglars needlessly destructive?
5. What does Dan Coleman mean when he says, "The standard procedure"? (line 95)
6. How would you complete the sentence on line 112 that begins . . . "but chances were that" . . . ?
7. Why does Celia try on her old evening gowns? Give as many reasons as you can think of.
8. What is the warehouse in the Bronx for?
9. How many burglars were there? What details do we know about them?
10. Did the burglars escape?
11. What important information do we learn from the talking objects?

PART **2** Second Reading

A   Exploring Themes

You are now ready to reread "The Lily-White Boys." Notice the way the story is structured in three distinct parts. Look carefully at the relationship between the couple and their talking objects.

1. How does the division of the story into three separate parts help express its central themes?

2. How do the candles on the Christmas tree foreshadow the later events of the story? Explain your answer, keeping in mind the candles' potential for danger.

3. In what way does the image of Mrs. Coleman's "high heels grind[ing] splinters of glass into the bedroom rug" (lines 126–127) reinforce one of the story's themes?

4. In what ways do the personalities of Mr. and Mrs. Coleman differ?

5. Why are the objects personified at the end of the story?

6. How would you characterize the Colemans' response to the burglary? Relate your answer to some of the thematic concerns of the story.

B   Analyzing the Author's Style

For more information on the literary terms in this section, turn to the explanations of *allusion* (page 297), *connotation* (page 300), *setting* (page 307), and *atmosphere* (page 298).

ALLUSION AND CONNOTATION

"The Lily-White Boys" is an intriguing and puzzling title that points to the layers of meaning in the story. On one level the story is about the warmth, joy, and family feeling that surround Christmas celebrations. However, on another level it's about the ease with which a person's sense of security can be shattered by violent forces that lurk beyond his or her control. The title sets up this tension from the start with its **allusion** to the lily-white boys in the British folk song sung at the party and through the **connotations** attached to the expression *lily-white*.

Allusion is when an author makes a brief reference to someone or something on the assumption that the reader understands the reference, making it unnecessary for it to be explained explicitly. In titling his story "The Lily-White Boys," William Maxwell is alluding to the English folk song "Green Grow the Rushes O," in which two lily-white boys are mentioned in the second verse. The complete verse referring to the boys is as follows:

I'll sing you two, O
Green grow the rushes, O
What are your two, O?
Two, two, lily-white boys,
Clothed all in green, O
One is one and all alone
And evermore shall be so.

Significantly, this song, with its religious overtones of God as *one and all alone*, is often sung at Christmas, which helps point the reader to the importance of the season.

1. In what ways does Maxwell embrace traditional Christmas rituals in the story?
2. How might the story also be read as a criticism of some aspects of Christmas today?

The **connotations** associated with the expression *lily-white* are integral to our understanding of the story's complexity. The connotation of a word is not its dictionary definition, but rather the associated meanings we place on the word. For example, the candles in the first paragraph are not merely "waxen lights" (their dictionary definition) but also carry associations such as warmth, good cheer, soft light, and fire.

The dictionary meaning of *lily-white* is "pure white like the color of a lily." So we speak of a lily-white complexion. But like many words, the expression also has both a positive and a negative connotation. On the positive side, it means "pure or spotless," as in a lily-white reputation; on the negative side, in the United States the term has come to imply a rich, segregated neighborhood, in which predominantly white inhabitants are protected from other races and from the unpleasant experiences more commonly associated with the world of the underprivileged.

3. How does the story reflect the positive connotations attached to the expression *lily-white*?
4. Which character(s) embody to some extent the negative connotations of *lily-white*? You may examine more than one character in your answer. Explain the reasons for your choice(s).

SETTING AND ATMOSPHERE

The **setting**—the time and place in which the action occurs—of "The Lily-White Boys" is crucial to an understanding of its themes. Setting also helps create **atmosphere** or mood in the story. In "The Lily-White Boys," the action unfolds in the course of one day, Christmas Day, but takes place in several locations with corresponding changes in atmosphere. For example, the opening scenes with their depiction of the luxurious apartment with its beautifully decorated Christmas tree surrounded by enchanted children, the gracious hostess orchestrating events, and the guests gathered around the piano in the candlelit, sweet-smelling living room, unite setting and atmosphere in a harmonious whole. This scene contrasts jarringly with the altered setting and atmosphere in the Colemans' burglarized home, where the contents are strewn everywhere and the house exudes violence and destruction.

1. How many settings are there in the story?
2. How are the settings described? Pick out descriptive phrases in the story that help bring each setting to life.
3. What atmosphere is conveyed by each setting? Give details to illustrate your answer.
4. How does each setting help us understand the themes of the story?
5. How does the description of the walk the Colemans take back to their home after the party help heighten the atmosphere and prepare us for the shock that awaits them?
6. What adjectives in lines 43–56 highlight the changed atmosphere in the Colemans' house?

C Judging for Yourself

Express yourself as personally as you like in your answers to the following questions.

1. Do you think the Follansbees felt themselves above the law? Why? Why not?
2. How old do you think the Colemans are? Give reasons for your answer.
3. Why do you think the burglars were so destructive?
4. Do you agree with the Elizabeth Arden perfume bottle that the Colemans will forget about the robbery after a while? Justify your answer.
5. Would you describe the Colemans as a cultured couple? Explain your answer.

D Making Connections

1. How common are burglaries in your country? What are the most frequent items stolen? Are most burglars caught? If they are, what is their punishment?
2. Are violent crimes common in your country? Explain why or why not.
3. What is your favorite holiday of the year? Explain how you celebrate it. Has it become overcommercialized?
4. Where do the wealthy people tend to live in your country? What kind of lifestyle do they enjoy?

E   Debate

Debate this proposition:

Crime pays.

PART 3   Focus on Language

A   Appositives

Writers use **appositives** to enhance and clarify their writing. Appositives are single words or phrases that give additional information about a particular noun or pronoun. They are generally separated from the noun or pronoun they describe by dashes, commas, or colons. For example: *The buildings of Manhattan,* **looming and ominous shapes,** *felt strangely alien as the Colemans walked home.* Here the appositive, *looming and ominous shapes,* focuses on the unpleasant nature of the surroundings on the Colemans' nocturnal walk. In this case, the appositive is set off from the buildings it describes by a comma. A dash creates a longer pause than a comma, thus putting more emphasis on the appositive, while a colon signals a more formal definition.

1. What appositive describes the Christmas tree decorations in the first paragraph? Which noun does the appositive describe? How is the appositive set off from that noun?

2. What appositives describe the house in lines 48–56? What is the effect of using appositives here?

3. Pick out the appositive in lines 96–105. What detail does it illustrate?

4. Find the appositives in lines 114–127 and say which noun or pronoun they refer to. How do these appositives reinforce the mood of the scene?

5. What appositive occurs in the last paragraph? What idea does it reinforce?

B   Placement of the Subject

There are several instances where the placement of the subject may cause difficulties.

1. The subject is omitted. For example:

    "Draw up an inventory of missing items," suggested the policeman.

    In this case, since *draw up* is an imperative, the subject is omitted and needs to be supplied by the reader.

2. The subject has appeared previously, but is not repeated, forcing the reader to supply it by looking back in the text.

    They will be melted down, said the brass fire irons, into unidentifiability. (line 158)

    In this case, the reader must go back to the previous paragraph, then choose between two possible antecedents—*precious stones* or *settings*—for the subject pronoun *they*. Here, the logic of the text dictates that the antecedent must be *settings*.

3. In the case of compound sentences (independent clauses joined by the coordinating conjunctions *and, but, so, yet, or, for, nor*), the subject is frequently mentioned only in the first part of the sentence and is omitted in the second part if the subject is the same. For example:

    The burglars had been frightened by somebody coming down the street, or a squad car perhaps, and had cleared out without taking anything. (lines 52–54)

    In the second clause, the subject (*burglars*) of the verb *had cleared out* has been omitted.

Identify the subject in the following phrases and sentences.

1. What should the subject of the participial phrase *ignoring the fire laws* be? (line 2)
    Note: The writer has used a dangling participial phrase, which is generally not recommended.
2. What is the subject of the participial phrase *bringing tears to the eyes of the susceptible*? (lines 7–8)
3. What is the subject of the sentence *Be a little careful*? (line 18)

4. What is the subject of the clause . . . *and, having done justice to all the familiar carols, were singing with gusto . . .*? (lines 21–22)

5. What is the subject of the clause . . . *and allowed to burn all the way down*? (line 70)

6. In the phrase *Its load lightened by a brief stop in the Bronx . . .* (line 128), what does the pronoun *its* refer to?

C Building Vocabulary Skills

Verbs can be categorized as regular and irregular verbs. Irregular verbs do not use -*ed* to form the past tense and the past participle. All the verbs in the chart appear exactly as they were used in "The Lily-White Boys." Complete the chart with the correct forms of the irregular verbs.

BASE FORM	PAST TENSE	PAST PARTICIPLE
break	broke	broken
buy		
choose		
		drawn
forget		
		ground
	hung	
know		
	lay	
	put	
sing		
	strung	
		swung
take		
wear		

PART 4 Writing Activities

1. Write an essay of two pages on crime in your country. Say what the most common crimes are and who generally commits them. Analyze the reasons for these crimes, and in your conclusion discuss what you think should be done to reduce the crime rate.

2. Imagine that you have returned home to a scene like the one that confronted the Colemans. In two to three paragraphs, depict the chaos as vividly as possible; then take another paragraph to describe your emotions. Try to incorporate appositives in your writing.

3. Many books and movies deal with crimes of different magnitudes. Dostoyevsky's great novel *Crime and Punishment* analyzes in depth the psychological toll a murder takes on the killer. In contrast, the movie *Ocean's Eleven* takes a light-hearted view of a Las Vegas casino heist, in which the viewer is invited to support the gang in its ingenious execution of their scheme. Write about a book or movie you know that centers on crime. Describe the crime, and say whether you hoped the perpetrator(s) would get away with it or not, and why.

4. "The Rocking-Horse Winner" (page 123) and "The Lily-White Boys" both lead us into the world of the supernatural. In the former, the house whispers and the horse mysteriously communicates with the boy, while in the latter, the objects in the house converse among themselves. Compare and contrast the supernatural element in both stories, and show how the supernatural helps further their respective themes.

19

The Catbird Seat

JAMES THURBER (1894–1961)

Born in Columbus, Ohio, James Thurber used his hometown as the setting for many of his humorous writings. His mild-tempered father and domineering mother served as the prototypes for his frequent explorations of the war between the sexes. After Thurber began working for the *The New Yorker* magazine in 1927, his career took off as he became widely known for his humorous essays, stories, cartoons, and illustrations.

Today Thurber is considered by many to be the greatest American humorist since Mark Twain. Beneath the humor of his work lies a concern with the consequences of marital humiliations, the destructive effects of technology, and the dangers of fascism. Thurber always admired the instinctive wisdom of animals and used them prominently in his work.

Thurber's large body of work, for which he won numerous awards, includes *My Life and Hard Times* (1933), *The Middle-Aged Man on the Flying Trapeze* (1935), *Further Fables for Our Time* (1940), *The Thurber Carnival* (1945), and *Thurber's Dogs* (1955).

THE CATBIRD SEAT

*A head filing clerk whose job is threatened takes drastic
and ingenious measures to protect himself.*

Mr. Martin bought the pack of Camels on Monday night in the most
crowded cigar store on Broadway. It was theatre time and seven or
eight men were buying cigarettes. The clerk didn't even glance at Mr. Martin,
who put the pack in his overcoat pocket and went out. If any of the staff at
F & S had seen him buy the cigarettes, they would have been astonished, [5]
for it was generally known that Mr. Martin did not smoke, and never had.
No one saw him.

It was just a week to the day since Mr. Martin had decided to rub out
Mrs. Ulgine Barrows. The term "rub out" pleased him because it suggested
nothing more than the correction of an error—in this case an error of Mr. [10]
Fitweiler. Mr. Martin had spent each night of the past week working out
his plan and examining it. As he walked home now he went over it again.
For the hundredth time he resented the element of imprecision, the margin
of guesswork[1] that entered into the business. The project as he had
worked it out was casual and bold, the risks were considerable. Something [15]
might go wrong anywhere along the line. And therein lay the cunning of
his scheme. No one would ever see in it the cautious, painstaking hand of
Erwin Martin, head of the filing department at F & S, of whom Mr. Fitweiler
had once said, "Man is fallible but Martin isn't."[2] No one would see his
hand, that is, unless it were caught in the act. [20]

Sitting in his apartment, drinking a glass of milk, Mr. Martin reviewed
his case against Mrs. Ulgine Barrows, as he had every night for seven
nights. He began at the beginning. Her quacking voice and braying
laugh had first profaned[3] the halls of F & S on March 7, 1941 (Mr. Martin
had a head for dates). Old Roberts, the personnel chief, had introduced [25]
her as the newly appointed special adviser to the president of the firm,
Mr. Fitweiler. The woman had appalled Mr. Martin instantly, but he
hadn't shown it. He had given her his dry hand, a look of studious
concentration, and a faint smile. "Well," she had said, looking at the
papers on his desk, "are you lifting the oxcart out of the ditch?"[4] As Mr. [30]
Martin recalled that moment, over his milk, he squirmed[5] slightly. He
must keep his mind on her crimes as a special adviser, not on her

---

1 **he resented the element of imprecision, the
   margin of guesswork** he did not like
   the fact that the tiniest detail could
   cause the plan to go wrong
2 **"Man is fallible but Martin isn't."** a humorous
   reference to the notion that usually only God
   cannot make a mistake

3 **profaned** treated something sacred
   with vulgarity
4 **"are you lifting the oxcart
   out of the ditch?"** are you
   attempting the impossible?
5 **squirmed** moved uncomfortably

peccadillos[6] as a personality. This he found difficult to do, in spite of entering an objection and sustaining it.[7] The faults of the woman as a woman kept chattering on in his mind like an unruly witness. She had, for almost two years now, baited him. In the halls, in the elevator, even in his own office, into which she romped now and then like a circus horse, she was constantly shouting these silly questions at him. "Are you lifting the oxcart out of the ditch? Are you tearing up the pea patch? Are you hollering[8] down the rain barrel? Are you scraping the bottom of the pickle barrel? Are you sitting in the catbird seat?"[9]

It was Joey Hart, one of Mr. Martin's two assistants, who had explained what the gibberish[10] meant. "She must be a Dodger fan," he had said. "Red Barber[11] announces the Dodger games over the radio and he uses those expressions—picked 'em up down South." Joey had gone on to explain one or two. "Tearing up the pea patch" meant going on a rampage;[12] "sitting in the catbird seat" meant sitting pretty,[13] like a batter with three balls and no strikes on him.[14] Mr. Martin dismissed all this with an effort. It had been annoying, it had driven him near to distraction, but he was too solid a man to be moved to murder by anything so childish. It was fortunate, he reflected as he passed on to the important charges against Mrs. Barrows, that he had stood up under it so well.[15] He had maintained always an outward appearance of polite tolerance. "Why, I even believe you like the woman," Miss Paird, his other assistant, had once said to him. He had simply smiled.

A gavel[16] rapped in Mr. Martin's mind and the case proper was resumed. Mrs. Ulgine Barrows stood charged with willful,[17] blatant,[18] and persistent attempts to destroy the efficiency and system of F & S. It was competent, material, and relevant to review her advent and rise to power. Mr. Martin had got the story from Miss Paird, who seemed always able to find things out. According to her, Mrs. Barrows had met Mr. Fitweiler at a party, where she had rescued him from the embraces of a powerfully built drunken man who had mistaken the president of F & S for a famous retired Middle Western football coach. She had led him to a sofa and somehow worked upon him a monstrous magic. The aging gentleman had jumped to the conclusion there and then that this was a woman of

---

6 **peccadillos** slight offenses
7 **entering an objection and sustaining it** In a court of law an attorney may object to a line of questioning by his opponent and the judge may sustain (agree with) the objection or overrule (disagree with) it.
8 **hollering** shouting
9 **sitting in the catbird seat** enjoying an advantageous position
10 **gibberish** meaningless language
11 **Red Barber** a sports broadcaster, born in Mississippi, who covered the Brooklyn Dodgers, a well-known baseball team
12 **going on a rampage** getting violently out of control
13 **sitting pretty** being in an advantageous position
14 **like a batter with three balls and no strikes on him** In baseball, this is a situation where a batter is likely to do well.
15 **had stood up under it so well** had successfully endured it
16 **gavel** a small hammer that a judge uses in the courtroom
17 **willful** deliberate
18 **blatant** offensively noticeable

singular attainments,[19] equipped to bring out the best in him and in the firm. A week later he had introduced her into F & S as his special adviser. On that day confusion got its foot in the door. After Miss Tyson, Mr. Brundage, and Mr. Bartlett had been fired and Mr. Munson had taken his hat and stalked out,[20] mailing in his resignation later, old Roberts had been emboldened to speak to Mr. Fitweiler. He mentioned that Mr. Munson's department had been "a little disrupted" and hadn't they perhaps better resume the old system there? Mr. Fitweiler had said certainly not. He had the greatest faith in Mrs. Barrows' ideas. "They require a little seasoning, a little seasoning, is all," he had added. Mr. Roberts had given it up. Mr. Martin reviewed in detail all the changes wrought by Mrs. Barrows. She had begun chipping at the cornices of the firm's edifice and now she was swinging at the foundation stones with a pickaxe.[21] 70 75 80

Mr. Martin came now, in his summing up, to the afternoon of Monday, November 2, 1942—just one week ago. On that day, at 3 P.M., Mrs. Barrows had bounced into his office. "Boo!" she had yelled. "Are you scraping around the bottom of the pickle barrel?" Mr. Martin had looked at her from under his green eyeshade, saying nothing. She had begun to wander about the office, taking it in with her great popping eyes.[22] "Do you really need *all* these filing cabinets?" she had demanded suddenly. Mr. Martin's heart had jumped. "Each of these files," he had said, keeping his voice even, "plays an indispensable part in the system of F & S." She had brayed at him, "Well, don't tear up the pea patch!" and gone to the door. From there she had bawled, "But you sure have got a lot of fine scrap[23] in here!" Mr. Martin could no longer doubt that the finger was on his beloved department. Her pickaxe was on the upswing, poised for the first blow. It had not come yet; he had received no blue memo from the enchanted Mr. Fitweiler bearing nonsensical instructions deriving from the obscene[24] woman. But there was no doubt in Mr. Martin's mind that one would be forthcoming. He must act quickly. Already a precious week had gone by. Mr. Martin stood up in his living room, still holding his milk glass. "Gentlemen of the jury," he said to himself, "I demand the death penalty for this horrible person." 85 90 95 100

The next day Mr. Martin followed his routine, as usual. He polished his glasses more often and once sharpened an already sharp pencil, but not even Miss Paird noticed. Only once did he catch sight of his victim; she swept past him in the hall with a patronizing "Hi!" At five-thirty he walked home, as usual, and had a glass of milk, as usual. He had never drunk anything stronger in his life—unless you could count ginger ale. 105

---

19 **singular attainments** unusual achievements
20 **stalked out** walked out proudly
21 **She had begun chipping at the cornices of the firm's edifice and now she was swinging at the foundation stones with a pickaxe.** She had started by slowly changing some aspects of the business and was now revolutionizing everything.
22 **popping eyes** wide eyes that stick out
23 **scrap** useless material
24 **obscene** vulgar, indecent

The late Sam Schlosser,[25] the S of F & S, had praised Mr. Martin at a staff meeting several years before for his temperate[26] habits. "Our most efficient worker neither drinks nor smokes," he had said. "The results speak for themselves." Mr. Fitweiler had sat by, nodding approval.

Mr. Martin was still thinking about that red-letter day[27] as he walked over to Schrafft's on Fifth Avenue near Forty-sixth Street. He got there, as he always did, at eight o'clock. He finished his dinner and the financial page of the *Sun* at a quarter to nine, as he always did. It was his custom after dinner to take a walk. This time he walked down Fifth Avenue at a casual pace. His gloved hands felt moist and warm, his forehead cold. He transferred the Camels from his overcoat to a jacket pocket. He wondered, as he did so, if they did not represent an unnecessary note of strain. Mrs. Barrows smoked only Luckies. It was his idea to puff a few puffs on a Camel (after the rubbing-out), stub it out in the ashtray holding her lipstick-stained Luckies, and thus drag a small red herring[28] across the trail. Perhaps it was not a good idea. It would take time. He might even choke, too loudly.

Mr. Martin had never seen the house on West Twelfth Street where Mrs. Barrows lived, but he had a clear enough picture of it. Fortunately, she had bragged to everybody about her ducky[29] first-floor apartment in the perfectly darling three-story red-brick. There would be no doorman or other attendants; just the tenants of the second and third floors. As he walked along, Mr. Martin realized that he would get there before nine-thirty. He had considered walking north on Fifth Avenue from Schrafft's to a point from which it would take him until ten o'clock to reach the house. At that hour people were less likely to be coming in or going out. But the procedure would have made an awkward loop in the straight thread of his casualness,[30] and he had abandoned it. It was impossible to figure when people would be entering or leaving the house, anyway. There was a great risk at any hour. If he ran into anybody, he would simply have to place the rubbing-out of Ulgine Barrows in the inactive file forever. The same thing would hold true if there were someone in her apartment. In that case he would just say that he had been passing by, recognized her charming house, and thought to drop in.[31]

It was eighteen minutes after nine when Mr. Martin turned into Twelfth Street. A man passed him, and a man and a woman, talking. There was no one within fifty paces when he came to the house, half-way down the block. He was up the steps and in the small vestibule[32] in no time, pressing the bell under the card that said "Mrs. Ulgine Barrows." When the clicking in the lock started, he jumped forward against the

25 **the late Sam Schlosser** the deceased Sam Schlosser
26 **temperate** moderate
27 **red-letter day** an excitingly memorable day
28 **red herring** a deliberately false clue
29 **ducky** cute (slang)

30 **But the procedure would have made an awkward loop in the straight thread of his casualness** But waiting until 10 P.M. would have overcomplicated his plan
31 **drop in** visit unexpectedly
32 **vestibule** the entrance hall of a building

door. He got inside fast, closing the door behind him. A bulb in a lantern hung from the hall ceiling on a chain seemed to give a monstrously bright light. There was nobody on the stair, which went up ahead of him along the left wall. A door opened down the hall in the wall on the right. 150 He went toward it swiftly, on tiptoe.

"Well, for God's sake, look who's here!" bawled Mrs. Barrows, and her braying laugh rang out like the report of a shotgun. He rushed past her like a football tackle, bumping her. "Hey, quit shoving!" she said, closing the door behind them. They were in her living room, which seemed to 155 Mr. Martin to be lighted by a hundred lamps. "What's after you?" she said. "You're as jumpy³³ as a goat." He found he was unable to speak. His heart was wheezing in his throat. "I—yes," he finally brought out. She was jabbering and laughing as she started to help him off with his coat. "No, no," he said. "I'll put it here." He took it off and put it on a chair near the 160 door. "Your hat and gloves, too," she said. "You're in a lady's house." He put his hat on top of the coat. Mrs. Barrows seemed larger than he had thought. He kept his gloves on. "I was passing by," he said. "I recognized—is there anyone here?" She laughed louder than ever. "No," she said, "we're all alone. You're as white as a sheet, you funny man. 165 Whatever *has* come over you? I'll mix you a toddy."³⁴ She started toward a door across the room. "Scotch-and-soda be all right? But say, you don't drink, do you?" She turned and gave him her amused look. Mr. Martin pulled himself together.³⁵ "Scotch-and-soda will be all right," he heard himself say. He could hear her laughing in the kitchen. 170

Mr. Martin looked quickly around the living room for the weapon. He had counted on finding one there. There were andirons³⁶ and a poker³⁷ and something in a corner that looked like an Indian club. None of them would do.³⁸ It couldn't be that way. He began to pace around. He came to a desk. On it lay a metal paper knife with an ornate handle. Would it be sharp 175 enough? He reached for it and knocked over a small brass jar. Stamps spilled out of it and it fell to the floor with a clatter. "Hey," Mrs. Barrows yelled from the kitchen, "are you tearing up the pea patch?" Mr. Martin gave a strange laugh. Picking up the knife, he tried its point against his left wrist. It was blunt.³⁹ It wouldn't do. 180

When Mrs. Barrows reappeared, carrying two highballs, Mr. Martin, standing there with his gloves on, became acutely conscious of the fantasy he had wrought. Cigarettes in his pocket, a drink prepared for him—it was all too grossly improbable. It was more than that; it was impossible. Somewhere in the back of his mind a vague idea stirred, 185 sprouted.⁴⁰ "For heaven's sake, take off those gloves," said Mrs. Barrows. "I always wear them in the house," said Mr. Martin. The idea began to

---

33 **jumpy** nervous
34 **toddy** an alcoholic drink
35 **pulled himself together** got control of himself
36 **andirons** a pair of metal supports for firewood

37 **poker** a metal rod for stirring a fire
38 **would do** were acceptable
39 **blunt** not sharp
40 **sprouted** began to grow

bloom, strange and wonderful. She put the glasses on a coffee table in front of a sofa and sat on the sofa. "Come over here, you odd little man," she said. Mr. Martin went over and sat beside her. It was difficult getting a cigarette out of the pack of Camels, but he managed it. She held a match for him, laughing. "Well," she said, handing him his drink, "this is perfectly marvellous. You with a drink and a cigarette."

Mr. Martin puffed, not too awkwardly, and took a gulp of the highball. "I drink and smoke all the time," he said. He clinked his glass against hers. "Here's nuts to that old windbag, Fitweiler,"[41] he said, and gulped again. The stuff tasted awful, but he made no grimace. "Really, Mr. Martin," she said, her voice and posture changing, "you are insulting our employer." Mrs. Barrows was now all special adviser to the president. "I am preparing a bomb," said Mr. Martin, "which will blow the old goat higher than hell." He had only had a little of the drink, which was not strong. It couldn't be that. "Do you take dope or something?" Mrs. Barrows asked coldly. "Heroin," said Mr. Martin. "I'll be coked to the gills[42] when I bump that old buzzard off."[43] "Mr. Martin!" she shouted, getting to her feet. "That will be all of that. You must go at once." Mr. Martin took another swallow of his drink. He tapped his cigarette out in the ashtray and put the pack of Camels on the coffee table. Then he got up. She stood glaring at him. He walked over and put on his hat and coat. "Not a word about this," he said, and laid an index finger against his lips. All Mrs. Barrows could bring out was "Really!" Mr. Martin put his hand on the doorknob. "I'm sitting in the catbird seat," he said. He stuck his tongue out at her and left. Nobody saw him go.

Mr. Martin got to his apartment, walking, well before eleven. No one saw him go in. He had two glasses of milk after brushing his teeth, and he felt elated. It wasn't tipsiness,[44] because he hadn't been tipsy. Anyway, the walk had worn off all effects of the whiskey. He got in bed and read a magazine for a while. He was asleep before midnight.

Mr. Martin got to the office at eight-thirty the next morning, as usual. At a quarter to nine, Ulgine Barrows, who had never before arrived at work before ten, swept into his office. "I'm reporting to Mr. Fitweiler now!" she shouted. "If he turns you over to the police, it's no more than you deserve!" Mr. Martin gave her a look of shocked surprise. "I beg your pardon?" he said. Mrs. Barrows snorted and bounced out of the room, leaving Miss Paird and Joey Hart staring after her. "What's the matter with that old devil now?" asked Miss Paird. "I have no idea," said Mr. Martin, resuming his work. The other two looked at him and then at each other. Miss Paird got up and went out. She walked slowly past the closed door of Mr. Fitweiler's office. Mrs. Barrows was yelling inside, but she was not braying. Miss Paird could not hear what the woman was saying. She went back to her desk.

---

41 **"Here's nuts to that old windbag, Fitweiler"** a disrespectful expression suggesting that his boss talks too much

42 **coked to the gills** filled with drugs (slang)

43 **bump that old buzzard off** kill that horrible man

44 **tipsiness** slight drunkenness

Forty-five minutes later, Mrs. Barrows left the president's office and **230** went into her own, shutting the door. It wasn't until half an hour later that Mr. Fitweiler sent for Mr. Martin. The head of the filing department, neat, quiet, attentive, stood in front of the old man's desk. Mr. Fitweiler was pale and nervous. He took his glasses off and twiddled them. He made a small, bruffing sound in his throat. "Martin," he said, "you have **235** been with us more than twenty years." "Twenty-two, sir," said Mr. Martin. "In that time," pursued the president, "your work and your—uh—manner have been exemplary." "I trust so, sir," said Mr. Martin. "I have understood, Martin," said Mr. Fitweiler, "that you have never taken a drink or smoked." "That is correct, sir," said Mr. Martin. "Ah, yes." Mr. Fitweiler **240** polished his glasses. "You may describe what you did after leaving the office yesterday, Martin," he said. Mr. Martin allowed less than a second for his bewildered pause. "Certainly, sir," he said, "I walked home. Then I went to Schrafft's for dinner. Afterward I walked home again. I went to bed early, sir, and read a magazine for a while. I was asleep before **245** eleven." "Ah, yes," said Mr. Fitweiler again. He was silent for a moment, searching for the proper words to say to the head of the filing department. "Mrs. Barrows," he said finally, "Mrs. Barrows has worked hard, Martin, very hard. It grieves me to report that she has suffered a severe breakdown. It has taken the form of a persecution complex **250** accompanied by distressing hallucinations."[45] "I am very sorry, sir," said Mr. Martin. "Mrs. Barrows is under the delusion,"[46] continued Mr. Fitweiler, "that you visited her last evening and behaved yourself in an—uh—unseemly[47] manner." He raised his hand to silence Mr. Martin's little pained outcry. "It is the nature of these psychological diseases," Mr. **255** Fitweiler said, "to fix upon the least likely and most innocent party as the—uh—source of persecution. These matters are not for the lay[48] mind to grasp, Martin. I've just had my psychiatrist, Dr. Fitch, on the phone. He would not, of course, commit himself, but he made enough generalizations to substantiate my suspicions. I suggested to Mrs. **260** Barrows, when she had completed her—uh—story to me this morning, that she visit Dr. Fitch, for I suspected a condition at once. She flew, I regret to say, into a rage, and demanded—uh—requested that I call you on the carpet.[49] You may not know, Martin, but Mrs. Barrows had planned a reorganization of your department—subject to my approval, of **265** course, subject to my approval. This brought you, rather than anyone else, to her mind—but again that is a phenomenon for Dr. Fitch and not for us. So, Martin, I am afraid Mrs. Barrows' usefulness here is at an end." "I am dreadfully sorry, sir," said Mr. Martin.

It was at this point that the door to the office blew open with the **270** suddenness of a gas-main explosion and Mrs. Barrows catapulted through

---

45 **hallucinations** fantastic images
46 **is under the delusion** falsely believes
47 **unseemly** improper

48 **lay** amateur, not professional
49 **call you on the carpet** criticize you severely

it. "Is the little rat denying it?" she screamed. "He can't get away with that!" Mr. Martin got up and moved discreetly to a point beside Mr. Fitweiler's chair. "You drank and smoked at my apartment," she bawled[50] at Mr. Martin, "and you know it! You called Mr. Fitweiler an old windbag and said you were going to blow him up when you got coked to the gills on your heroin!" She stopped yelling to catch her breath and a new glint came into her popping eyes. "If you weren't such a drab, ordinary little man," she said, "I'd think you'd planned it all. Sticking your tongue out, saying you were sitting in the catbird seat, because you thought no one would believe me when I told it! My God, it's really too perfect!" She brayed loudly and hysterically, and the fury was on her again. She glared at Mr. Fitweiler. "Can't you see how he has tricked us, you old fool? Can't you see his little game?" But Mr. Fitweiler had been surreptitiously[51] pressing all the buttons under the top of his desk and employees of F & S began pouring into the room. "Stockton," said Mr. Fitweiler, "you and Fishbein will take Mrs. Barrows to her home. Mrs. Powell, you will go with them." Stockton, who had played a little football in high school, blocked Mrs. Barrows as she made for[52] Mr. Martin. It took him and Fishbein together to force her out of the door into the hall, crowded with stenographers and office boys. She was still screaming imprecations at Mr. Martin, tangled and contradictory imprecations. The hubbub finally died out down the corridor.

275

280

285

290

"I regret that this has happened," said Mr. Fitweiler. "I shall ask you to dismiss it from your mind, Martin." "Yes, sir," said Mr. Martin, anticipating his chief's "That will be all" by moving to the door. "I will dismiss it." He went out and shut the door, and his step was light and quick in the hall. When he entered his department he had slowed down to his customary gait, and he walked quietly across the room to the W20 file, wearing a look of studious concentration.

295

300

---

50 **bawled** shouted very loudly
51 **surreptitiously** secretly
52 **made for** attempted to attack

PART 1 First Reading

A   Thinking About the Story

Did you sympathize with Mr. Martin's antagonism toward Mrs. Barrows? Do you think Mrs. Barrows did anything wrong? Explain your answers.

B   Understanding the Plot

1. What is Mr. Martin planning to do when he buys his unaccustomed pack of cigarettes?

2. What does Mr. Fitweiler's reference to Mr. Martin—"Man is fallible but Martin isn't"— tell us about Mr. Martin's character? (line 19)

3. What animals does Mr. Martin compare Mrs. Barrows to? What do these animals have in common?

4. What is the situation of a baseball player who is "sitting in the catbird seat"? How does the comparison that he is "like a batter with three balls and no strikes on him" (lines 47–48) help reinforce your answer?

5. Why is it important to the success of Mr. Martin's plan that he has "maintained always an outward appearance of polite tolerance" toward Mrs. Barrows? (line 53)

6. What exactly does Mr. Martin accuse Mrs. Barrows of doing?

7. How did Mrs. Barrows initially come to the attention of Mr. Fitweiler?

8. When did Mr. Martin decide to take action against Mrs. Barrows?

9. Why is it important for Mr. Martin to follow his routine on the day he plans to "rub out" Mrs. Barrows?

10. What is the "red herring" Mr. Martin drags across the trail? (line 121) What is the purpose of this red herring?

11. Why do the lights in Mrs. Barrows's apartment building make Mr. Martin uncomfortable?

12. Why does he keep his gloves on but take his hat and coat off?

13. What goes wrong with Mr. Martin's scheme?

14. What idea "sprouted" and then began "to bloom" in Mr. Martin's mind? (lines 185–188) How does he implement this idea?

15. What does Mr. Fitweiler decide to do about Mrs. Barrows? How did he come to that decision?

PART 2 Second Reading

A Exploring Themes

You are now ready to reread "The Catbird Seat." Look at how Thurber draws Mr. Martin with minute descriptive details and sets him against Mrs. Barrows in an archetypal battle of the sexes.

1. When Mr. Martin reviews his case against Mrs. Barrows (lines 21–100), what role does he adopt for himself in his imagination, and in what setting does he see himself playing this role? What particular words and expressions does he use to help him sustain this imaginary role?
2. What kind of relationship between men and women is Thurber poking fun at in the story?
3. What makes this story funny? Give examples from the story, and explain the different elements Thurber uses to create the humor.
4. From reading "The Catbird Seat," what can you infer about Thurber's attitude to modernization? Justify your answer.
5. What parallels does Thurber draw between the characters of Mr. Fitweiler and Mr. Martin?

B Analyzing the Author's Style

For more information on the literary terms in this section, turn to the explanations of *understatement* (page 309) and *humor* (page 303).

UNDERSTATEMENT AND HUMOR

In creating Mr. Martin, James Thurber has his character constantly understate or de-emphasize his position in order to create **humor** through the contrast between what he says and the actual dramatic situation he is describing. **Understatement** also serves to reinforce the aspects of Mr. Martin's personality crucial to his makeup. In fact, the males in general are given to understatement in this story, a trait that unites them in comic brotherhood against the loud, exaggerated ranting of Mrs. Barrows.

For example, when we first encounter Mr. Martin, he is thinking about his decision to *rub out* Mrs. Barrows. (line 8) Taken literally, *rub out* means "erase a mistake," as a clerk might erase a wrong entry in a file. Although Mr. Martin is planning to kill Mrs. Barrows, he cannot bring himself to use violent language.

1. In what way is "project" an understatement? (line 14) What word could be substituted?

2. Mr. Martin describes the immediate consequences of Mrs. Barrows's appointment as "confusion got its foot in the door." (line 69) What confusion is he referring to here? What more direct phrase could he have used?

3. Explain Mr. Roberts's understated comment to Mr. Fitweiler, and say what he really meant to convey. (line 73) What does Mr. Fitweiler reply? Convey his answer in more forceful language.

4. In a deliberate and humorous reversal, Mr. Martin unexpectedly sheds his naturally understated speech and talks very plainly in the style of Mrs. Barrows when he says:

   a. "Here's nuts to that old windbag, Fitweiler." (line 196)

   b. "I'll be coked to the gills when I bump that old buzzard off." (lines 203–204)

   c. "I'm sitting in the catbird seat." (line 211)

   How might he have phrased these three sentences in his naturally understated manner?

5. When Mr. Fitweiler tells Mr. Martin that Mrs. Barrows has accused him of behaving in an "unseemly manner" (line 254) and has demanded that he be "called on the carpet" (lines 263–264), what do you think she really said?

C   Judging for Yourself

Express yourself as personally as you like in your answers to the following questions.

1. Do you think that Thurber was fair to Mrs. Barrows in the way he portrayed her? Justify your answer.

2. In your view, did F & S appear to need some restructuring? How would you characterize the business?

3. Were you confident that Mr. Martin would triumph over Mrs. Barrows? Explain your answer.

4. Did you feel that Mr. Martin acted ethically toward Mrs. Barrows at the end?

5. What do you think life at F & S will be like in the future?

D Making Connections

1. How is progress viewed in your culture? Do you think that all progress is automatically good?

2. If a woman has a domineering personality, how is she viewed in your country? Are the same standards applied to an aggressive man?

3. What are the main reasons workers are fired in your country? Discuss how you would feel if you were fired from a job. How do you think you would handle it?

4. Have you ever tried to change something that you felt was wrong? Did you succeed?

5. Have sporting terms influenced your language? If your answer is yes, give as many examples as you can.

E Debate

Debate this proposition:

The end justifies the means.

PART 3 Focus on Language

A Noun Clauses

A **noun clause** is a dependent clause that functions as a noun. It can act as either the subject of a clause or as the object of a transitive verb or a preposition. Since it is a dependent clause, it cannot stand alone in a sentence but must be accompanied by an independent (main) clause, and like all clauses it has its own subject and verb.

> *He mentioned **that Mr. Munson's department had been "a little disrupted"**. . . .* (lines 72–73)

The noun clause is the object of the transitive verb *mentioned*.

> ***That Mr. Munson's department had been "a little disrupted"** came as no surprise to the staff at F & S.*

The noun clause is the subject of the verb *came*.

A noun clause may also come after a clause beginning with the neutral *it*.

> *. . . it was generally known **that Mr. Martin did not smoke** . . .*
> (line 6)

This sentence could also be written in the following way:

> ***That Mr. Martin did not smoke*** *was generally known.*

The following examples from "The Catbird Seat" indicate other ways noun clauses can be used.

1. Noun clauses are most commonly introduced by the word *that*, which may sometimes be omitted.

   > *"You called Mr. Fitweiler an old windbag and said **you were going to blow him up when you got coked to the gills on your heroin!"** (lines 275–277)

   The noun clause is the object of the verb *said*. It also includes the dependent adverbial clause *when you got coked to the gills on your heroin*.

2. Noun clauses may also be introduced by the following words: *whether, if, where, when, why, how, who, whom, whose, what,* and *which*.

   > *"Can't you see **how he has tricked us, you old fool?"*** (line 283)

   The noun clause is the object of the verb *see*.

   Note: The above list of words may also introduce adjectival and adverbial clauses. For information on and practice with adjectival clauses, see page 80; for adverbial clauses, see page 242.

3. If one noun clause is linked to another clause by *and, but,* or *or,* the second clause is also a noun clause.

   > *Mrs. Barrows said **that Mr. Martin had visited her last evening** and **had behaved himself in an unseemly manner.***

   The two noun clauses are the object of the verb *said*.

Follow the instructions concerning the following sentences from the story.

1. It was fortunate, he reflected as he passed on to the important charges against Mrs. Barrows, that he had stood up under it so well. (lines 51–52)
   a. Underline the noun clause.
   b. Which clause does it relate to?
   c. Rewrite the sentence, placing the noun clause at the beginning.

2. "Why, I even believe you like the woman," Miss Paird, his other assistant, had once said to him. (lines 53–55)
   a. Underline the noun clause.
   b. What word is missing from the noun clause but is implied?
   c. Which clause is the noun clause dependent on?
   d. Is the noun clause the subject or the object of the verb in that clause?

3. It was at this point that the door to the office blew open with the suddenness of a gas-main explosion and Mrs. Barrows catapulted through it. (lines 270–272)
   a. How many noun clauses are in this sentence? Underline them.
   b. What word is omitted but understood? Where would you place it?
   c. Which clause do the noun clauses relate to?

4. "You may describe what you did, after leaving the office yesterday, Martin," he said. (lines 241–242)
   a. Underline the noun clause.
   b. Which clause does it relate to?
   c. Is it the subject or the object of the clause?

5. It was his idea to puff a few puffs on a Camel (after the rubbing-out), stub it out in the ashtray holding her lipstick-stained Luckies, and thus drag a small red herring across the trail. (lines 119–122)
   a. Are there any noun clauses in this sentence?
   b. If your answer is yes, underline them/it. If your answer is no, explain why not.

6. Make up five noun clauses of your own relating to the story, using the previous examples as models. Start your noun clauses with the following words: *that, who, where, why,* and *how.* At least one noun clause should be the subject of the main clause and one the object, and one should come after the neutral *it.* One sentence should contain two noun clauses.

B   Building Vocabulary Skills

1. The following two-word verbs appear in "The Catbird Seat."

   went over (line 12)
   worked out (line 15)
   stood up (line 52)
   ran into (line 136)
   turn (you) over (line 221)

The above verbs have at least two meanings. Find the verbs in the story and in your dictionary. Then complete the following sentences with the correct expression from the list. You will use each expression twice: once as it is found in the story and once with an alternate meaning. On the line at the end of each sentence, write a synonym for the expression to show you understand it.

   a. She often _____ at her gym during her lunch break. _____

   b. He _____ his teacher when he least expected to see her. _____

   c. If I catch you shoplifting again, I'm going to _____ to the police.

   _____

   d. The employee _____ her proposal at least twice before submitting it to her boss.

   _____

   e. After drinking too many beers at the party, the driver _____ a parked car. _____

   f. No matter how many times I tried to introduce my friend to eligible partners, it never _____ .

   _____

   g. When my mother was a child, all the students _____ when the teacher entered the room. _____

   h. In order to prevent you from getting sores, I must _____ in your bed every two hours.

   _____

   i. This house _____ in spite of the two hurricanes that battered it last season.

   _____

   j. When the play _____ with the first-night audience, the producers knew they had a hit on their hands.

   _____

2. Thurber makes use of two expressions in "The Catbird Seat" that contain the color red. Mr. Martin fondly remembers a special occasion as a *red-letter day*. (line 111) He also thinks it would be a good idea to drag a *red herring* along the trail and so divert the police's suspicions from himself. (line 121)

Use your dictionary to find out the meaning of the following expressions. Then write sentences using each expression appropriately.

red-blooded	a green thumb
out of the blue	yellow journalism
in the black	white-collar

Can you add any expressions of your own?

3. The following expressions from the story are commonly used in a legal context.

crimes (line 32)	charges (line 51)
peccadillos (line 33)	gavel (line 56)
enter an objection (line 34)	blatant (line 57)
sustain the objection (line 34)	summing up (line 81)
witness (line 35)	death penalty (line 100)

With a partner, complete the paragraphs below with the appropriate expressions. Use each expression only once.

The judge formally read the _____ to the defendant. "These are serious _____, not mere _____," he said sternly. "You could even get the _____." At this, the courtroom erupted in noisy protest. "Order in the court," shouted the judge as he hammered on his table with his _____.
The prosecuting attorney then began his examination of the first _____.

"Your Honor," interjected the defense counsel, "I wish to _____. The prosecutor is harassing this person and is showing a _____ disregard for the rules."

"I will _____," said the judge. "Now let's get on with the case. I want the _____ by the end of the week at the latest so that we can all get home in time for the holidays."

PART 4 Writing Activities

1. Have you ever been the victim of a domineering personality? Perhaps it was at work, at school, or in the family. Write an essay of two pages outlining your relationship to the person, and say what he or she did to you. Describe how you felt and what measures you took to deal with the situation.

2. "Like attracts like" or "Opposites attract." Which of these statements is true for you? Write a two-page essay considering the advantages or disadvantages of your choice when it comes to personal relationships. State whether you think the advantages outweigh the disadvantages or vice versa. Try to include various types of noun clauses in your piece.

3. From William Shakespeare's play *The Taming of the Shrew* to the current animated TV program *The Simpsons,* many books, movies, TV programs, and cartoons have dealt with the war between the sexes. Write an essay of two pages analyzing how men and women are presented in a work you have seen or read about the gender war. Say whether you think a war of the sexes is the natural outcome of the society we live in.

4. In both "The Boarding House" (page 143) and "The Catbird Seat," a trap is set that is crucial to the success of a central character's scheme. In an essay, compare and contrast the plots of the two stories and their main characters, bringing out their similarities and differences.

20

Everyday Use

ALICE WALKER (b. 1944)

Born in Georgia, the eighth child of poor tenant-farmer parents, Alice Walker soon demonstrated her exceptional abilities. After graduating as valedictorian of her local high school, Walker went on to study at Spelman and Sarah Lawrence colleges. She became involved in the civil rights movement in the South, working to register black voters, a time she recreated in her novel *Meridian* (1976). Over the years her political activism has embraced feminism, environmentalism, racism, the antinuclear movement, and female genital mutilation in Africa.

Walker is an accomplished poet, novelist, short-story writer, essayist, and biographer. Her first book of poems, *Once,* was published in 1968, but it was her novel *The Color Purple* (1982) that catapulted her to fame. She won the Pulitzer Prize for it in 1983. Steven Spielberg went on to make a movie of the book. Her two collections of short stories, *In Love and Trouble* (1973) and *You Can't Keep a Good Woman Down* (1982), focus on the twin ills of sexism and racism that have plagued black women. Her novel *By the Light of My Father's Smile* (1998) celebrates the centrality of human sexuality, while *Now Is the Time to Open Your Heart* (2004) centers on a woman's journey into self.

EVERYDAY USE

FOR YOUR GRANDMAMA

Family tensions come to a head in a dispute over the ownership of some quilts.

I will wait for her in the yard that Maggie and I made so clean and wavy yesterday afternoon. A yard like this is more comfortable than most people know. It is not just a yard. It is like an extended living room. When the hard clay is swept clean as a floor and the fine sand around the edges lined with tiny, irregular grooves, anyone can come and sit and look up 5 into the elm tree and wait for the breezes that never come inside the house.

Maggie will be nervous until after her sister goes: she will stand hopelessly in corners, homely[1] and ashamed of the burn scars down her arms and legs, eying her sister with a mixture of envy and awe. She thinks her sister has held life always in the palm of one hand,[2] that "no" is a 10 word the world never learned to say to her.

You've no doubt seen those TV shows where the child who has "made it" is confronted, as a surprise, by her own mother and father, tottering[3] in weakly from backstage. (A pleasant surprise, of course: What would they do if parent and child came on the show only to curse out 15 and insult each other?) On TV mother and child embrace and smile into each other's faces. Sometimes the mother and father weep, the child wraps them in her arms and leans across the table to tell how she would not have made it without their help. I have seen these programs.

Sometimes I dream a dream in which Dee and I are suddenly brought 20 together on a TV program of this sort. Out of a dark and soft-seated limousine I am ushered into a bright room filled with many people. There I meet a smiling, gray, sporty man like Johnny Carson[4] who shakes my hand and tells me what a fine girl I have. Then we are on the stage and Dee is embracing me with tears in her eyes. She pins on my dress a large orchid, 25 even though she has told me once that she thinks orchids are tacky[5] flowers.

In real life I am a large, big-boned woman with rough, man-working hands. In the winter I wear flannel nightgowns to bed and overalls during the day. I can kill and clean a hog as mercilessly as a man. My fat keeps me hot in zero weather. I can work outside all day, breaking ice to get 30 water for washing; I can eat pork liver cooked over the open fire minutes after it comes steaming from the hog. One winter I knocked a bull calf straight in the brain between the eyes with a sledge hammer and had the meat hung up to chill before nightfall. But of course all this does not show on television. I am the way my daughter would want me to be: a 35

---

1 **homely** unattractive
2 **has held life always in the palm of one hand**
   has always gotten what she wants from life
3 **tottering** walking unsteadily

4 **Johnny Carson** an American comedian, host of the *Tonight Show* on television from 1962 to 1992
5 **tacky** vulgar, tasteless

hundred pounds lighter, my skin like an uncooked barley[6] pancake. My hair glistens in the hot bright lights. Johnny Carson has much to do to keep up with my quick and witty tongue.

But that is a mistake. I know even before I wake up. Who ever knew a Johnson with a quick tongue? Who can even imagine me looking a strange white man in the eye?[7] It seems to me I have talked to them always with one foot raised in flight, with my head turned in whichever way is farthest from them. Dee, though. She would always look anyone in the eye. Hesitation was no part of her nature.

"How do I look, Mama?" Maggie says, showing just enough of her thin body enveloped in pink skirt and red blouse for me to know she's there, almost hidden by the door.

"Come out into the yard," I say.

Have you ever seen a lame animal, perhaps a dog run over by some careless person rich enough to own a car, sidle up[8] to someone who is ignorant enough to be kind to him? That is the way my Maggie walks. She has been like this, chin on chest, eyes on ground, feet in shuffle,[9] ever since the fire that burned the other house to the ground.

Dee is lighter than Maggie, with nicer hair and a fuller figure. She's a woman now, though sometimes I forget. How long ago was it that the other house burned? Ten, twelve years? Sometimes I can still hear the flames and feel Maggie's arms sticking to me, her hair smoking and her dress falling off her in little black papery flakes. Her eyes seemed stretched open, blazed open by the flames reflected in them. And Dee. I see her standing off under the sweet gum tree she used to dig gum out of; a look of concentration on her face as she watched the last dingy gray board of the house fall in toward the red-hot brick chimney. Why don't you do a dance around the ashes? I'd wanted to ask her. She had hated the house that much.

I used to think she hated Maggie, too. But that was before we raised the money, the church and me, to send her to Augusta to school. She used to read to us without pity; forcing words, lies, other folks' habits, whole lives upon us two, sitting trapped and ignorant underneath her voice. She washed us in a river of make-believe,[10] burned us with a lot of knowledge we didn't necessarily need to know. Pressed us to her with the serious way she read, to shove us away at just the moment, like dimwits,[11] we seemed about to understand.

Dee wanted nice things. A yellow organdy dress to wear to her graduation from high school; black pumps[12] to match a green suit she'd made from an old suit somebody gave me. She was determined to stare down[13] any disaster in her efforts. Her eyelids would not flicker for

---

6 **barley** a honey-colored grain
7 **looking a strange white man in the eye**
   looking directly at a white man I didn't know
8 **sidle up** move sideways, trying not to be seen
9 **feet in shuffle** very slow walk, barely lifting
   the feet up

10 **make-believe** pretense
11 **dimwits** stupid people
12 **pumps** shoes
13 **stare down** stare until the other person looks
   down

minutes at a time. Often I fought off the temptation to shake her. At sixteen she had a style of her own: and knew what style was.

I never had an education myself. After second grade the school was closed down. Don't ask me why: in 1927 colored asked fewer questions than they do now. Sometimes Maggie reads to me. She stumbles along[14] good-naturedly but can't see well. She knows she is not bright. Like good looks and money, quickness passed her by. She will marry John Thomas (who has mossy teeth in an earnest face) and then I'll be free to sit here and I guess just sing church songs to myself. Although I never was a good singer. Never could carry a tune.[15] I was always better at a man's job. I used to love to milk till I was hooked in the side in '49. Cows are soothing and slow and don't bother you, unless you try to milk them the wrong way.

I have deliberately turned my back on the house. It is three rooms, just like the one that burned, except the roof is tin; they don't make shingle roofs anymore. There are no real windows, just some holes cut in the sides, like the portholes in a ship, but not round and not square, with rawhide[16] holding the shutters up on the outside. This house is in a pasture, too, like the other one. No doubt when Dee sees it she will want to tear it down. She wrote me once that no matter where we "choose" to live, she will manage to come see us. But she will never bring her friends. Maggie and I thought about this and Maggie asked me. "Mama, when did Dee ever *have* any friends?"

She had a few. Furtive boys in pink shirts hanging about on washday after school. Nervous girls who never laughed. Impressed with her they worshiped the well-turned phrase,[17] the cute shape, the scalding humor that erupted like bubbles in lye.[18] She read to them.

When she was courting[19] Jimmy T she didn't have much time to pay to us, but turned all her faultfinding power on him. He *flew* to marry a cheap[20] city girl from a family of ignorant flashy people. She hardly had time to recompose herself.

When she comes I will meet—but there they are!

Maggie attempts to make a dash for the house, in her shuffling way, but I stay[21] her with my hand. "Come back here," I say. And she stops and tries to dig a well in the sand with her toe.

It is hard to see them clearly through the strong sun. But even the first glimpse of leg out of the car tells me it is Dee. Her feet were always neat-looking, as if God himself had shaped them with a certain style. From the other side of the car comes a short, stocky man. Hair is all over his head a foot long and hanging from his chin like a kinky[22] mule tail. I hear Maggie suck in her breath. "Uhnnnh," is what it sounds like. Like when you see the wriggling end of a snake just in front of your foot on the road. "Uhnnnh."

---

14 **stumbles along** hesitates and mispronounces
15 **carry a tune** sing in tune
16 **rawhide** untreated skin of an animal
17 **well-turned phrase** an apt phrase
18 **lye** a strong alkaline solution used for washing
19 **courting** going out with
20 **cheap** vulgar
21 **stay** stop
22 **kinky** tightly twisted, curled

Dee next. A dress down to the ground, in this hot weather. A dress so loud it hurts my eyes. There are yellows and oranges enough to throw back the light of the sun. I feel my whole face warming from the heat waves it throws out. Earrings gold, too, and hanging down to her shoulders. Bracelets dangling and making noises when she moves her arm up to shake the folds of the dress out of her armpits. The dress is loose and flows, and as she walks closer, I like it. I hear Maggie go "Uhnnnh" again. It is her sister's hair. It stands straight up like the wool on a sheep. It is black as night and around the edges are two long pigtails that rope about like small lizards disappearing behind her ears.

"Wa-su-zo-Tean-o!" she says, coming on in that gliding way the dress makes her move. The short stocky fellow with the hair to his navel is all grinning and he follows up with "Asalamalakim, my mother and sister!" He moves to hug Maggie but she falls back, right up against the back of my chair. I feel her trembling there and when I look up I see the perspiration falling off her chin.

"Don't get up," says Dee. Since I am stout it takes something of a push. You can see me trying to move a second or two before I make it. She turns, showing white heels through her sandals, and goes back to the car. Out she peeks next with a Polaroid. She stoops down quickly and lines up picture after picture of me sitting there in front of the house with Maggie cowering[23] behind me. She never takes a shot without making sure the house is included. When a cow comes nibbling around the edge of the yard she snaps it and me and Maggie *and* the house. Then she puts the Polaroid in the back seat of the car, and comes up and kisses me on the forehead.

Meanwhile Asalamalakim is going through motions with Maggie's hand.[24] Maggie's hand is as limp as a fish, and probably as cold, despite the sweat, and she keeps trying to pull it back. It looks like Asalamalakim wants to shake hands but wants to do it fancy. Or maybe he don't know how people shake hands. Anyhow, he soon gives up on Maggie.

"Well," I say. "Dee."

"No, Mama," she says. "Not 'Dee,' Wangero Leewanika Kemanjo!"

"What happened to 'Dee'?" I wanted to know.

"She's dead," Wangero said. "I couldn't bear it any longer, being named after the people who oppress me."

"You know as well as me you was named after your aunt Dicie," I said. Dicie is my sister. She named Dee. We called her "Big Dee" after Dee was born."

"But who was *she* named after?" asked Wangero.

"I guess after Grandma Dee," I said.

"And who was she named after?" asked Wangero.

"Her mother," I said, and saw Wangero was getting tired. "That's about as far back as I can trace it," I said. Though, in fact, I probably could have carried it back beyond the Civil War through the branches.

23 **cowering** bending low in fear
24 **going through motions with Maggie's hand**
   shaking Maggie's hand unenthusiastically

"Well," said Asalamalakin, "there you are."

"Uhnnnh," I heard Maggie say.

"There I was not," I said, "before 'Dicie' cropped up[25] in our family, so why should I try to trace it that far back?"

He just stood there grinning, looking down on me like somebody 165 inspecting a Model A car. Every once in a while he and Wangero sent eye signals over my head.

"How do you pronounce this name?" I asked.

"You don't have to call me by it if you don't want to," said Wangero.

"Why shouldn't I?" I asked. "If that's what you want us to call you, 170 we'll call you."

"I know it might sound awkward at first," said Wangero.

"I'll get used to it," I said. "Ream it out again."[26]

Well, soon we got the name out of the way. Asalamalakim had a name twice as long and three times as hard. After I tripped over it two 175 or three times he told me to just call him Hakim-a-barber. I wanted to ask him was he a barber, but I didn't really think he was, so I didn't ask.

"You must belong to those beef-cattle peoples down the road," I said. They said "Asalamalakim" when they met you, too, but they didn't shake hands. Always too busy: feeding the cattle, fixing the fences, putting up 180 salt-lick shelters, throwing down hay. When the white folks poisoned some of the herd the men stayed up all night with rifles in their hands. I walked a mile and a half just to see the sight.

Hakim-a-barber said, "I accept some of their doctrines, but farming and raising cattle is not my style." (They didn't tell me, and I didn't ask, 185 whether Wangero (Dee) had really gone and married him.)

We sat down to eat and right away he said he didn't eat collards[27] and pork was unclean. Wangero, though, went on through the chitlins[28] and corn bread, the greens and everything else. She talked a blue streak[29] over the sweet potatoes. Everything delighted her. Even the fact 190 that we still used the benches her daddy made for the table when we couldn't afford to buy chairs.

"Oh, Mama!" she cried. Then turned to Hakim-a-barber. "I never knew how lovely these benches are. You can feel the rump[30] prints," she said, running her hands underneath her and along the bench. Then she 195 gave a sigh and her hand closed over Grandma Dee's butter dish. "That's it!" she said. "I knew there was something I wanted to ask you if I could have." She jumped up from the table and went over in the corner where the churn[31] stood, the milk in it clabber[32] by now. She looked at the churn and looked at it. 200

---

25 **cropped up** appeared suddenly
26 **Ream it out again.** Say it again. (literally, squeeze out)
27 **collards** a leafy green vegetable popular in the South
28 **chitlins** traditional Southern African-American dish made from pigs' intestines
29 **talked a blue streak** spoke a lot without stopping
30 **rump** backside
31 **churn** a vessel used to make butter
32 **clabber** sour milk

"This churn top is what I need," she said. "Didn't Uncle Buddy whittle [33] it out of a tree you all used to have?"

"Yes," I said.

"Uh-huh," she said happily. "And I want the dasher, [34] too."

"Uncle Buddy whittle that, too?" asked the barber.

Dee (Wangero) looked at me.

"Aunt Dee's first husband whittled the dash," said Maggie so low you almost couldn't hear her. "His name was Henry, but they called him Stash."

"Maggie's brain is like an elephant's," Wangero said, laughing. "I can use the churn top as a centerpiece for the alcove table," she said, sliding a plate over the churn, "and I'll think of something artistic to do with the dasher."

When she finished wrapping the dasher the handle stuck out. I took it for a moment in my hands. You didn't even have to look close to see where hands pushing the dasher up and down to make butter had left a kind of sink in the wood. In fact, there were a lot of small sinks; you could see where thumbs and fingers had sunk into the wood. It was beautiful light yellow wood, from a tree that grew in the yard where Big Dee and Stash had lived.

After dinner Dee (Wangero) went to the trunk at the foot of my bed and started rifling [35] through it. Maggie hung back [36] in the kitchen over the dishpan. Out came Wangero with two quilts. They had been pieced [37] by Grandma Dee and then Big Dee and me had hung them on the quilt frames on the front porch and quilted them. One was in the Lone Star [38] pattern. The other was Walk Around the Mountain. [39] In both of them were scraps [40] of dresses Grandma Dee had worn fifty and more years ago. Bits and pieces of Grandpa Jarrell's Paisley shirts. And one teeny faded blue piece, about the size of a penny matchbox, that was from Great Grandpa Ezra's uniform that he wore in the Civil War.

"Mama," Wangero said sweet as a bird. "Can I have these old quilts?"

I heard something fall in the kitchen, and a minute later the kitchen door slammed.

"Why don't you take one or two of the others?" I asked. "These old things was just done by me and Big Dee from some tops your grandma pieced before she died."

"No," said Wangero. "I don't want those. They are stitched around the borders by machine."

"That'll make them last better," I said.

"That's not the point," said Wangero. "These are all pieces of dresses Grandma used to wear. She did all this stitching by hand. Imagine!" She held the quilts securely in her arms, stroking them.

---

33 **whittle** carve
34 **dasher** the part of the churn that stirs up the milk
35 **rifling** searching vigorously
36 **hung back** held [herself] back
37 **pieced** sewn by joining together pieces of material
38 **Lone Star** a special quilting pattern
39 **Walk Around the Mountain** a special quilting pattern
40 **scraps** small pieces of material

"Some of the pieces, like those lavender ones, come from old clothes her mother handed down [41] to her," I said, moving up to touch the quilts. Dee (Wangero) moved back just enough so that I couldn't reach the quilts. They already belonged to her.

"Imagine!" she breathed again, clutching them closely to her bosom.   245

"The truth is," I said, "I promised to give them quilts to Maggie, for when she marries John Thomas."

She gasped like a bee had stung her.

"Maggie can't appreciate these quilts!" she said. "She'd probably be backward enough to put them to everyday use."   250

"I reckon she would," I said. "God knows I been saving 'em for long enough with nobody using 'em. I hope she will!" I didn't want to bring up [42] how I had offered Dee (Wangero) a quilt when she went away to college. Then she had told me they were old-fashioned, out of style.

"But they're *priceless*!" [43] she was saying now, furiously; for she has a   255
temper. "Maggie would put them on the bed and in five years they'd be in rags. Less than that!"

"She can always make some more," I said. "Maggie knows how to quilt."

Dee (Wangero) looked at me with hatred. "You just will not   260
understand. The point is these quilts, *these* quilts!"

"Well," I said, stumped. [44] "What would *you* do with them?"

"Hang them," she said. As if that was the only thing you *could* do with quilts.

Maggie by now was standing in the door. I could almost hear the   265
sound her feet made as they scraped over each other.

"She can have them, Mama," she said, like somebody used to never winning anything, or having anything reserved for her. "I can 'member Grandma Dee without the quilts."

I looked at her hard. She had filled her bottom lip with checkerberry   270
snuff [45] and it gave her face a kind of dopey, hangdog look. It was Grandma Dee and Big Dee who taught her how to quilt herself. She stood there with her scarred hands hidden in the folds of her skirt. She looked at her sister with something like fear but she wasn't mad at her. This was Maggie's portion. This was the way she knew God to work.   275

When I looked at her like that something hit me in the top of my head and ran down to the soles of my feet. Just like when I'm in church and the spirit of God touches me and I get happy and shout. I did something I never had done before: hugged Maggie to me, then dragged her on into the room, snatched the quilts out of Miss Wangero's hands   280
and dumped them into Maggie's lap. Maggie just sat there on my bed with her mouth open.

---

41 **handed down** passed on
42 **bring up** mention
43 **priceless** so valuable no price can be put on them
44 **stumped** very puzzled
45 **checkerberry snuff** finely crushed tobacco

"Take one or two of the others," I said to Dee.

But she turned without a word and went out to Hakim-a-barber.

"You just don't understand," she said, as Maggie and I came out to the car. 285

"What don't I understand?" I wanted to know.

"Your heritage," she said. And then she turned to Maggie, kissed her, and said, "You ought to try to make something of yourself,[46] too, Maggie. It's really a new day for us. But from the way you and Mama still live 290 you'd never know it."

She put on some sunglasses that hid everything above the tip of her nose and her chin.

Maggie smiled; maybe at the sunglasses. But a real smile, not scared. After we watched the car dust settle I asked Maggie to bring me a dip of 295 snuff. And then the two of us sat there just enjoying, until it was time to go in the house and go to bed.

---

46 **make something of yourself** improve yourself

PART 1 First Reading

A   Thinking About the Story

Were you moved by the changing relationship between Maggie and her mother? Did you sympathize with Dee's need to leave her rural life and family? Explain your answers.

B   Understanding the Plot

1. What details depict the family's rural lifestyle? Give as many as possible.
2. How is Dee different from Maggie? List as many ways as you can.
3. In what ways (both stated and implied) is Dee different from her mother in lines 27–44?
4. What is unusual about Dee's behavior on the day of the fire?
5. Is the narrator correct when she thinks: "No doubt when Dee sees it [the house] she will want to tear it down"? (line 93–94) Explain your answer as fully as possible.
6. Why did Jimmy T, the man Dee courted, flee to the city?
7. Why does Dee greet her mother in a strange language, and why has she changed her name to Wangero Leewanika?

8. What is the mother's opinion of Hakim-a-barber? Support your answer as fully as possible.

9. What is the difference between Dee and Hakim-a-barber regarding the meal they ate?

10. Why does Dee want the butter churn? Is it still being used? How much does she know of its history?

11. How has Dee's attitude toward the quilts changed?

12. What does Dee mean when she says to Maggie, "It's really a new day for us"? (line 290)

PART 2 Second Reading

A Exploring Themes

You are now ready to reread "Everyday Use." Consider the ways in which Alice Walker reveals a great deal of psychological, biographical, and physical information about the characters.

1. Explain how the title and the dedication reflect a central theme of the story.

2. In what ways is the TV show the narrator talks about in lines 12–44 relevant to the mother/daughter theme of the story? Explain your answer as fully as possible.

3. How does the discussion between Dee and her mother regarding the origin of Dee's name reflect their different attitudes toward their heritage? What other examples in the story illustrate their differences?

4. What is the effect of breaking the narrative into four parts? How does each part contribute to our understanding of the story?

5. What is Dee searching for in her life? Give as many examples as possible from the text to explain your answer.

6. What do the quilts represent in the story?

B Analyzing the Author's Style

For more information on the literary terms in this section, turn to the explanations of *characterization* (page 298) and *point of view* (page 306).

CHARACTERIZATION: Round Characters

The narrator/mother, Dee, and Maggie are fully fleshed **round characters,** who are presented to us in all their human complexity. We see them filtered through the mother's eyes, with Alice Walker using numerous devices to bring each character alive. In an interesting twist, the narrator analyzes and describes her daughters to us before we meet them in person. The characters' actions, personalities, and physical characteristics are revealed in a mix of scenes set in the near future, present, and past, with each scene unpeeling another aspect of their evolving, complicated, triangular relationship. Unlike with **flat characters,** we cannot always predict with certainty the women's actions or responses as they confront one another on the day of Dee's visit.

Narrator/Mother

The narrator is a tough, self-aware, ironic woman, who depicts herself and her difficult mother/daughter relationship with disarming honesty.

1. Pick out all the descriptions that convey the mother's physical strength.
2. What details point to the tense relationship the mother has had with Dee over the years?
3. The mother may be uneducated due to the discrimination that prevailed in the South, but she is intelligent and perceptive. Give some examples that support this statement.
4. In what important ways does the mother change by the end of the story?

Maggie

We learn from her mother that plain, scarred Maggie has a nervous personality, especially in the presence of her sister, whom she eyes *with a mixture of envy and awe.* (line 9) According to her mother, Maggie believes that her sister is a person who always gets what she wants, that *"no" is a word the world never learned to say to her.* (lines 10–11)

1. Pick out as many descriptions as possible connected with Maggie that reinforce her mother's assessment of Maggie's appearance, personality, and relationship with her sister.
2. In what ways does Maggie embody her heritage?
3. How does Maggie change by the end of the story? What contributes to this change?

Dee

Like Maggie, Dee too is first drawn for us in her absence. Before meeting her, we learn a good deal about her values, her appearance, her past, and her relationship with her mother and sister.

1. Draw up as complete a list as possible to support what we learn about Dee before we ever see her.
2. When Dee steps out of the car, her dress is described in glowing detail. What aspects of Dee's appearance and personality are reflected in her clothing?
3. Given what we know about Dee, does Hakim-a-barber seem a suitable mate for her? Support your answer.
4. In the scene after dinner, which of Dee's actions reinforce Maggie's perception that her sister can always have what she wants?
5. What lesson must Dee learn by the end of her visit?

POINT OF VIEW: First-Person Narration

"Everyday Use" is presented through **first-person narration,** which means that the story is told by a narrator using the pronoun "I." Consequently, the point of view is *partial*, or incomplete, as we see the characters, interpret their actions, and delve into their personalities solely through the eyes of the narrator/mother.

1. Does the fact that the narrator's point of view is limited mean that she is unable to give an unbiased and accurate picture of the characters and events? Justify your answer.
2. Whom is the narrator addressing in lines 12 and 49? Explain your answer.
3. Is the narrator clearly more sympathetic to one character than the other? Explain your answer.
4. What is the tone of the narrator? Give examples to support your answer.
   Note: For information on tone, see page 309.
5. In what ways might the story have been different if narrated through Dee's eyes?

C   Judging for Yourself

Express yourself as personally as you like in your answers to the following questions.

1. Do you sympathize with Dee's drive to improve herself? What kind of life do you think she lives?
2. Do you think Dee is unreasonable in her desire for Maggie and her mother to be different?
3. Is Maggie's life likely to change after her marriage?
4. In your opinion, who should get the quilts—Dee or Maggie? Explain your answer.
5. Is Dee's adoption of an African name and dress likely to satisfy her search for roots?
6. In your view, has the narrator been a good mother? Justify your answer.

D   Making Connections

1. In your culture, how are traditions kept alive?
2. Do people move around a lot in your country? Is mobility considered to be a positive or a negative attribute?
3. Are reality television shows popular in your country? Why? Why not?
4. What foods are considered typical in your culture? Do they have a special significance?

E   Debate

Debate this proposition:

Tradition stands in the way of progress.

PART 3   Focus on Language

A   Prepositional Phrases

A **prepositional phrase** is a preposition followed by a noun or pronoun object and any modifiers. A few of the more common prepositions in English include *after, at, before, during, in, like, of, on, through, under, until,* and *with*. Prepositional phrases almost always have an adverbial or adjectival function. Writers use these phrases to clarify, contextualize, heighten, and sharpen their words. For example, in describing the scene where Maggie is on fire, Walker increases the horror when she writes about *her dress falling off her **in little papery flakes*** (lines 57–58). Here, *in little papery flakes* functions as an adverbial phrase of manner and draws our attention to the severity of Maggie's burns.

In the dream sequence the narrator imagines that she is ushered ***out of a dark and soft-seated limousine . . . into a bright room . . .*** (lines 21–22). In this instance, the two prepositional phrases act as adverbial phrases of place, locating the narrator more firmly in the contrasting locations. Later, Dee's young friends are depicted as *furtive boys **in pink shirts** hanging about **on washday after school*** (lines 98–99). In this sentence, the prepositional phrase *in pink shirts* is used adjectivally to flesh out the description of the boys; two prepositional phrases, *on washday* and *after school*, are used adverbially to position the scene more securely in time.

Note 1: In the expression *hanging about* (line 98), *about* acts as the particle of the two-word verb *hang about*, not as a preposition introducing a prepositional phrase. *About* is an integral part of the idiomatic expression and cannot be omitted without changing the meaning.

Note 2: The preposition *like* can be used adjectivally or adverbially. It is used adjectivally after the verb *to be*, as well as after linking verbs such as *seem* and *look*. For example: *my skin [is] **like an uncooked barley pancake.*** (line 36) Otherwise, it is used adverbially. For example: *[Her hair] stands straight up **like the wool on a sheep.*** (lines 124–125)

Note 3: Sometimes an adverbial intensifier can precede a prepositional phrase. For example, the sound Maggie makes on first spotting Hakim-a-barber is one that might be made on seeing *the wriggling end of a snake **just in front of your foot** on the road.* (lines 115–116) The adverb *just* intensifies the prepositional phrase *in front of your foot.*

Note 4: Also possible are two- and three-word prepositions, such as *according to, because of, except for,* and *in addition to.*

1. Pick out and underline the prepositional phrases in lines 1–11. Say whether they are adjectival or adverbial. If the prepositional phrase is adjectival, say which noun or pronoun it modifies.

   Note: There are some verbs that take a specific preposition before a noun. For example, the verb *wait* (lines 1 and 6) takes *for* plus a noun, which is sometimes called a "prepositional object," and should not be included as a prepositional phrase in this exercise.

2. Pick out the prepositional phrases in the following sentences and say whether they are adjectival or adverbial: *In real life I am a large, big-boned woman with rough, man-working hands. In the winter I wear flannel nightgowns to bed and overalls during the day.* (lines 27–29) If the prepositional phrase is adverbial, say what kind of adverbial phrase it is (for example, time, place, manner).

3. Underline the prepositional phrase in the following sentence and circle its intensifier: *Even after Dee's arrival, Maggie tried to disappear indoors, but her mother determinedly stopped her.*

4. In line 88, is *on* a preposition or a particle? Explain your answer.

5. Are the prepositional phrases *like the portholes* (line 91) and *like a kinky mule tail* (line 114) adjectival or adverbial?

6. How many prepositional phrases are there in this sentence? *She stoops down quickly and lines up many pictures of me sitting there in front of the house, with Maggie cowering behind me in a quivering heap.* Explain your answer.

Complete each sentence with an apt prepositional phrase, bearing in mind the plot and themes of the story.

1. The narrator sat _____, anticipating Dee's arrival.

2. The narrator was a big-boned woman _____.

3. After the accident, Maggie always walked _____.

4. Dee's hair hung _____.

5. _____, Dee was determined to get the churn top and the quilts.

6. _____, Maggie and her mother enjoyed sitting outside together.

B   Verbs of Movement

Alice Walker uses the following verbs to depict the uncertain way Maggie walks: *shuffle, scrape, drag, and sidle.*

With the aid of a dictionary or the glossary, define the verbs, and write sentences that illustrate their meaning. Then draw up a list of five verbs that describe what you imagine to be Dee's manner of walking, define these verbs, and write sentences that illustrate their meaning.

C   Building Vocabulary Skills

1. The following two-word verbs appear in "Everyday Use."

stare down (lines 74–75)	crop up (line 163)
tear down (line 94)	go on (line 188)
throw out (line 120)	hang back (line 220)
follow up (line 129)	hand down (line 242)
give up (line 146)	bring up (lines 252–253)

Complete the sentences that follow with the correct verb. You may need to change its form and/or tense. Use each verb only once.

Note: When a two-word verb is separable, the noun can be placed either between or after the two parts of the verb. For example: *The narrator struggled to fight off her fears* can also be written *The narrator struggled to fight her fears off.* If we use a pronoun instead of a noun, it will always be placed between the verb and its particle. For example: *The narrator struggled to fight them off.*

a. Dee finally _____ her plan to take home the quilts, and left in a temper.

b. The narrator was surprised to find she was for the first time able to _____ Dee _____ in their confrontation over the quilts.

c. The narrator hopes that Dee never _____ the question of the quilts again.

d. Even before their first house had burned down, Dee always wanted to _____ it _____.

e. Maggie and her mother _____ sitting outside long after Dee had left them.

f. When the subject of the butter churn _____ in conversation, Dee couldn't remember who had whittled it.

g. As the sun was setting, it _____ a pale pink glow.

h. Dee was a determined young woman who always _____ her goals with concrete actions.

i. Whenever Dee was around, Maggie was used to _____ and making herself inconspicuous.

j. Because of their association with her ancestors, Maggie treasured the quilts that _____ to her.

2. The expression *used to* is used in two different ways in the story.

> *I see her [Dee] standing off under the sweet gum tree she* **used to dig** *gum out of . . .* (lines 59–60)

Here, *used to* means that in the past Dee frequently dug gum out of a particular tree, but she doesn't do so any longer. In this case, *used to* is followed by the base form of the verb *dig*.

> *"She can have them, Mama," she said, like somebody* **used to** *never* **winning** *anything, or* **having** *anything reserved for her.* (lines 267–268)

Here, *used to* means that she (Maggie) is accustomed to never getting what she wants. In this case, *be/get used to* is followed by the gerund. Note that in the example, the phrase *used to never winning anything* is a reduction from [*who was*] *used to never winning anything*.

What is the difference between the following pairs of sentences?

> *"These are all pieces of dresses Grandma* **used to wear."** (line 238–239)
>
> *Grandma* **was used to wearing** *dresses even when she did hard physical labor.*

> *I* **used** *to love* **to milk** *[cows] till I was hooked in the side in '49.* (lines 85–86)
>
> *I* **was used to milking** *cows from a very young age.*

Write three sentence pairs relating to the story that include both meanings of *used to*.

PART 4 Writing Activities

1. Write an essay of two to three pages on the role of roots in a person's life. First consider what factors constitute roots, such as country of birth, hometown, knowledge of ancestors, culture, arts and crafts, traditions, or religion. Next say whether you think roots are important. If they are, explain what you are doing to maintain or strengthen your roots, and if they are not, give your reasons.

2. Choose a sibling or other close family member, and create an extended word portrait of that person. Be sure to include both physical and psychological attributes, and convey your relationship with your relative in all its dimensions. Try to use prepositional phrases to enliven and contextualize your writing.

3. In "Everyday Use," Dee admonishes Maggie at the end to make something of herself. Reflect on where you are in life right now, and write several paragraphs on what you can do to improve your current situation. Say whether anyone in your family is encouraging and helping you.

4. Literature and the movies have often scrutinized the difficult relationship between siblings. In the movie *Marvin's Room,* two sisters, played by Meryl Streep and Diane Keaton, meet after many years of estrangement. In the course of the movie they learn to work through their deep-seated feelings of anger and resentment at each other, while responding to the needs of Streep's troubled adolescent son, played by Leonardo DiCaprio. Similarly, in his play *True West,* the American playwright Sam Shepard examines the intense rivalry of two adult brothers when they are closeted for a week in their absent mother's house. Choose any work of art whose plot centers on a conflict between siblings. Write an essay explaining the background to the conflict and its psychological underpinnings, and say whether the siblings reconciled in the end.

EXPLANATION OF LITERARY TERMS

One of the keys to appreciating literature is an awareness of the literary devices that writers use to enrich their language and create complexity within a story. To understand the *plot* (the elements of character, time, place, and action in a story) and the *themes* (the underlying connections that reveal the inner truths of the story), you should be familiar with such stylistic devices as *metaphor, simile, symbol,* and *point of view.* As you read the short stories in this book, you will be directed to the following explanations of literary terms.

Alliteration

In alliteration a consonant—usually the first one in a word—is repeated in succeeding words to produce a certain effect. Poets most frequently use alliteration; the full effect of the sounds is heard when the verse is read aloud.

When EPICAC (page 23) pens his first love poem to Pat, he waxes poetic with his softly repeated **w** sound followed by the soothing repetition of **th:** "*Where willow wands bless rill-crossed hollow, there, thee Pat, dear, will I follow . . . .*" (lines 118 119)

Katherine Mansfield in the following sentence from "Miss Brill" (page 199) repeats the short, sharp **st** sound to reinforce the jerky, uncertain movements of a small child in the park, as well as the agitated walk of its mother:

> *And sometimes a tiny staggerer came suddenly rocking into the pen from the trees, stopped, stared, as suddenly sat down "flop" until its small high-stepping mother, like a young hen, rushed scolding to its rescue.* (lines 53–56)

For practice with alliteration, see "Powder" (page 94).

Allusion

Allusion is a device that authors use when they make a passing reference to among other things art, religion, myth, literature, music, and history. Allusions are never directly explained since the reader is presumed to be familiar with the object of the allusion. Writers frequently use allusions to make implied connections or contrasts. For example, if a writer refers to an action as "crossing the Rubicon," informed readers will understand that it means taking an action from which there is no return, just as Julius Caesar launched a civil war when he crossed the Rubicon River in 49 B.C.

In "Disappearing" (page 189) when the narrator says to her husband, "You're no Cary Grant" (line 24), the assumption is that the reader will know that Cary Grant is an actor who personifies exceptional good looks that are in distinct contrast to the husband's very plain appearance.

For practice with allusion, see "The Lily-White Boys" (page 254).

Anachronism

Anachronism refers to a situation in which people say, do, or see something that is inconsistent with the time they live in. For example, a boy playing with World War II mementos in a story set in 1914 would constitute an anachronism. Similarly, teenagers in the 1990s could not use 1940s slang without being thoroughly inconsistent with their time. And a nineteenth-century character looking up and spotting an airplane would be an anachronism.

For practice with anachronism, see "The Kugelmass Episode" (page 64).

Atmosphere

Atmosphere refers to a dominant *feeling* in a story. It points to the mental and moral environment of the story and is different from the *setting,* which describes the physical environment in which the characters operate. Frequently the setting helps create the atmosphere.

Nadine Gordimer charges the atmosphere with fear and horror in "An Intruder" (page 69). When Marie leads her husband into the desecrated rooms, it is as though *evil had come out of the walls, as the black beetles did in the kitchen.* (lines 256–257)

Ann Petry in "Like A Winding Sheet" (page 229) evokes the tension in a factory with her description of the unbearable noise the workers must endure every day.

> *The machines had started full blast. The whirr and the grinding made the building shake, made it impossible to hear conversations. The men and women at the machines talked to each other but looking at them from just a little distance away, they appeared to be simply moving their lips because you couldn't hear what they were saying.*
> (lines 88–92)

For practice with atmosphere, see "The Lily-White Boys" (page 255).

Characterization: Round and Flat Characters

The English novelist and critic E. M. Forster divided characters into categories of round and flat. Round characters are fully formed, complex people who may act unpredictably and who in the course of the story struggle and change, finally achieving a greater self-knowledge. Flat characters, in contrast, are one-dimensional, predictable people who do not change or in any way increase their self-awareness by the end of the story.

"The Rocking-Horse Winner" (page 123) and "The Catbird Seat" (page 261) contain examples of flat characters. In "The Rocking-Horse Winner," D. H. Lawrence presents the gardener in a static fashion. His conversation is limited to respectful references to his social superiors and never reveals his thoughts or feelings. At no time does he demonstrate awareness of his possible role in the boy's tragedy. Similarly, in "The Catbird Seat," James Thurber portrays a woman whose behavior never varies: she is a human caricature, expressing herself in a high-pitched, hysterical fashion in every situation, never stopping to contemplate the human consequences of her actions.

By contrast, the young narrator in "My Oedipus Complex" (page 157) is an example of a round character. As the story progresses, we learn much about his inner thoughts and feelings and accompany him on his journey of growth, sharing with him his painfully gained independence and self-knowledge.

For practice with flat characters, see "The Kugelmass Episode" (page 63) and with round characters see "Everyday Use" (page 289).

Colloquialism

Colloquial English is informal or conversational language. It echoes the natural, unforced speech rhythms and vocabulary of everyday speech. Colloquial language is frequently livened with slang. The sentences are short and often bend the rules of grammar. In several of the stories, colloquialisms go hand in hand with *dialect*. (See *Dialect*.)

The characters in "The Kugelmass Episode" (page 51) express themselves very informally all the time. In the following examples, the original dialogue is given first, then a more formal version in brackets. At his first meeting with the magician Persky, Kugelmass immediately asks him, *"What's your scam?"* (line 61) ["What are you scheming?"] Persky later assures Kugelmass, *"You could carry on all you like with a real winner. Then when you've had enough you give a yell, and I'll see you back here in a split second."* (lines 76–78) ["You could have as much sex as you like with your dream woman. Then when you've had enough, call me, and I'll bring you back immediately."]

Daphne Kugelmass is no less informal when she confronts her husband with *"Where the hell do you go all the time? . . . You got a chippie stashed somewhere?"* (lines 207–209) ["Where in the world do you go all the time? Have you got another woman hidden away somewhere?"] Even Emma Bovary catches the mood of informality when she complains about her husband to her lover. *"Oh, Kugelmass,"* Emma sighed. *"What I have to put up with. Last night at dinner, Mr. Personality dropped off to sleep in the middle of the dessert course. I'm pouring my heart out about Maxim's and the ballet, and out of the blue I hear snoring."* (lines 179–182) ["Oh, Kugelmass, I have to endure so much. Last night at dinner, my boring husband fell asleep in the middle of the dessert course. I was explaining how I really felt about Maxim's and the ballet when suddenly I heard him snoring."]

For practice with colloquialism, see "EPICAC" (page 31) and "Like a Winding Sheet" (page 239).

Connotation

Connotation is the associations or implications of a word rather than its denotative (literal) meaning. It evokes ideas, qualities, or emotions related to the word. For example, the word *eagle* literally means a large bird of prey, while its connotation, especially in the United States, reflects the concept of liberty. However, when referring to a person as *a snake,* the image aroused reflects the negative qualities frequently associated with a snake. And while we may own a number of houses, we perhaps call only one of those buildings our home, with the qualities of warmth, security, and love associated with the latter. The story "Mother" (page 103) revolves around the connotations we have of the word *mother,* while "Powder" (page 89) challenges the connotations we traditionally hold of the word *father.*

For practice with connotation, see "My Oedipus Complex" (page 171) and "The Lily-White Boys" (page 255).

Dialect

Dialect is a variety of speech different from the standard language of the culture. It usually corresponds to such differences among population groups as geographical location, social class, or age. Writers use dialect to make their characters authentic. In the examples here the original dialogue is given first, followed by a more standard version in brackets. The characters in "Like a Winding Sheet" (page 229) speak with a distinctive black working-class voice. When a wife senses that something is wrong, she asks her husband, *"Whatsa matter? . . . You get bawled out by the boss or somep'n?"* (lines 276–277) ["What's the matter? Did your boss get angry and yell at you or did something else happen?"] He replies irritably, *"What you got to be always fooling with your hair for?"* (lines 283–284) ["Why are you always arranging your hair?"]

Similarly, the mother's speech in "Everyday Use" (page 279) reflects her region and education, unlike her daughter Dee, who has jettisoned her background. When talking to Dee she says, *"You know as well as me you was named after your aunt Dicie. . . . Dicie is my sister. She named Dee . . . ."* (lines 152–153) ["You know as well as I that you were named after your aunt Dicie. Dicie is my sister. She is named Dee."]

For practice with dialect, see "Like a Winding Sheet" (page 239).

Dialogue

Stories vary widely in the amount and type of dialogue, or conversation, that is present. A story like "Teenage Wasteland" (page 209) has a great deal of dialogue which reflects the characters and their situations and which helps push the plot along rapidly. At the other end of the spectrum is "The Story of an Hour" (page 13), whose action moves at a leisurely pace and whose very sparse dialogue is mainly used to reinforce the wife's epiphany on the death of her husband that she is free. Similarly, in "The Boarding House" (page 143), dialogue in no way drives the plot, and is kept to a minimum as we enter the heads of the main characters and are privy to their innermost thoughts. In a story like "Disappearing" (page 189), the narrator carries on an interior conversation in which the natural cadences of everyday speech are reproduced, while in "EPICAC" (page 23) the narrator sets the scene of his betrayal with a lot of narrative background, and only a quarter of the way through the story do the characters directly address each other in a reenactment of the story.

For practice with dialogue, see "The Kugelmass Episode" (page 63).

Ellipsis

Ellipsis means that parts of sentences or words are left out but can nevertheless be understood or inferred. A writer may use ellipsis to give the reader the impression of being in direct, unfiltered contact with the thoughts or feelings of a character or narrator. For example, in "The Kugelmass Episode" (page 51), when a wife reminds her husband of her father's forthcoming birthday, she says, *"My whole family will be there. We can see the twins. And Cousin Hamish. You should be more polite to Cousin Hamish—he likes you."* (lines 216–217) The sentence "And Cousin Hamish" is elliptical; the words *will be there* are omitted but understood. In turn, her husband's elliptical reply, *"Right, the twins"* (line 218) contains a wealth of unspoken hostility toward his wife and her family and a clear lack of interest in what she is saying.

In "An Intruder" (page 69) there is an odd encounter between James and a man who appears out of his past. Their elliptical conversation reflects the mysterious, unsettling nature of this past, as well as James's lapses of memory.

> *James. . . . What's the matter? Colin—'*
> *'Look, old man, I'm sorry, but I'm afraid—'*
> *'Colin, Colin. The Golden Horn Inn, Basutoland.'*
> *He continued to look into the man's face as if at an amiable lunatic, while the man's expression slowly changed to a strange; coquettish smile. 'Oh I see. Well, that's all right, James.'*
> (lines 171–176)

For practice with ellipsis, see "Disappearing" (page 194).

Epiphany

Epiphany is a literary device in which a character experiences an unexpected flash of understanding about the true nature of a person or situation, deeply altering his or her perception of that individual or event. James Joyce, in particular, refined the use of epiphany, and this device is closely associated with him.

An example of epiphany occurs in "My Oedipus Complex" (page 157) when the narrator's father, on overhearing his son muttering to himself about the new baby, realizes in a moment of sudden intuition that he and his son share the same feelings toward the baby. This recognition helps forge a close new relationship between them. (lines 351–362)

Marie, too, in "An Intruder" (page 69) has an epiphany at the end of the story, which will alter her life significantly: . . . *and this time, while she was speaking, she began to know what else he would never remember, something so simple that she had missed it.* (lines 278–279)

For practice with epiphany, see "The Story of an Hour" (page 18).

Fable

A fable is a short story, often with animals in it, that is told to illustrate a moral. The moral is the lesson to be drawn from the story and is usually stated clearly at the end. Famous fabulists include Aesop, La Fontaine, and more recently, James Thurber.

For practice with fable, see "The Rocking-Horse Winner" (page 138).

Flashback

The flashback is a narrative technique in which a narrator or character interrupts the present time and returns to the past.

Through this device, some aspect of character or incident is illuminated. Movie directors commonly employ flashbacks to condense the story and highlight the significance of certain events. Barbra Streisand does this most effectively in *Prince of Tides* where the central character, played by Nick Nolte, is forced to relive a childhood rape, a reenactment that is crucial to his recovery as an adult. The Chinese martial arts movie *Hero* is narrated almost entirely in flashback as a nameless warrior recounts to his king how he killed three assassins who intended to murder the sovereign. In an unexpected twist, the king contradicts his subject, and in a separate series of flashbacks relates what he surmises really happened. A third series of flashbacks portrays yet another reality.

Virginia Woolf manipulates time in "The Legacy" (page 39), when a husband, on reading his wife's diary after her death, relives past events as if they were occurring in the present. In one such example, he reenacts a political dinner at which he and his wife were present many years ago. *He could see her now sitting next to old Sir Edward; and making a conquest of that formidable old man, his chief.* (lines 120–121)

For practice with flashback, see "Mother" (page 106).

Humor

Humor takes many forms. It ranges from the exaggerated situations, snappy lines, sarcasm, and parody (comical imitation) in "The Kugelmass Episode" through the sharp irony of "Can-Can" and "The Boarding House, to the gentle irony of "My Oedipus Complex." (See *Irony*.) Humor equally embraces the jaunty colloquialisms of "EPICAC" and the comic characterizations and ingeniously funny plot of "The Catbird Seat." Black humor, as seen in the ending of "The Kugelmass Episode," combines comedy with horror, while Shakespearean humor often encompasses puns or clever word play, and farcical humor relies on closely timed physical responses to a situation.

For practice with humor, see "EPICAC" (page 31), "The Kugelmass Episode" (page 64), "The Boarding House" (page 151), "My Oedipus Complex" (page 169), and "The Catbird Seat" (page 271).

Imagery

Imagery is used by writers to create vivid pictures that our senses (sight, touch, smell, hearing, and taste) respond to. The most effective writing contains striking and fresh images and avoids commonly used comparisons. Adjectival or descriptive writing is a dominant element of imagery. Often the language is figurative (not literal) and takes the form of *metaphors* and *similes*. (See *Metaphor* and *Simile*.) The scene in "Everyday Use" (page 279) where Dee first dazzles her family in a sunburst of color relies on visual, tactile, and auditory imagery for its effect.

> *A dress down to the ground, in this hot weather. A dress so loud it hurts my eyes. There are yellows and oranges enough to throw back the light of the sun. I feel my whole face warming from the heat waves it throws out. Earrings gold, too, and hanging down to her shoulders. Bracelets dangling and making noises when she moves her arm to shake the folds of her dress out of her armpits. The dress is loose and flows, and as she walks closer, I like it.* (lines 117–123)

For practice with imagery, see "The Boarding House" (page 152), "Disappearing" (page 195), and "Like a Winding Sheet" (page 240).

Inference

Frequently writers are interested in suggesting rather than explaining a theme or detail. This enables the writer to be subtle or indirect, leaving the reader to infer, or deduce, the writer's meaning. For example, in "My Oedipus Complex" (page 157) when the wife refers to her husband's precious war memorabilia as "toys" (line 294), she is suggesting that these are childish pleasures. Similarly, when the central character in "Miss Brill" (page 199) takes out her fur in the opening paragraph, shakes out the moth powder, and rubs the life back into its eyes, the reader is left to infer that she has not worn the fur for a long time.

For practice with inference, see "The Model" (page 183) and "Teenage Wasteland" (page 220).

Irony

Irony occurs when a person says one thing but really means something else. It also exists when a person does something that has the opposite effect from what he or she intended. It can be used to convey both the seriousness and humor of situations. For example, when Josephine in "The Story of an Hour" (page 13) begs her sister to open the door, saying, *"You will make yourself ill"* (line 69), the irony lies in her ignorance of the fact that her sister has indeed never been happier in her life. Another example of irony is found in "My Oedipus Complex" (page 157) when a small boy's prayers regarding his father's safe return from the war are answered, yet he finds himself in a worse position as a result of his father's presence. And the scene in which the mother in "Everyday Use" (page 279) dreams of her television encounter with her daughter is suffused with irony, as the unreality of her dream clashes with her real-life situation.

For practice with irony, see "Can-Can" (page 7) and "The Boarding House" (page 151).

Metaphor

A metaphor is an implied comparison in which one element is described in terms of another to create a connection. Unlike a *simile,* in which the two parts of the comparison are united by *like* or *as,* a metaphor is more indirect, and the reader has to work at understanding the two elements involved. (See *Simile.*) For example, it is said of the boy in "The Rocking-Horse Winner" (page 123) that *his eyes were blue fire.* (lines 212–213) In this instance, the two elements being compared are the boy's eyes and fire. The image is further compounded by the addition of the color blue to both parts of the comparison. In "Teenage Wasteland," we are left at the end with the metaphor of the ball in Daisy's waking dream. The ball that soared through the hoop but fell to the ground with a thud represents Donny's young life. And there is a sustained metaphor in "Miss Brill" (page 199) in the slowly unraveling scene in the park where Miss Brill imagines that she and all the other people there are characters in a play, and the plot is unfolding before her eyes. (lines 96–119)

For practice with metaphor, see "The Story of an Hour" (page 18), "An Intruder" (page 78), and "A Short Digest of a Long Novel" (page 118).

Oxymoron

An oxymoron is a figure of speech that brings together two seemingly contradictory elements—usually words or phrases—for effect. Oxymorons are a frequent device in poetry and are also used to heighten prose, enhance humor, or reveal a deeper truth. Some common examples include *bittersweet, tough love, being cruel to be kind,* and *jumbo shrimp.* Oxymorons may embrace social commentary, as in the well-known example *military intelligence.* In "My Oedipus Complex" (page 157), the young narrator refers to the war as being "the most peaceful period of my life." (line 19)

For practice with oxymoron, see "The Boarding House" (page 154).

Personification

Personification is a figure of speech in which animals or things are given human characteristics. Like *metaphors* and *similes,* personification heightens our imaginative response to what is being described. (See *Metaphor* and *Simile*.) For example, in "My Oedipus Complex" (page 157), the narrator observes, *Dawn was just breaking with a guilty air.* (line 130) Here dawn, a natural phenomenon, is characterized as displaying the behavior of a person who has done something wrong.

Personification pervades the following scene in "The Rocking-Horse Winner" (page 123) in the form of the whispering house, which torments its residents and which stands for the parents who are never satisfied with what they have.

> *"But what are you going to do with your money?" asked the uncle.*
> *"Of course," said the boy, "I started it for mother. She said she had no luck, because father is unlucky, so I thought if **I** was lucky, it might stop whispering."*
> *"What might stop whispering?"*
> *"Our house. I **hate** our house for whispering."* (lines 291–296)

For practice with personification, see "The Story of an Hour" (page 19) and "EPICAC" (page 31).

Point of View

Point of view refers to the specific character or narrator through whose eyes all or part of the story unfolds. What the narrator or character knows or is ignorant of affects his or her view of the action. When reading a story, it is important to be alert to the narrator's prejudices, which influence the way he or she perceives the action and tells the story.

Stories are usually narrated in the first or third person. A story narrated in the first person means that it is told by a narrator using the pronoun *I*. In first-person narration the point of view of the narrator is necessarily subjective and incomplete since he or she is not granted a full view of the action and does not have access to other characters' thoughts. "My Oedipus Complex" (page 157), which is filtered through the limited vision of a five-year-old boy, is narrated in the first person.

A story narrated in the third person is told by a narrator using the pronouns *he, she,* and *they*. A third-person narrator may be either **omniscient** (the narrator is not a participant in the story and has a complete view of the characters and events) or **limited omniscient** (the narrator can penetrate the thoughts of only one or two characters and provides a subjective view of characters and events). An omniscient narrator relentlessly unfolds the events in "The Rocking-Horse Winner" (page 123), and a limited omniscient narrator controls the perspective in "The Catbird Seat." (page 261)

Very rarely are stories narrated in the second person using the pronoun *you* as a direct address to the reader. One example is when the narrator in "EPICAC" (page 23) informally pulls the reader into the action when he says: *You can call him a machine if you want to.* (line 14)

For practice with point of view, see "The Legacy" (page 47), "Teenage Wasteland" (page 220), and "Everyday Use" (page 291).

Repetition

Repetition can be a most effective way of creating atmosphere or of pointing to a theme in a story. It can take the form of repetitive language as in the insistent, sinister refrain of *"There must be more money"* in "The Rocking-Horse Winner" (page 123); or of the striking alliterative repetition of consonants in "A Short Digest of a Long Novel" (page 113) when a father suggests that his daughter's hair is like *"maple polished to a golden grain"* (lines 6–7); or of repeated events as in the parallel walks a small boy takes with his father and mother in "My Oedipus Complex" (page 157), which highlight the different ways the boy relates to each parent.

For practice with repetition, see "Powder" (page 95).

Setting

The setting of a story refers to the time and place in which the action unfolds. It can also include the society being depicted, as well as its values. The setting helps us understand the characters and themes of a story. For example, the snowy setting in "Powder" (page 89) acts both as a backdrop to the rash actions of the father and as a reflection of the changing emotions of the boy. Likewise, the raw depiction of factory life in "Like a Winding Sheet" (page 229) is integral to the theme of the brutalization of a man. And in "Miss Brill" (page 199), Katherine Mansfield devotes most of the story to the main character's view of scenes in a park. This focus heightens our awareness of the character's role as a lonely observer.

For practice with setting, see "The Lily-White Boys" (page 255).

Simile

A simile is an explicit comparison that contains the words *like* or *as.* It is usually quite easy to identify the two elements of the comparison. Imaginative writers combine two unlikely components to make up the simile, allowing the reader to appreciate the unexpectedness as well as the aptness of the comparison. For example, in "The Boarding House" (page 143),

Mrs. Mooney's personality is brilliantly evoked when James Joyce describes her as *deal[ing] with moral problems as a cleaver deals with meat.* (lines 64–65) Similarly, Polly's conflicting moral and physical attributes are encapsulated in the comparison of her pretty, wayward eyes that make her *look like a little perverse madonna.* (line 45) Another example of an evocative simile is found in "My Oedipus Complex" (page 157) when the narrator wakes up feeling *like a bottle of champagne* (lines 125–126), which suggests that his mood is as bright and bubbly as the celebratory drink.

For practice with similes, see "The Story of an Hour" (page 18), "An Intruder" (page 78), "A Short Digest of a Long Novel" (page 118), and "Miss Brill" (page 206).

Symbol

A symbol may be a person, an object, or an action that represents something else because of its association with it. It is frequently a visible sign of something invisible. For example, newly fallen snow is recognized as a symbol of purity. Symbols may be general—the lion is a symbol of courage and strength, an olive branch is a symbol for peace, a cross represents Christianity, and a red rose stands for romantic love—or they may be particular, arising out of the story itself and connected to a central theme. In "The Legacy" (page 39) a black coat is a generally accepted emblem of mourning, whereas the symbol of the fur in "Miss Brill" (page 199) is peculiar to this story only and has no wider reference.

For practice with symbol, see "Can-Can" (page 7) and "The Rocking-Horse Winner" (page 138).

Synecdoche

Synecdoche is a figure of speech in which a part is used to describe the whole or the whole is used for a part; the special is used for the general or the general for the special. Writers often employ synecdoche as a dramatic shorthand to focus sharply on an element of the story, as well as to express something in a striking fashion. For example, in "Mother" (page 103) Grace Paley writes: *She'd just quit the shop for the kitchen.* (lines 26–27) Here, the kitchen represents the house, so in a condensed way we learn that a mother gave up her job in the sweatshop for a life as a homemaker. On the other hand, a policeman might refer to himself as *the law,* a generalized expression standing for a special representative.

For practice with synecdoche, see "Miss Brill" (page 205).

Tone

The tone of a story refers to the attitude of the writer toward the characters and/or theme of the story. For example, the tone may be humorous, sarcastic, ironic, cheerful, pessimistic, angry, unfeeling, compassionate, or satirical. A compassionate humor is the prevailing tone in "My Oedipus Complex" (page 157); a warm understanding suffuses "Powder" (page 89); an angry pessimism pervades "The Rocking-Horse Winner" (page 123); sharp irony laces the ending of "The Kugelmass Episode" (page 51); and a deep sympathy with the central character is evident in "Disappearing" (page 189).

For practice with tone, see "The Boarding House" (page 151).

Understatement

Understatement occurs when a writer deliberately de-emphasizes the dialogue or action. There may be diverse reasons for doing this. In "Can-Can" (page 3), the writer uses irony to distance and defuse the passions of the central characters, while in "The Lily-White Boys" (page 247), the quietly understated scene in which the wife tries on her dresses amidst the ruin left by the robbers is wonderfully effective in conveying her restrained reaction to the event. In contrast, James Thurber in "The Catbird Seat" (page 261) uses understatement to heighten the comedy of the story's plot and characters.

For practice with understatement, see "The Catbird Seat" (page 271).

TEXT CREDITS

Woody Allen. "The Kugelmass Episode" from *Side Effects* by Woody Allen. Copyright © 1977 by Woody Allen. Reprinted by permission of Random House, Inc.

Kate Chopin. "The Story of an Hour." First published in *Vogue, IV* (December 1894).

Nadine Gordimer. "An Intruder" from *Livingstone's Companions* by Nadine Gordimer. Copyright © 1965, 1966, 1967, 1968, 1969, 1971 by Nadine Gordimer. Reprinted by permission of Viking Penguin, a division of Penguin Group (USA) Inc. and Random Century Group, London, and Russell and Volkening as agents for the author.

James Joyce. "The Boarding House" from *Dubliners* by James Joyce. Copyright © 1916 by B. W. Heubsch. Definitive text Copyright © 1967 by the Estate of James Joyce. Reprinted by permission of Viking Penguin, a division of Penguin Group (USA) Inc.

D. H. Lawrence. "The Rocking-Horse Winner" from *Complete Short Stories of D. H. Lawrence* by D. H. Lawrence. Copyright © 1933 by the Estate of D. H. Lawrence, renewed © 1961 by Angelo Ravagli and C. M. Weekley, Executors of the Estate of Frieda Lawrence. Reprinted by permission of Viking Penguin, a division of Penguin Books (USA) Inc. and Laurence Pollinger Ltd., London.

Bernard Malamud. "The Model." Reprinted by the permission of Russell & Volkening Inc. as agents for the author. Copyright © 1982 by Bernard Malamud. Originally appeared in *The Atlantic,* August 1983.

Katherine Mansfield. "Miss Brill" from *The Short Stories of Katherine Mansfield* by Katherine Mansfield. Copyright © 1923 by Alfred A. Knopf, a division of Random House, Inc., and renewed 1951 by John Middleton Murry. Used by permission of Alfred A. Knopf, a division of Random House, Inc.

William Maxwell. "The Lily-White Boys" from *The Paris Review,* Issue 100, 1986. Copyright © 1986 by William Maxwell, reprinted with the permission of The Wylie Agency, Inc.

Frank O'Connor. "My Oedipus Complex" from *The Collected Stories of Frank O'Connor* by Frank O'Connor. Copyright © 1981 by Harriet O'Donovan Sheehy, Executrix of the Estate of Frank O'Connor. Used by permission of Alfred A. Knopf, a division of Random House, Inc., and Writer's House, LLC on behalf of the proprietors.

PHOTO CREDITS